NO KNOWN GRAVE

This tale of Bomber Command – part biographical, part history, part fiction – is the story of Titch Wilkins, a composite of three real life characters, one lost with no known grave. He could be any of hundreds of 'tail end Charlies', and their childhood may have been as tragic, their youth as innocent. The flying sequences happened most nights to some aircrew or other in Bomber Command, and the material came from lengthy talks in 'ops' rooms, barrack huts, bars and long country walks with surviving crew members.

NO KNOWN GRAVE

NO KNOWN GRAVE

by

Don Roberts

Magna Large Print Books
Long Preston, North Yorkshire,
BD23 4ND, England.

British Library Cataloguing in Publication Data.

Roberts, Don
    No known grave.

    A catalogue record of this book is
    available from the British Library

    ISBN   0-7505-2435-9

First published in Great Britain in 1998 by J & K H Publishing

Copyright © Donald H Roberts (1998)

Cover illustration © Andy Walker by arrangement with
P.W.A. International Ltd.

The moral right of the author has been asserted

Published in Large Print 2005 by arrangement with
Mrs Ann Roberts

Magna Large Print is an imprint of Library Magna Books Ltd.

Printed and bound in Great Britain by
T.J. (International) Ltd., Cornwall, PL28 8RW

CONTENTS

INTRODUCTION

'No Known Grave'. Part biographical, part history, part fiction. The flying sequences were real, they happened most nights to some aircrew or other in Bomber Command – 50,500 aircrew did not live to tell the tale. Titch Wilkins did. With a different name but in similar circumstances – he is alive today. He could be any of the hundreds of 'tail end Charlies', and who knows, their childhood may have been as tragic – their youth as innocent. That was the state of the times – poverty was the norm for many – chastity and innocence were cherished for fear of family rejection and public scorn rather than moral or religious rectitude. A time when children struggled to grow to adulthood with the memory of the Great War and the no less great depression only a yesterday away.

Titch Wilkins is a composite of three real life characters, one lost with no known grave. The material for the story came from lengthy talks in 'ops' rooms, barrack huts, bars and long country walks I had with the characters. The existence of God and a life after death was a topic between us. We were curious and could not believe the platitudes of the clergy. Each time we returned from an 'op' or heard of a friend 'getting the chop' we wondered – we were happy to believe that there was something, though surely not just sitting up on a cloud with a harp. The fantasy experienced by Titch seemed a reasonable answer to 'the end' – though of course we hoped it was not the end. The word re-cycle is common since concern for the environment became the norm – re-cycling of waste an every day thing. Is it beyond our imaginings that God should re-cycle our souls, or psyches – that 'life' went on? Somehow. How young we were.

DHR. Perth 1997

A DEDICATION

To my wife Ann for her forbearance and patience, and the many cups of tea she tirelessly brewed – my daughters for listening to me with patience. And the 'tail end Charlies' who may read this and perhaps see themselves, or a comrade from their youth within its pages, and remember the reargunner's motto. 'VIGILANTIA ET VIRTUE'

PREFACE

My brief short life is over.
My eyes no longer see.
No summer walks,
No Christmas trees.
No pretty girls for me.
I've got the chop!
I've had it!
My nightly Ops are done.
But in a hundred years or more.
I'll still be twenty one.

Anon. 1944

Note. *My information is that the foregoing was found among a litter of papers strewn over a table of a Nissen Hut vacated the night before by a Non-Commissioned Officer crew of a Lancaster Bomber shot down over Berlin in the winter of 1944-45. I include it in the manuscript as a preface, and a tribute, to the Titch Wilkins' of RAF Bomber Command, and their contemporaries.*

D.H.R. 1996

PROLOGUE

July 17th 1943

A four-engined Lancaster bomber flies low over the moonlit water of the English Channel. Its wheels are retracted and three of its four engines are silent. Three propellers stand stark and stiff in the light of the setting moon; the fourth airscrew spins invisibly in the damp pre-dawn air. The only engine functioning sounds sick; it coughs, and backfires. The plane is losing height. The rear turret is turned to beam – the rear gunner is half out of the open doors, one gloved hand clutches a turret strut while the other holds the Mae West life jacket inflation tube to his mouth. The gunner's cheeks are puffed as he blows a lungful of air into the mouthpiece to partially inflate the jacket. Pale moonlight glittered on the polished aluminium of gaping, jagged wounds in the bomber's fuselage and wings.

There was a brief silence when power is cut from the single engine – the bomber touches the water and bounces with the report of a gun. There is a roar from the single engine as the pilot applies the throttle to counter the aircraft's rearing. A wing tilts and dips into the belly of an oncoming wave. The Lancaster slews violently – with a crash and a fountain of white water the giant plane falters and the rear gunner is catapulted into the

15

sea yards from his plane. Broken water surges around the aircraft as it settles lazily – the plane's tail points towards the moon in an obscene gesture; the fuselage black and sinister begins its death plunge. For a moment the letters AR 'D' stand out stark and red in the soft light; a bright jagged strip of fuselage fabric flaps in the wind like a nonchalant hand waving a farewell. Soundlessly the bomber sinks beneath the waves with water pouring into the rear turret as the fins and rudders of the aircraft disappear. Grey water covered the spot and a wave rolled over the thin film of oil that marked the bomber's grave. In a moment all signs of the crash were erased, until an inflated round yellow dinghy erupted to the surface in a cascade of white water. It tilts on its side and is half drawn beneath the waves before its mooring line snaps and it catapults again to the surface to float bottom uppermost. A southerly wind catches the taut yellow topsides and blows it gently to the north; moonlight shines wanly on the wet black rubber of its underbelly. Nothing is left, not even a battered piece of flotsam. Nothing, nothing but a body wallowing grotesquely in the trough of a wave.

The rear gunner floats face down in the water until a wave breaks over him – the water recedes and the body is face uppermost. It is fully-clothed in flying kit. Helmet, goggles and oxygen mask. A fur-lined 'Irvin' suit is zipped to the throat. The Mae West buoyancy jacket is half inflated, the inflation tube hands limp in the water; an unclipped oxygen mask flops from side to side as the waves move the body. The corrugated rubber

16

oxygen tube hung limp as the flaccid phallus of a geriatric stallion.

Blood flowed dark and syrupy from a jagged wound on the gunner's cheek; the ooze night black in the pale moonlight. It ran down the gunner's face into the water – the flow stops. A wave washed the wound clean – flesh gapes wet and swollen, like lips of a drooling lecher, the colour a ripe pink; sensual yet repulsive. An exposed jagged piece of cheek bone shines like a single tooth, unnaturally white and clean. Waves rolled the body sluggishly – the moon sank below the horizon as the eastern sky showed a glimmer of light.

F

Chapter One

The letters painted on the leather flying helmet were plainly seen, 'T I T C H' – crudely painted in faded white paint across the forehead. They were smeared – the paint had chipped and peeled a little – part of the 'C' is missing, but there was no mistaking the name. It was the name of the wearer, Titch. Flying goggles are partly over the eyes and an oxygen mask was unclipped on one side and was askew – it showed a portion of the face. There was a deep gash of a cut down the left cheek that was not bleeding – pink sea-washed flesh was exposed; a large blue black bruise showed just beneath the goggles. A piece of bone protruded from the gash, white and clean; like a

17

baby's first tooth.

Two large gulls fought for the right to sit on the head. There was a squawk and a flurry of wings – a feather flew; the victor folded its wings and with arched back gave a victory squawk and began pecking at the lenses of the goggles, then at the torn flesh of the body's cheek. The other gull sat in the water and watched its rival.

The figure hovering over the floating corpse looked on with a look of incredulity. 'Titch' Wilkins hardly realised the body being attacked by the gull was his, and that he was dead. His dress was that of his corpse – he reached up with a gloved hand and touched his cheek and felt the jagged wound and the protruding bone, but there was no pain. He watched in amazement.

The gull's yellow beak pecked at the jagged flesh of the cut. Titch kicked at the bird in disgust, but his heavy flying boot passed through the creature's body and it remained undisturbed, pecking at the dead face. A wave washed over the body; the bird rose effortlessly and water splashed over the face; there was no doubting it now; it was him. The gull settled again on the head. The oxygen mask moved lazily revealing more of the features. He was totally convinced, he was dead. Drowned?

Titch Wilkins looked around him. There was nothing but an empty sea – not a sign of his aircraft 'The Dog'. Lancaster AR-D Dog that is. The pale dawn light looked cold and unfriendly – though strangely he was warm enough. The sea about him was a series of well-rounded ridges that moved like living things. Small white caps appeared and died, but all the time the low swell rolled, lifting the body up and down with the motion; the gull squawked – it pecked again at the face tearing a lump of flesh away.

There was no sign of Keith, Titch's friend and pilot. Warrant Officer Keith Gale DFC DFM. Quite a hero was Keith – now he too was dead; or was he? Titch looked around again. Nothing – no dinghy – no debris; not even a patch of oil to show where old 'Dog' had disappeared. Disappeared with Keith and the bodies of the Flight Engineer and Navigator.

Titch was alone out there – somewhere in the English Channel. He looked into the distance and saw the blurred outline of a coast. Kent he supposed it was – or was it France; Titch was completely disoriented. He remembered Keith hoped to make Kent with the wounded Navigator and Flight Engineer. They had died minutes after leaving the French coast. Too late to bale out then – too late to turn back; too low anyway. Too late for anything but keep going; and hope, and perhaps pray.

'We'll press on for home old friend and belly-land on Romney Marsh. Flat as a pancake there.' Keith made it sound so easy. But then he always did – Titch smiled grimly at the memory of it.

They had been losing height since enemy flak knocked out 'The Dog's' starboard inner engine over the target just after their bombing run and badly wounded the two crew members. The pilot brought things under control while Mac the Wireless Operator did his best for the wounded Engineer and Navigator but he could do little for them.

'Reckon they've just about bought it, Keith.

19

Whole bloody sides shot away. Both of 'em... Poor bastards... Poor fuckin' bastards!' Titch remembered Mac had sobbed at this before he continued. 'Merve's got his back all shot away too.' The Australian's voice broke again. 'Holy bloody cow! What a bloody mess.' Titch smiled that grim smile again, Mac's Sydney accent was thick enough to cut with a knife. The German 88mm shell had nearly blasted the life out of Merve and Leo as it had out of the engine.

A Lancaster can fly well on three engines – everything else was working. They should make it home. That was until Titch spotted the two Focke Wolf 190s zeroing in on them from astern up. Two of the Luftwaffe's 'Wild Boar' nightfighters. Fighter aircraft that generally flew in daylight, but on a night like this, a night of full-moon and low unbroken cloud, it was a night made for them; they flew without the aid of radar and made their kills visually.

The enemy planes came straight out of the glare of the moon and had the bomber silhouetted against the blanket of cloud that spread as far as the moonlit scene reached. The silver covering stretched away into the distance making bombers appear like black beetles crossing a white linen table cloth; 'The Dog' was in the nightfighter's sights.

Titch waited breathlessly – his gut shrank – his anus contracted and oozed moisture, and his mouth went dry. Fear gripped him, his scalp tingled and his heart raced enough to burst; raced in deep rapid throbs that he felt in his head and his guts. He knew they were a sitting duck –

it had to be a shoot out; evasive action could only cope if there was the cover of darkness. The moon shining on the cloud made it almost as bright as day; and that cloud was seven or eight thousand feet below them. Not a hope of reaching it in time.

Titch screamed 'Corkscrew Port!' as he opened fire with his four Brownings in a long burst of tracer and armour piercing bullets. He caught the first FW right on its nose; it blew up about 100yds astern of them; its cannon tracer missing Titch by only feet. It was the second 190 that clobbered them – it got in a long burst of cannon and machine gun fire that blasted both the bomber's port engines before it broke away with smoke trailing from its stern from Aussie Meldrum's, he was the Mid-upper Gunner, and Titch's own guns. Then the hydraulics packed up – the gun turrets went dead; probably flaps, undercarriage and bomb doors too; not that that mattered, they had dropped their bombs thank God – but the flaps and undercarriage? Time to worry about them when they had to land.

Keith Gale, the Lancaster's pilot, battled the controls and fought alone with the two port engine's fire extinguishers. He pulled 'The Dog' out of a dive and struggled to maintain height, but it was no good. The engine fires were out but the altimeter had crawled round the dial to three thousand feet as they approached the French coast.

The pilot ordered them, the Bombardier, Wireless Operator, Mid-upper Gunner the rear gunner to bale out. 'It'll lighten the plane chaps,' he said. 'I'll make the Kent coast and get these poor blighters home.'

Three of them went – Titch didn't blame them. They had only been a crew for three months. Only their third 'Op' together, they knew each other pretty well but Keith and Titch had been together since 1940. On their second tour of operations together flying bombers they were – then there were the other times, and always together. Titch couldn't leave his friend to fly those wounded home on his own; besides, a nightfighter might jump him over the water; not that the rear gunner could do more than warn him.

The moon lit up the English Channel like daylight – water spread into the distance in a million polished pewter corrugations, cold, lonely and deadly, yet mysteriously inviting. No – Titch couldn't leave him – they had been through too much together, but the rear gunner didn't tell his pilot he was still with him until they were over the 'drink'. Keith raved over the intercom; swore even. It was about the only thing that was working except that one engine; the intercom that is, and that sounded sick; so did the engine.

The pilot raved – calling Titch an imbecile sub-human rear gunner, his favourite term of endearment. Then he was silent. Titch heard his breathing, then a sort of sob. 'Thanks, Rupert, old friend.'

Keith was the only one who ever called him Rupert. Then only when they were by themselves. Keith and Mary that is – Mary is Titch's girl, a WAAF on the same base – everybody else called him Titch. They always had – not surprising really; he was only five foot two inches with his boots on.

It was all the pilot said. 'Thanks, Rupert, old friend.' Just the one time – Titch heard the words again as his body floated at his feet. He said nothing up there alone in the tail turret – there was no need; they understood each other. Not a word passed between them until Keith said he thought the Engineer and Navigator were dead.

'Their eyes are open and they look bloody awful, Rupert. What do you reckon?'

'Don't ask me. I'm only a dumb sub-human rear gunner remember. Just drive this bloody thing and get us home.'

Keith laughed at that – his old laugh. Minutes passed in silence, but for the engine noise – it was broken by Keith's voice over the spluttering intercom.

'I can't hold Old Dog to the coast, Rupert. I'm down to 300ft. We'll have to ditch, old chum.'

'Whatever you say, Keith. Just do it gently. Remember I am only a little man and very delicate.' Keith laughed again – a short nervous laugh. Titch knew he was scared – so was he; he can't swim.

'You coming up front, Rupert?'

'No thanks. I'd be lost up there. I'll take my chance down this end. Just make it nice and gentle.'

There was no time for an answer. But Keith didn't make it gentle. Titch had turned his turret manually to beam and opened the doors ready for a quick exit. He had already pulled his goggles over his eyes, and pressed the quick release of his parachute harness. With an effort, he wriggled it free from under him and let it fall into the sea. The harness was bulky and would slow him up – he needed freedom of movement to scramble clear of the turret once they hit the water. The gunner even stuck his backside out into the breeze in case he was trapped when they ditched, and he prayed. He was inflating his Mae West when they struck the water like a battering ram at over 80 miles an hour, and no flaps. The giant plane bounced once – the nose lifted – the single engine roared a burst of power; the port wing dipped and caught the underside of a wave. With the drag it caused and the surge of power of the remaining starboard engine it slewed nearly 90°. Titch was thrown hard against the supports of the gun turret on impact. A vivid, scorching flame of light shattered his eyes – he felt his body telescope within himself in the split second it took for his mind to explode into a void of nothingness and he was catapulted backwards out of the turret to fall into the cold grey water.

Titch didn't see the old Lanc's tail lift as it plunged into the depths. Neither did he see the dark water of the English Channel as he hit it and went under. He didn't see, or feel, a thing after that explosion in his head. He doesn't feel a thing now. Time doesn't drag for him – he is without feeling. He feels neither heat nor cold, hunger nor thirst, boredom, excitement, fear, happiness, sadness; nothing.

The body at his feet rose and fell, he wonders, 'Is this the heaven I was taught to expect as a kid? If it's hell then it isn't too bad; certainly it isn't hot, and "Old Nick" or his demons haven't showed up yet; but neither has Saint Peter...? Then where the heck am I?' Titch began to think all those parsons that lectured him and the boys at school and in church about going to heaven if they were good, or the other place if they weren't, had got it all wrong. About heaven and hell, anyway.

His thoughts were disturbed when another pair of gulls arrived to feed on his corpse.

When light appeared in the east on the fifth day, Titch saw that he, his body that is, was almost on the beach. Waves were breaking over the bloated gory mess that had been, is still he supposed, Flight Sergeant Rupert Montgomery Wilkins, DFM, RAFVR, Air Gunner, Number 156282. Known to officialdom as 'Wilkins 282. Flight Sergeant'.

A wave bigger than its fellows rolled the sodden mess over onto its back and pointed what was left of his face to the sky. The gulls had had a party – the face is unrecognisable. Another wave carried it. IT! That was all he was now? An it? Carried it further up the beach. The next wave slopped to a halt a foot away; the tide was on the turn. Soon the bundle of rotting leather flying suit, Mae West, and bloated, rotting flesh and bone was high and dry on the beach; then the first gull arrived.

It was Corporal Jenkins of the Royal Hampshire Regiment who spotted the 'Object' first. He leaned on a sandbag parapet of the hidden cliff-top weapon pit and peered through the regulation binoculars trying to figure out what it was he was looking at. After five long minutes he gave up and called his sergeant in the camouflaged dugout behind him.

'Hey Sarg. Sum'fin's washed up on the beach art'side the bloody minefield. Could be a Jerry mine?' There was a worried question in his voice.

The rugged figure of Sergeant Thomas in full battle order propped his rifle against a sandbag and took over the field glasses. He studied the distant bundle for some minutes.

'Nar… Looks like a soddin' seal. Saw one once when I was on 'oliday wiv the missus in Cornwall.' He looked again. 'It h'aint a'movin though. The ones I see'd waggled their tails a bit, and their flippers. That there h'aint a'movin'.' He looked hard for another long minute. 'Could be a body though? 'Eard as 'ow one was washed up in "D" Company's sector a couple of weeks ago. A soddin' German it was. Shot down by one of our blokes. Air Force I mean. You stoopid sods couldn't 'it a bull's arse wiv a bleedin' cricket bat.' He looks at the object yet again. 'Buggered if I know. I'll give the captain a call. 'E's paid to know 'abart these f'ings an' 'e.'

It took Captain Billings ten minutes to reach the concealed weapon pit grumbling with every step at being disturbed from his breakfast, another two to examine the corpse through his own binoculars. The tide was well out, and the light was better; there were twenty or more gulls fighting to breakfast on the decaying body.

'I do believe you are right Sergeant. It is a body, and outside the minefield. Those gulls are a give away.' He gazed hard into the distance. 'A job for

26

the Engineers I think. I'll get in touch.' He snapped his field glasses closed and tucked them into the leather case. 'On the other hand...' He pushed back his steel helmet as he thought. 'Keep an eye on it. You might bring up a Bren gun and cover it. One never knows. It might be some devilish trick of the Hun. Carry on then Sergeant and do keep in touch.' Almost as an afterthought he added, 'I say... Have your chaps had breakfast?' He didn't wait for a reply but strode off briskly to enjoy his own meal.

Titch gazed around him. He realised with a smile he was looking at the little coastal resort of Broadstairs, in the county of Kent – a place he had been sent to convalesce after an illness at school when he was about 12. He recognised the Lifeboat House and the shops and boarding houses that lined the hill from the beach leading up to the town. The cliffs below the town were a dirty white in the dull morning's light, just as he remembered them – further along were the rocks he used to scramble over looking for crabs, mussels and winkles. 'Yes' he concluded, 'It is Broadstairs for sure.'

He saw a party of five approaching – they were picking their way carefully through a defensive minefield. The whole south and east coasts of England were littered with defensive minefields against the German invasion that was expected in 1940. The army was on guard – it could still happen, even in 1943.

The five as they came closer were seen to be an officer, a very young second lieutenant, a sergeant and two sappers of the Royal Engineers and a middle-aged corporal of the Royal Army Medical Corps. The two sappers were carrying a stretcher and the corporal a heavy satchel of medical equipment. Titch smiled when he saw the red cross on the side of it.

'A bit late for that mate!' he shouted.

The stocky medic didn't hear him – the corporal plodded behind the others in a single file; each man stepped in the foot prints of the man in front. Titch smiled to himself again. 'At least the corporal can give them the first aid if one of them treads on a mine. And he is last. Crafty old bastard.'

Angry gulls screeched their fury when their meal was disturbed – they flew off and settled just yards away still squawking. The five soldiers gathered round what was left of Titch. They looked at what had been his face. The officer and one of the sappers turned away to vomit noisily.

'My God. The poor devil. One of our chaps too by the look of the Mae West.' The young Lieutenant was wiping his mouth with a khaki handkerchief. 'What do you think, corporal? More in your line than mine, what?' He gave a nervous laugh. 'Nasty business.' Titch agreed with him but they didn't hear him. They didn't see him. This puzzled him until he remembered that he was dead; he remembered trying to kick the gull.

So he was a ghost? Well, a spirit, anyway; an invisible spirit? He made a mischievous swipe at the officer's tin helmet; his hand passed through the young man's head unnoticed. They really didn't know he was there.

The two sappers opened the stretcher and laid

it on the firm sand and stood up – they were afraid to touch the decomposing heap. Titch called out needlessly, 'I won't bite ch'know.' Then chided himself for his foolishness. Sergeant Roberts of the Royal Engineers snorted in disgust. 'Come on you two dim sods. I see'd worse at Dunkirk. Roll the poor bugger onto the stretcher. NO!...' He gave a startled cry. 'Don't try ter lift 'im. 'E'll fall apart if yer do. 'E'se that rotten. Roll 'im, like I says.'

The second sapper broke away to vomit – the sergeant took his place and three pairs of hands lifted and rolled the body onto the stretcher. As it turned onto the canvas base there is a noise of escaping gases and a young sapper passed out in dead faint. Titch laughed – not that they could hear him.

The RAMC corporal soon got the sapper on his feet and the two young chaps made light work of carrying what was left of Titch. Like I say, 'He was only five foot two with his boots on.' A rough blanket covered the body from head to toe. The five with their sodden grisly load picked their way through the minefield on the return journey. Titch was compelled to float along invisibly at the side of the stretcher.

There was an army ambulance waiting at the top of the Lifeboat ramp. The stretcher was pushed inside and the door slammed shut. Not a word was said by any of them – too relieved to be rid of their burden Titch supposed; he didn't blame them; it wasn't a nice job. The ambulance ground its way up the hill passing tank traps, barbed wire entanglements and houses fortified and empty except for helmeted troops. Each house was pitted with rifle slits like grim sterile lips – civilians were nowhere to be seen; all evacuated to places away from the threatened beaches.

Two Army medicos examined the body, or what was left of it. A young captain and a middle-aged major. 'No Identity Discs old man? Odd. I thought all the chaps are supposed to wear them.' It was the younger of the two who spoke; the captain. Titch was standing, hovering really, hovering close by, within an inch of his body, watching and wondering. 'Will it always be the same?' he wondered. 'My body is like a shadow. I can't shake it off.' Such were the rear gunner's thoughts as the doctors divested the corpse of its outer clothing.

'Perhaps the cord rotted and the wretched things got lost. Dog Tags, the Yanks call them.' The second doctor replied. He was an older man; medal ribbons on the breast of his battledress blouse hanging on a peg showed him to be a veteran of the Great War. The younger man, the captain, looked puzzled. 'How odd. Dog Tags. An apt name really. Worn round the neck, I mean. Never really thought of it before, must remember. Dog Tags?' He said the last in almost a whisper as he struggled with the buttons of Titch's battle dress. The older man grunted and carried on with the grisly task of trying to identify the body.

Titch wanted to tell them that his ID discs' cord broke as he was showering before take off. He had placed them on the hook of the shower door and had forgotten them – they were probably still there.

'Not a sausage to tell us who he is or where he

comes from. I thought he might have a letter or something that would help.' The captain dropped Titch's soiled battledress onto the floor.

'Of course there is nothing you stupid twerp. Don't we always empty our pockets before take off so that Jerry doesn't know where we belong?' Titch sighed his disbelief but his words fell on deaf ears. 'I should know better, but I'll learn. They say we are dead a long time, I wonder?' Titch smiled grimly.

'List him as "UNKNOWN". And death from drowning after a head injury. There are no signs of gunshot wounds. Probably knocked unconscious when the plane hit the water. That should suffice for the records. Cover the poor blighter and let's get back to the mess for a cuppa before sick parade.' It was the older man who spoke. The captain made a note on a clipboard then covered the corpse with a sheet.

Surprising how quickly the army can arrange things when they have to. The nearest RAF station was informed and a burial party, chaplain and all, were on the scene in double quick time. Titch watched as his body was crated, just a plain white wood coffin much like a packing case, draped in the RAF Ensign and with due ceremony, a volley of shots, a discordant Last Post blown by a pimple-faced young airman bugler and the earthly remains of Flight Sergeant Rupert Montgomery Wilkins were committed to the chalky soil of Kent in the churchyard of St Peter's Church in Broadstairs. Titch could see the little flint stoned church from where he hovered over his coffin.

After the first sods were dropped with a hollow thump on the coffin lid the funeral party left. The RAF Chaplain lingered talking to the local Rector.

'Has the chap a name? For the Parish Register you understand.' It was the Rector who spoke.

'No. No identification I'm afraid. Just a Flight Sergeant. An Air Gunner. RAF of course. Got a DFM too, poor devil.'

Titch looked at the RAF Padre. Again he wanted to explain about his Dog Tags.

'DFM? I don't quite understand?' The old Rector looked nonplussed – Titch wanted to kick him. He was a tall skinny character with long thin white hair, as white as the grubby surplice he wore, and a pointed red nose that had a dew drop suspended from the end of it. Surely everyone knew what a DFM was – or did they? The RAF Chaplain explained. 'The Distinguished Flying Medal. He must have put up a good show at some time. The ribbon was on his battledress beneath his Air Gunner's brevet. They are both buried with him.'

'I say. How sad… And you say he was in a terrible state when they found him. His body I mean. Burnt was it?'

'No. Poor devil. He was washed up on the beach. Been in the water some days apparently. The gulls made a havoc of his face, poor chap. Completely unrecognisable, or so the Medical Officer informed me.'

'How ghastly.' The Rector paused and wiped a dew drop from the end of his nose with a none-too-clean handkerchief. 'What about his people.

Will they be informed?'

The padre paused and looked at his colleague. 'Just that awful telegram. He will be another "Missing. Believed Killed in Action", poor chap. Later, when the war is over he will be registered. "No Known Grave". Probably have his name carved in stone somewhere. Damned sad.'

'They'll be wasting their time there,' Titch smiled at the thought. 'Mary is the only one who cares, and Keith of course, but he's gone for a Burton too, like me. Mary's on the Squadron. She'll be the first to know, bless her.' He grunted a short laugh, 'It'll give the old Adj a jolt when he reads "No next of kin" on my records.' The thought of his name being carved in stone somewhere tickled him. 'Titch Wilkins immortalised in stone. Bloody marvellous.' He threw back his head and laughed.

'Then what must I enter in the Register, do you think?' The old Rector was insistent on getting his records right. The Padre thought for a moment. 'An unknown RAF Flight Sergeant. Air Gunner. And do mention the DFM there's a good chap. Damn it, he has earned it.'

'Of course.'

They began to move away – Titch called out. 'Thanks Padre!' But the reverend did not hear him – Titch watched as the pair disappeared through the little lych-gate that he knew led to the Rectory. Titch remembered he had tea there at a church fête. The time he was convalescing; strawberries and cream it was, and sticky buns and burpy lemonade. He recalled he had been asked to sing and was given a half-crown by the local squire. But that was a long time ago – not that long really when he thought about it.

An old sexton appeared and began piling the soil onto the coffin, each spadeful sounding loud on the hot afternoon air as it landed on the pine lid. The old man was bent and worn with toil, but worked away and did not upset Titch's recollections. It seemed it was all he had to do now; think. Think about his life and all he had done, or had not done. Perhaps that's what it is all about.

Titch looked about him. He was surprised to see figures standing and sitting around like him. A dozen or more close by, others sparsely scattered and stretching into the distance; some in clothing from a forgotten era. A few were quite close to him, just feet away. Most seemed lost in thought, others, those that were close to each other, chatted quietly. Titch wondered. Perhaps?

The young rear gunner looked about at his neighbours; they were a mixed bunch and for the most part seemed content with their own thoughts. Titch's mind cleared; he found his thoughts sinking inwards. He watched lazily the old sexton piling soil on his coffin and allowed his mind to drift into hidden recesses of memory, surprised at discovering his earliest experiences. Strange? As strange as recalling clearly the words his long-dead mother had spoken as he suckled her breast. Experiences of his very early life, even the day he was born. Titch's recollections were as if it was all just yesterday.

Chapter Two

Christmas Day of 1916 was cold; the mantle of snow was deep, making the dark dingy streets of Wandsworth take on a picture of an exquisite fairyland; in reality they were dreary in the extreme. A pale sun was doing its best to pierce the grey clouds – the early morning scene had a purity broken only by the track of a cart, and a steaming pile of horse turds deposited there by the milkman's pony just moments before. The pile showed black – the steam, grey against virgin snow. Under the beguiling disguise the inner suburb of South London stretched for narrow street after narrow street – mile after mile; each mean row of houses a mirror image of the other.

The winter of 1916-17 was the worst recorded so far that century. From early November rain had fallen almost daily – the countrysides of war-weary England and Europe were a morass of boot- and hoof-trodden mud – wheel ruts were rivers of ooze; Allied and German trenches on the Western Front were continually flooded. No-Man's Land was a sea of flooded shell holes and drowning mud, filled with torn and broken bodies of men and horses; conditions for the troops on both sides of the battle lines in Flanders were appalling.

In December it froze – hard. Ridges of frozen solid ruts twisted ankles and bruised feet already covered with chilblains that itched, broke and festered. Swollen fingers cracked and oozed pus in tattered woollen gloves. Soldiers' hands were so inflamed and sore they could hardly hold a rifle. Frost bite was a common condition among the front line troops already worn down with the fighting, malnutrition and the privations of trench warfare. In mid-month it snowed to add further misery. Men on both sides died where they stood at their posts – frozen with their weapons in their hands.

For British soldiers Christmas Day in the Flanders' trenches was celebrated with tins of 'Bully Beef' and ubiquitous army biscuits washed down with weak unsweetened tea, and a tot of rum if the troops were lucky. There was no truce as had happened earlier on in the war. The High Commands of both sides did not want their soldiers to fraternise with the enemy – it was war; that entailed hate to be effective.

Civilians – German, Belgian, French and British suffered only marginally less than their sons, husbands and brothers in France. They froze over their miserable little smoky fires of low-grade coal, when they could get it. The poor creatures sniffed and coughed – men cursed, women wept and children cried. Food rationing was severe on both sides – German U-Boats were sinking Allied shipping daily; food was not getting to the British ports and farms could not produce enough to feed the millions of hungry mouths. The very young and the elderly died of the cold and starvation. Politicians snug in their warm club rooms urged their people to work

36

harder – to make further sacrifices; their soldiers and sailors, to fight harder to bring victory, and the casualty lists from The Front grew longer. Then there were the Zeppelins and Botha bombers that bombed Britain indiscriminately night after night; they spared neither soldier nor civilians, women nor children in their quest to terrorise the nation into surrender.

Into all this cold, confusion, heartache, hunger and loss Titch Wilkins was born; in the early hours of Christmas Day 1916. He was an under-sized sickly child.

'Poor little sod. 'E'll be dead in a mumf,' was the comment of the cockney mid-wife that attended the birth. Titch was hardly the most exciting Christmas present for the young mother. But she was wrong – the mid-wife I mean. Titch survived and was baptised into the Anglican Church and given the name Rupert Montgomery Wilkins. He discovered why years later. His birth certificate stated 'Illegitimate'. Father 'Unknown'.

Titch was five before he realised he had never had a birthday. The celebration of Christ's birthday always outshone his own – from the beginning it seemed his life was going to be one where he missed out.

Titch Wilkins grew up believing his mother was a widow – a war widow; Titch believed his father had been killed in The Great War.

'My dad was killed in the war. In the Navy I 'fink.' It was the reply he gave to enquiries. He didn't know where he got the notion for his mother died when he was only three; a victim of poverty and the influenza epidemic of 1919.

She had been a beautiful woman, a girl really –
only 22 when she died. Four years of poverty,
worry and neglect had stripped her of her
youthful beauty; disease and near starvation took
every vestige of youth from her. She was little
more than skin and bone when a neighbour
heard her baby's cries and found the mother
dead – a shrivelled old lady at 22.

At little more than three years old Titch Wilkins
was an orphan – orphaned in 1919 when Britain
and the world was recovering from The Great
War. When people all over Europe were dying of
influenza – dying like they never died during the
War. Twenty-six million people – from the Urals
of Bolshevik Russia to the west coast of Ireland;
even onto America. Influenza took them by the
thousands, high born or low – rich or poor, but
especially the poor; their resistance was low after
years of near starvation.

Titch was an orphan with no family to care for
him. Mother and child had lived in one dingy
room above a coal merchant's office overlooking
a railway siding and a coal dump. The mother
had been rejected by her family before Titch was
born – he discovered that later, too.

The boy's earliest memories were of puffing
shunting engines and the reek of coal smoke. The
first taste he could recall was of marmalade tart
– the sickly white pastry flecked with coal dust
that gritted on his baby teeth. You see, Titch and
his mother were poor – desperately poor. His
mother was unable to find employment because
of him. What little money she had earned was by
taking in sewing for people as poor as herself. So

poor that when she died she was buried in a pauper's grave; her son was admitted to the Wandsworth Parish Work House.

At hardly four years of age, Titch was not the youngest resident of the Parish Charity House – because of the numbers of younger children he was considered old enough to be placed in 'The Men's Ward'.

'Shove 'im in wiv the blokes. 'E'll sort 'is self out there.' The attendant in charge was concerned with filling vacant beds rather than caring for children. Six or seven little boys lived with what Titch remembered were very old men who slathered, smoked, coughed and spat great revolting globs of phlegm. They drooled over him and stole the meagre food that was placed in front of him twice a day. They pinched his cheek or tickled his chin with hard gnarled old hands with filthy broken finger nails. Each day was the same – especially the food. A nauseous wad of near solid glutinous cold porridge – a mug of luke-warm tea and a thick slice of unbuttered bread in the morning; an equally nauseous dollop of cold pease pudding and fatty bacon for the evening meal. His protests of 'I don't like it' fell on deaf ears – except those of his hungry neighbours who snatched away his plate before he could change his mind. 'Give it 'ere kid.' If he hesitated a painful pinch soon got a response. Titch soon learned to eat it, though he was never to like it.

Other memories were of rough ill-fitting clothes that chafed his baby skin enough to draw blood and a long, cold dormitory. Long dark, cold walks to the foul smelling lavatory – a urine soiled seat and filth encrusted pan, and the hard old newspaper supplied for toilet paper. Disgusting blobs of sputum unseen underfoot were stepped on with small bare feet, and the sight of unshaven grey faces that leered and grinned at him through broken decayed teeth as he groped his way to his cold bed.

'Come 'ere kid. Let an ol' bloke warm yer' was an oft heard remark that sped his small feet to the shelter of his hard mattress. Titch's audio recollections were of coughing, spitting and the trumpeting of old anuses as the inmates broke wind in chorus. His sense of smell offended by nauseous odours of putrefying bowels, foul beer and tobacco-sodden breath, and heavy sweat reeking air thick with stale cigarette and pipe tobacco smoke.

Life was cold, hard, loveless and very lonely. Most nights Titch cried himself to sleep in a cold hard bed – often to receive a cuff across his head in an attempt to silence him. He learned to weep soundlessly. He woke to a cold water wash and the frightening figure of a work house attendant towering over him searching his hair and private parts for lice. He got them once – lice I mean. His head was shaved and he was bathed in a tub of near boiling water laced with carbolic acid. It got into every orifice of his small, infant body. Anus, penis, mouth, ears but worst of all; his eyes. He screamed blue murder and got a hiding that made him scream the more.

Threats of, "old still yer little bleeder or I'll murder yer!' did little to comfort him. But he healed and learned not to cry, or not to be seen crying. With the other children he had tasks to perform each day like emptying spittoons, picking up litter and taking messages – after all it was a Work House and charity. The inmates, young and old, were constantly reminded of that.

It lasted weeks, perhaps months; it seemed endless to the child, until some compassionate soul decided to send him to an orphanage, 'The Swaffield Anglican Boy's School' at Annerly, a south east suburb of London in sight of the towers of The Crystal Palace. The school seemed to him to be in the country – it had a farm where the older boys in the senior school milked cows and tended chickens and other farm animals; or worked in the extensive vegetable gardens. There was what appeared to Titch then to be a huge orchard laden with fruit. Wherever it was, after the Work House, it was heaven. For the first time in months Titch was warm and able to eat and enjoy the food he received. Love, what little there was, was spread thinly over the many children impartially.

Titch was one of fifty or so in the Infant School under the strict care of a Matron Story. A tall kindly old lady in a starched dark blue dress and a stiff white pinafore that crackled when she moved. She hobbled about on what must have been very sore feet encased in brightly polished high, tightly-laced, soft leather boots that bulged from what Titch later realised were a crop of bunions. She wore gold rimmed pince-nez glasses on the top of a button nose and her hair was covered with a lace mob cap.

With all her kindness Matron Story ruled her brood with a 'rod of iron', or a hard right hand

41

anyway. She often had a bunch of keys concealed in the palm of her hand that added weight to her persuasion; many a therapeutic cuff Titch got from it.

'Watch it young Robert.' The lady's counselling received an instant response. She had an equally no nonsense group of uniformed nurses to help her – all with equally heavy hands, right or left, they dealt out justice with equal partiality.

The children slept in a great long dormitory with whitewashed walls and white cracked ceilings. Titch remembered that well. He would lay in his hard little bed and look up at the ceiling and make pictures from the cracks in the plaster 15ft above his young head. Fantastic shapes evolved and he often fell asleep to dream of the dragons or birds, or perhaps ships, that he would conjure up from the labyrinth of cracks in the dormitory ceiling. There was a corner where if he looked hard and twisted his head around he could make out his mother's face. She was smiling – those nights he slept well – singing softly a lullaby; the only one he ever remembered his mother singing. There were other times when for some reason he couldn't find her among the twisted cracks – he was convinced then that she had left him – convinced that she did not love him; those nights he cried himself to sleep, but silently.

It was a happiness of sorts – happier than being in the Work House. Titch was perhaps the smallest child there, though not the youngest. His name Rupert dubbed him 'The Little Bear', Rupert Bear; after the comic strip character of the day. He didn't mind at first, but as he grew he hated the name and was relieved when he was called 'Titch'; the name stuck. He was always the smallest of any group he was with. Wherever he has been they called him Titch. Titch Wilkins – he almost forgot the Rupert Montgomery.

There was little enough to do 'hovering' as he was over his grave. Not that he was ever bored. Like I said, 'He felt nothing'. It was interesting for him to relive his life. For reasons he could not explain he can somehow see times that he couldn't possibly remember; like the dingy streets of Wandsworth and the terrible winter that he was born into. There was time to look about him too – the little church yard of St Peters was well inhabited with spirits similar to himself; all 'hovering' as it were over their graves. He saw a young policeman, and several men who looked like fishermen. An old lady and a young girl, and a tiny baby that seemed to sleep all the time. There was a portly old gent, and an elderly military looking man dressed in a Norfolk jacket and corduroy breeches, and wearing a monocle in his right eye. There was a little communication – Titch could see though not hear that people did talk to each other. Did I say people? They looked like people. Anyway there seems to be some sort of chatter going on, but nothing in his direction.

About a month after his burial, it was raining; two men rugged up against the rain and the south west wind that was blowing up the English Channel stopped and looked at the pile of chalky dirt that covered Titch.

'This is it 'Arry. Seven 'undred and ninety four.

43

On a red painted peg.' The taller one looked at the wooden peg driven into the ground at the foot of the grave. 'Must be 'im. The grave is new.'

'Yeah. 'Ere 'ammer the bloody f'ing in and let's get out of the bloody rain.'

The man called Harry produced a wooden cross and his companion a large hammer – with six blows the cross was hammered into the spot where they believed Titch's head to be. If Titch thought they would have heard him he would have shouted 'Ouch!' just to see the look on their faces, but of course he didn't. The two stood back a pace to admire their work.

'That'll do n'til they fix a permanent 'ead stone. Poor bastard. One o'them rear gunners I expect. Tail end Charlies they calls 'em. Wash 'em out of their turrets with 'oses they tells me. They never last long in that job. Poor sods.'

'Yeah. Wonder w'ot 'e got the DFM for. They don't give them away fer nuffin' y'now... I knowed a bloke. 'Is son got one. 'E was...'

They passed out of earshot and disappeared around the side of the church. Titch looked at their handy work. It was a nicely-made cross painted white and in black letters were

AN UNKNOWN RAF FLIGHT SERGEANT. AIR GUNNER. DFM

'So that's me. Unknown – I might have known it.' Titch sighed. If he had been able to he would have cried. A soft voice, hardly more than a whisper made him turn. It was an old lady in the clothes of seventy years before. Titch had seen her sitting quietly on her grave but she seemed to ignore him.

44

'Even if you could it is pointless crying. In a little while we are all unknown here. People soon forget and one's grave becomes neglected. But life, I mean death, goes on.'

Titch looked across at her. She was very old, or had been in her life – she had a nice old face and was sure she was only trying to be friendly.

'How long have you been here then, Madam?' He felt he ought to call her Madam; she was sitting on a very ornate tombstone what must have cost a few bob.

'Sixty-six years, come Michaelmas. See, the date is on the stone.'

After all the usual language of where she had lived and what she had been, Titch saw

Elizabeth Mary Burnet. Spinster. Born 1802. Died 1883.

'Eighty-one you were?...You had a good innings if you don't mind me saying so. You must have seen a lot happen in your day.'

'I suppose I did one way or another. Spent most of my life in Africa. The Cape. Went there as a young girl to marry a missionary. Poor chap was speared by the Zulu before I arrived. Stayed on and became a teacher in the Colony. Wonderful times they were.'

She talked on for some minutes about her life in The Cape as she called it. About the Zulu wars, and the balls and parties she went to with the officers in the garrison.

'I had hoped to marry a young captain of "The Garrison Artillery" until I discovered he had a wife in England. The cad. He was a disgrace to the Queen's uniform. The talk of the colony he

45

was for a while. I came home in sixty-three and lived in the Rectory here. A nephew of mine, my sister's son, was the Rector then. The Reverend St John Barrington-James. He is buried over in the far corner near the church. A charming man he was then. I kept house for him until I was knocked over by the weekly stage coach that used to call here on the London run. Got kicked by one of the horses and a wheel ran over me. I was as dead as mutton when they picked me up. But like you say. I had a good innings.' She paused a moment and Titch saw her smile. 'I like that phrase. A good innings. A cricket term isn't it? Yes... A good innings ... I suppose I had that. It was indeed exciting one way and another.'

It was dark by the time she had finished her story – the rain had stopped but the wind was still blowing. It was going to be a rough night. Titch thought of the chaps on the squadron – surely there would be no 'Op' tonight. RAF Bomber crews and German civilians could sleep soundly tonight; soundly and safe. For tonight.

He was wrong – it was dark and overcast and the wind was still whipping the trees in the church yard, but he heard the engines as the bomber stream headed east. 'Lucky bastards... What am I saying? I could get killed.' He laughed, 'Stupid bugger. You're already dead.'

He listened until the last bomber passed out of earshot and only the wind sounded around him and thought... "Old 'Bomber" Harris is sending his blokes out again, poor buggers. Out to face the darkness and fear – what a life; no time for reminiscing up there. And yet we had our good times – if only we were not shot at, and people didn't get hurt; civilians, I mean. Well women and children anyway.'

Things took a turn for the worse for Titch in 1924. It was a good year for Britain, though – the nation was recovering from the war; shops were full of goods and people were happy. Wimbledon was on again and England was winning the Cricket Test Matches. Young women – 'Flappers'; they called them, were wearing shorter skirts and had their hair 'bobbed', and the Charleston was the dancing craze. There was even an absurd rumour that 'Talking Pictures' were being invented, but it was a bad time for Titch.

He graduated from the Infants School to 'Kate's House'. The name given to the intermediate school that housed the boys between the Infants and Senior school. Here he came under the dubious care of the Ms's Palmer and Curtis. The two ladies who he was later sure were more than a little fond of the gin bottle, and he suspected enjoyed a rather perverted existence where small boys were the unwitting pawns.

Of the two, Sister Curtis, she insisted on the title, was the one the boys most feared. She was a tall thin individual with an elongated face, protruding front teeth, a beak of a nose and sunken eyes that seemed to the small boys in her charge to shine like those of a snake. A starched white cap topped a mop of mouse-coloured hair streaked with dirty grey. A severe uniform of a black dress and a white pinafore reaching down to heavy black shoes protruding at an angle of

47

45°. A bunch of keys hung from a leather belt – a two foot length of cane held in hands with inordinately long claw-like fingers completed the picture of this witch-like female.

Her partner Sister Palmer was almost the exact opposite. Small and plump with a round face and watery blue eyes, and a red button nose that always needed a wipe. A thing she did by wiping her arm across it with a sniff. The poor woman was always close to tears – she followed the lead of her colleague in all things, from beatings to the perversions and cruelties against Titch and his fellow inmates. Her uniform was a light blue dress covered with a white regulation pinafore, but she wore a veil as a head covering. Even in the coldest weather Sister Palmer's arms were bare revealing well-muscled forearms and small muscular hands – she too had a length of cane that she used with abandon on small buttocks equal to her tall partner.

Again there were 50 or so boys separated into two dormitories. The firm of Palmer and Curtis enforced a discipline by recruiting bullies in the group to keep order by sheer brutality, while they did the minimum of supervision for their meagre wages. They each had a room, really a partitioned cubicle, at the end of the two dormitories. The walls were of match board and served only as a visual screen – every sound penetrated, from their snores to the drunken laughter and the noise of their perversions that were fortunately beyond the boys' understanding. The moans and grunts that emanated from those women during their orgies of gin or sin were frightening for a seven-year-old.

On occasion, all would be woken and made to form a line and remove their cotton nightshirts. Fifty or sixty little boys would stand shivering while the two women walked past them stopping occasionally and lifting the tiny penis of a boy on the tip of the cane they always carried. There would be ribald comments and gin-sodden giggles the children failed to understand, but all felt the cold and embarrassment of the exercise.

After the second time Titch had personally been subjected to such close scrutiny he was avoided. The first 'inspection' caused him to urinate over Ms Palmer who was gazing intently as his small organ. It was erect because of the need to urinate – it protruded gamely like an undersize hat peg. The worthy sister held it delicately on the end of her cane; she laughed drunkenly. It was an accident – Titch was suffering from cold and shame, and a desperate physical need; his bladder sphincter rebelled at the combination of the three. 'Ow! You 'orrible little sod. You pissed on me! Look! The little shit pissed on me!' Her voice was loud with indignation – she was soaked before she could leap clear yelling her obscenities of disgust and alarm. Titch got a beating across his back and buttocks for the offence, as he did on the second occasion. The second was deliberate – neither women risked a third wetting, ever.

There followed three years of this and other perversions. Nights when the boy's childish slumbers were shattered by the women's drunken screams or fighting. Nights when even more was happening than Titch's young mind could comprehend. There were dark cold nights when out of sheer

49

perversity the whole dormitory were made to get out of bed and stand shivering for an hour or more beside their beds. Often their guardians would fall into a drunken sleep forgetting about them – the more timid would fall asleep on their feet. The braver souls risked the women's wrath and slipped between their cold sheets with no little dread.

Titch learned that if he coughed during the night he was hastily moved to the far end of the dormitory – away from the ladies' sleeping quarters.

'Get that barking dog away from me. Can't sleep a wink with him yapping all night!'

Titch's coughing was louder and more prolonged than his friends' whose coughs were genuine. The further he was away from those ogres the better.

The other side of life was more pleasant. They all attended school and took the usual three 'Rs'. Titch enjoyed that part of the routine, perhaps because he was free for a few hours from the attentions of 'The Witches' as the boys called their guardians. Free from the women's attention, but not of their bullies who carried on their activities in the school yard, and reported any 'unkind' remarks made. Their naked parades revealed many a little bum crisscrossed with bruises from the ever-handy canes.

During the years at 'Kate's' Titch formed a friendship with Freddy Silk. He had never had a friend before, not a real friend – Freddy and he were great chums. They first became aware of each other while they waited outside Sister

Curtis' cubicle door for a dose of whacks with that ever-present length of bamboo. The sin that Titch had committed was trivial enough, but Freddy was accused of taking a pinch of sugar from the ladies' sugar bowl when he was given the task of clearing the 'Staff' table. Whoever the thief was, and Freddy claimed it was not him, he left the clear marks of a grubby finger and thumb indented in the sugar. Freddy proclaimed his innocence and got an extra whack.

'For lying. You 'orrible little beast.'

He got another six when the woman's hand got within range of Freddie's teeth. The yell of pain from the tormentor was a joy to hear.

'You 'orrible little sod. Me 'and is bleedin'.' And it was; Titch was delighted. But poor Freddy – his little bum was black and blue for days, and throughout it all he did not cry. Not in front of Sister Curtis anyway – later, well he was only eight years old. A lad after Titch's heart was Freddy; they were pals from that day.

Freddy was a little older than Titch, and bigger, but utterly useless in a fight, at first. You see, Freddy had scruples. He never hit a man when he was down. He shaped up to an opponent boxer style, and always fought according to the rules. He got licked every time. Not Titch – fists, boots, elbows, nails, teeth and head butts. He was small – he had to fight dirty to survive, and survive he did. Bullies knew if they fought Titch Wilkins it was all or nothing. Freddy was a good pupil – between them they stood up to the bullies then and later; two against two – on some occasions three and four against them; they were an unbeatable combination.

One of the perquisites of a friendship with Freddy was that he had a grandfather and a lovely old grandmother. This old couple would visit Freddy occasionally and bring him all sorts of goodies. Sticky sweets and buns, fruit and fizzy lemonade; the boys shared it all. Other boys had visitors too and Titch would sit with them afterwards as they gorged themselves on the parcels – he would accept gratefully an apple core no matter how nibbled, or perhaps a sweet or a segment of an orange, all grudgingly given. Not with Freddy – what was his was Titch's; what little Titch got through dint of his wits he shared equally with Freddy. Did any boy have such a chum? Titch's life was bliss when he was allowed to join his friend when his grandparents visited one Christmas Day and received his very own Christmas present; a 'Boys Own Annual'.

'Ooo! Tar ... I ain't never 'ad a birf'day present before.'

The old couple were open-mouthed. 'Birf'day! Is it yer birf'day young Titch.'

'Yes Mrs Silk. Sorry.'

'Sorry, be buggered. 'Ere lad.' The grandfather dug into his trouser pocket and produced a silver sixpence. ''Ere's a tanner... If we'd 'er known I would'a made it a bob. But I 'ad a short week this week. Eh, muvver?' he looked sadly at his old wife; a road labourer's wages were poor and bad weather had stopped them working.

Titch accepted the sixpenny piece – wealth indeed; wealth that he secreted in the knotted corner of his dirty handkerchief. That sixpence

52

was transferred from dirty handkerchief to clean for weeks until it was stolen from him in a fight – someone was kind enough to hold his coat.

The British Broadcasting Corporation made their first broadcast from Savoy Hill on New Years' Day, 1927. That year, Al Jolson starred in Holly-wood's first talking picture; the song 'Sonny Boy' became popular. Malcolm Campbell travelled at 174mph in his car 'Bluebird' to set the world land speed record, and 3,000 Japanese were killed in a giant tidal wave. Charles Lindbergh made the first solo flight across the Atlantic in May, the same month Freddy Silk and Titch, and a dozen other boys, left the tender care of 'The Witches' for the world of 'The Senior' boys. Titch did not know it; it was from the frying pan into the fire.

The pair managed to stay together and were immediately detailed to work on the poultry section of the farm – Titch because he was so small; Freddy because he bribed the senior boy who was giving the orders with an orange from the latest visit of his grandparents. It was a 'blood orange' too – these were especially favoured by the boys.

'I'll 'ave anuvver next visitin' day young Fred or it's the pig pen fer you. Bo'fe of yer!' The monitor's threat was no bluff.

It was spring so rising at 5.30 in the morning was no hardship – winter was another story. They made their beds and swept the floor around their bed space. A cold wash and they all trooped to do their various pre-school chores. Some to the kitchens others to the laundry, bake house, boiler room and, of course, the farm.

Farm boys ran in ranks of four, about 20 of them, the half mile to the farm. Milkers, fodder boys, pig keepers and poultry boys – a quick change into rubber boots and a brown overall, all much too big for Titch, and into the work. They soon learned their roles under the heavy hand of the monitors, bigger older boys who wielded a power almost of life and death over them; or so it seemed.

The chicken houses were mobile sheds set in a field – the birds had to be let out by opening the little doors at the ends of the sheds – feed and water carried to them; eggs collected were brought back to the Farm Manager, an obese individual, a Mr Hardbutler. And woe betide any boy caught eating raw eggs. 'Fatty Arbuckle' the boys called this petty tyrant behind his back – he had a very heavy hand, and a heavier boot. All work to be done in an hour – then back to the school, at the double, to wash and have breakfast of porridge, bread and dripping with unsweetened tea; evenings, the chores repeated.

Eight thirty every morning saw them 'On Parade' in their four 'Houses'. Each House named after a former headmaster of the school. Freddy and Titch were in 'Thrower House', named after the Rev Thomas Thrower BA deceased. The House colours were red and green and showed in the ties they wore for school and church.

The boys stood in four ranks and dressed off and numbered military style to the commands of the uniformed school officer of the day. There were six or seven of these gentlemen who worked in shifts looking after the monitors who ruled the lesser fry. The men were all old soldiers who believed suffering built character, they made the boys suffer. Everything was done by numbers, and at the double; except the school parade morning and afternoon. This was done at 'The quick march' behind the school band. It was a mile to the classrooms and the boys marched there every day rain or shine with the school band playing and every boy in step, or else; three Sunday church services were heralded in the like manner. Boys answered to the ever-ready cane for any infringement of the many rules – they all began with, 'Boys will not...' Punishment was swift and severe if they did.

The boys were worked from 5.30 in the morning to 8 o'clock at night – 9 o'clock when hay making was in progress. An hour's break at midday for a rough but wholesome lunch, and an hour after tea always of bread and jam – on Sundays a slice of slab fruitcake was additional.

Boys knew the day of the week by the lunch menu. Tuesday was always stew – generally mutton stew, with more stew than mutton. Friday it was fishcake and peas – peas so hard they were taken by the boys and used in improvised peashooters. Sunday was roast meat with vegetables and a dessert of stewed fruit and custard. Wholesome food no doubt but hardly an epicure's delight served as it was on bare tables by the dining room boys whose perquisite was to scrape the cooking dishes – it explained why these lads were plumper than their friends, and why the jobs were well sought after.

The lad's clothing was uniform. Rough, hard-wearing Norfolk style jackets and long shorts made of a coarse yarn chaffed the backs of legs. Heavy boots pinched and blistered feet. Rough woollen stockings chaffed ankles. Eton-type collars were worn on Sundays for church – these were unpopular; the stiff starched linen wore necks to bleeding point. Winters were dreaded. There was little heating of the common room and none in the dormitories and toilets. Water pipes froze – feet, fingers and toes itched and festered with chilblains. Hands, wrists and ankles were raw with chapped skin lesions. Colds were endemic with the effects of catarrh lingering for weeks. Catarrh so revolting the weekly handkerchief allowed per boy was nauseating sodden slime in hours. All this was suffered by children who knew no difference – who knew deep in their subconscious that the alternative to this charity was living under London bridges or in open parks.

Monitors were a terror. Chosen for their size and ability to intimidate smaller boys; they became bullies. Certainly they maintained discipline of sorts, but through terror.

What Titch Wilkins lacked in size, he developed in cunning. He had to survive, and he did. It became a battle of wits to outsmart the bullies – either that or a showdown in the dormitory at night.

The music teacher and choir master-cum-organist discovered Titch had a good voice. Titch found himself in the school choir – in a year he was the leading chorister, the master's favourite; until the man was dismissed for an offence that puzzled his pupil. But that's another story.

Titch loved the singing. Easter, Christmas and Harvest Festivals were a joy for the boy, anthems and carols nectar for his musical palate, though he was never taught music. He hardly knew the difference between a crotchet and a quaver, but he could descant on the high notes, and hold them for as long as required. A perquisite was it got him off farm chores every Friday for choir practice, and all day Sundays when he was freed from the filth of the hen houses and the bullying monitors.

But there was more to orphanage life than singing – behind the scenes, in the dormitories, lavatories and bathrooms it was every boy for himself, and heaven help the weak. This was where the bullies reigned supreme – where they really got down to their bastardry. Beatings were frequent, and intimidation rampant. In cold weather older boys made their smaller juniors sit on the hard cold wooden segments on the toilet pedestals to warm them before their tormentor could compose himself in greater comfort, but that was a minor humiliation; small boys were made to commit greater indignities that shocked and revolted them. Titch's turn came early in his move to the senior school. On a warm summer night after lights-out he was ordered to masturbate an older boy. The beneficiary was a tall solid overweight youth of 14. Dull of wit and flabby, but a notorious bully. The act was demonstrated enthusiastically before an audience of ten or more; Titch was held by a monitor and compelled to watch.

'Go on. Watch or I'll smash yer face in.' Titch

looked at the pimply faced 14 year old holding his head a foot from the genitals of the senior monitor. Titch vomited his disgust to the glee of the older boys. He ran from the dorm retching and stumbling to wash himself. On his return, pale, sick and frightened, he fell over a fire bucket full of sand. His damp hand reached out to save himself and landed palm down in the grit. Titch got to his feet and wiped his hand perfunctorily on his night shirt.

In the few dark paces back to the dormitory he felt the grit between his fingers and thought nothing of it. He had no choice but return to the bed of the bully and perform – he did, with the vigour demonstrated earlier, albeit he had his eyes tight shut and he held his breath throughout the exercise.

'Do it proper or we'll 'ave yer 'ere all bloody night doin' it ter all of us.'

There was laughter from the group and a scream from the bed but Titch held on – the bully was sore for a week. Titch was never asked to perform again – the beating he got from the bully was worth the discomfort caused to the perpetrator. Besides, the young was a flabby individual and what with the pain in his private regions and his poor physical condition his punches were feeble and relatively painless, but Titch yelled appropriately so honour was satisfied.

This and other beatings inspired Titch and Freddy to retaliate. A group of younger boys led by the pair made a solemn pact to stick together and avenge any one of them who was bullied or beaten. They did, on several occasions, with bloody noses on both sides, until the bullies steered a wide course of the determined and united little group – surprising what six small boys with boots too heavy for their feet, could do to an overbearing bully.

In the two years Freddy and Titch were together in their senior school they established themselves as a formidable pair, and remained so until the diphtheria epidemic. Both boys went down with it – Titch Wilkins was just 12 years old; just one of many sufferers.

Titch did not learn that Freddy had died until he returned from hospital – the boy was devastated; he had lost the only thing he loved, his best friend. Titch prayed hard to the God he had been taught to love, asking to be taken and his friend allowed to be returned to his loving grandparents.

'Please, God. Bring Freddy back. If you want a little bloke take me. Please.' There was no reply to his plea. The morning after the prayer Titch woke to find himself in the dorm of Thrower House, and Freddy still dead. From that day he wondered about God.

What with the illness and Freddy's death, Titch was weak and constantly ailing and did not respond to the treatments offered. He did not know it of course but the school doctor was worried and believed the lad had contracted tuberculosis. He hadn't, but the authorities were not going to take a chance – there had been too many deaths and questions were being asked. Titch was packed off to a home in Broadstairs to convalesce.

There followed the happiest period in the boy's 12 years of life. It was summertime – there was the sea, the sands and lovely rocks to be explored for all the things dear to a boy's heart, and he learned to read. Really read, and understand and enjoy what he was reading. Miss Margaret Cuthberson the home's kindly school teacher took Titch under her wing, seeing, she believed, a lad of true potential. She showed him stories like Robinson Crusoe, Treasure Island, Rob Roy and David Copperfield. Titch learned of the existence of authors like Rider Haggard, Jack London and Mark Twain – a fascinating wonder world opened for Titch at the hands of this talented young teacher. School ceased to be a chore to be endured – the boy devoured the knowledge Miss Cuthberson imparted with relish. Sometimes after school the pair would walk the cliffs and lay on the cropped grass and talk of books and people. As summer waned into autumn afternoons were spent around the small fire in Miss Cuthberson's bed-sitter reading, talking and often toasting muffins on the hot coals.

During that summer and autumn, conversation came easy – even for Titch, and he was afraid of adults; his experience with them hardly endeared him to the species. Margaret Cuthberson was different – she listened. No adult had listened to Titch before; really listened; she did. Titch found himself talking about his mother, the work house, school and Freddy, and ... oh, lots of things. Things that he had never spoken of before.

One rainy afternoon they were toasting muffins when Margaret asked Titch about his father. The lad was distressed when he could tell her nothing; or very little.

''E was killed in the war Miss.' Titch paused and looked at her – she was looking at him – interested; not minding his slum cockney accent.

'I f'ink,' Titch added almost apologetically, and that was about the truth of it. Titch didn't know, but she seemed to understand.

There was a photograph of a young man in the uniform of an officer in the Royal Flying Corps, a good looking fellow – he had pride of place on the sideboard, and there was another of him, smaller, on the mantlepiece above the fire. He was bare headed and leaning nonchalantly on the wing of a bi-plane – pilots wings and a medal ribbon stood out boldly against the dark khaki of his tunic. The Military Cross, Miss Cuthberson said it was.

'Where is 'e now, Miss?'

As soon as Titch said it he sensed he had said the wrong thing. He knew what had happened to him, but he couldn't take his words back.

'Sorry, Miss. I shouldn't 'ave asked.'

Kindly Margaret Cuthberson reached over and touched his hand – she had never done that before and Titch was surprised how soft her hand was, and warm.

'That's alright, Rupert.' She used his real name and somehow it sounded good. 'He was killed you see. Like your father. He was shot down over the enemy lines on The Western Front in 1916. We were engaged to be married.'

She turned away to hide a tear – Titch pretended he hadn't noticed. But he was crying too, silently. For the first time for a long time

61

Titch Wilkins cried and did not hide his tears. Miss Cuthberson wiped her eyes and looked at him – her eyes seemed to melt – she reached out and gathered him in her arms and they wept together. She for the love she had lost – Titch? He wasn't sure what he was crying for. His mother perhaps – or the father he had never known? Or was it for her? Titch felt he understood, in his childish way, the loneliness she felt; he was a little surprised that loneliness was not confined to him.

Smoke from the burning muffin on the brass toasting fork caught their attention and they drew apart. They laughed and while Titch scraped the charred muffin clean, Miss Cuthberson buttered those they had already toasted. It was one of many afternoons they spent together in the autumn of 1929 – quiet, happy times when they would talk and sometimes read to each other. She in her cultured precise English, Titch? Why, he couldn't do better than the cockney English he had learned in the Work House and School. Dropping his 'H's' and generally ending a statement with a question. 'Know wot I mean then?' Both of them knew he was little better than a slum boy. Titch believed later they both knew he was capable of something better. She was very patient – she taught him much, but above all she taught Titch an appreciation of the English language, and a confidence in talking to people. Perhaps more than anything Margaret Cuthberson gave Titch a determination to improve himself, and to be a worthwhile person.

When he timidly said one day that he was 'Only a little bloke', she smiled her answer. 'It really doesn't matter how tall you are, Rupert. What matters is how big you are … inside, I mean. In your heart, and in your mind.' It was one of the many pieces of advice Titch stored in his young memory.

Saint Peter's Church in the town saw Titch briefly in the choir for their harvest festival in the autumn and he sang as he had never sung before, or since, now he came to think of it.

The memory of it flooded Titch's mind – he looked from his grave through the trees to the grey flints of the small parish church. He saw above the church spire the soft blue sky of an English summer. That Sunday of the Harvest Festival it was a rainy autumn day. How long ago? Titch counted the years.

'My God. Only 14, but more than half a life time away. My life time?'

Titch Wilkins sang that day in 1929 for the lady who had done so much for him. Him, Titch Wilkins a kid from the slums, an orphan and a bastard. During the service the boy's eyes were riveted on the trim figure half-hidden behind the pulpit. That he was singing for her she was sure; it was wonderful for them both.

Too soon, Titch was completely well and had to return to Annerly and was unable to re-visit Broadstairs for some years. Miss Cuthberson wrote to him and he had a card from her at Christmas wishing him a Happy Birthday. The boys were forbidden to write letters and he had not even the penny halfpenny for the postage anyway, so Titch never answered her letter. She became for him a glimpse of the life he dreamed of for when he grew up. A dream locked away deep inside him along with the other happy memories of his mother, Freddy Silk and Broadstairs.

These memories were thought provoking for Titch, standing as he was on his grave.

'I suppose life was grim now I come to think about it, but were we all unhappy?' He asked himself the question looking over the graves around him. 'I never thought about it. And I don't suppose the other kids did either. Happiness or sadness? I don't know. It was just life for me and the others. We knew no other life. We were all in the same boat so to speak. Orphans or simply kids abandoned as un-wanted. Lucky to have a roof over our heads and food to eat.' He smiled grimly to himself. 'Sometimes we laughed and sometimes we cried. But we never questioned our lot. It was…' he paused to find the words to express the feelings of a child. 'Whatever it was, it was life.' The thought satisfied him and he dismissed further speculation as futile.

Perhaps if Titch had been asked he might have chosen to be buried in St Peter's Churchyard, but he wasn't – it just happened. He was glad it was this little seaside town where he was washed up; if it had to happen he couldn't have wished for a better place. Titch didn't fancy slopping around in the drink for all eternity, or whatever the time he will be left hovering over this corpse of his. Perhaps till the Day of Judgment that Titch had heard so much about in church – he thought of Keith Gale out there at the bottom of the Channel, but he had Merve and Leo for company, so he won't be so bad.

Chapter Three

The British Prime Minister was Mr Ramsey Mac-Donald – the world depression after the Wall Street crash of 1929 was still a hardship. Unemployed men walked the streets of cities all over Britain, America and Europe. Crippled ex-soldiers sold matches at street corners and groups of them paraded the gutters playing musical instruments hoping to collect enough for a meal, a smoke or a glass of beer; the song 'Buddy, can you spare a dime' became popular and meaningful. Ordinary people of the world worried where the next meal was coming from, and Dame Nellie Melba died. The same year England lost the Test Cricket Series and it poured with rain for the Derby – at Aintree near Liverpool, four horses fell and died on the rain soaked course during the Grand National Steeple Chase, and Titch Wilkins left the cold confines of Swaffield Boys Home for the colder world beyond its gates. On New Year's Day, 1931 our young hero found himself entering the employment field as a 'Lift boy messenger' in Park Lane Mansions, a luxury block of service flats set on London's prestigious Park Lane overlooking Hyde Park.

He was made to attend the interview with his prospective employer in the company of the deputy headmaster, a Reverend William Jones who repeatedly told his charge how lucky he was to be given such a wonderful opportunity to enter the world of 'service'. As the train rumbled through the dreary suburbs of South East London, 14 year-old Titch detected the veiled threat that if he did not perform well at the interview there would be grave consequences for him.

The Reverend Jones sat like a gaunt crow opposite Titch in the grubby third class carriage of the city-bound train – he was smoking his third cigarette since taking his seat by the window. There were just the two of them, but the air in the closed compartment was cold, stuffy and heavy with tobacco smoke. Titch's gaze alternated from the dreary scene of the backs of mean terraced houses of the working class to the pale and pock-marked face of the middle-aged cleric. The man's grey unhealthy pallor contrasted with his dull black clerical attire that showed patches of green aging. Brown rheumy eyes peered at Titch through the thick lenses of his wire-framed spectacles – the thick glass seemed to exaggerate the unhealthy dark shadows and heavy bags under the parson's eyes. The sober-looking man of God had not removed his cleric's black low-crowned bowler hat – tufts of dirty grey hair stood out stiff around large hairy ears. His white parson's collar was soiled – there were food stains on his black clerical shirt – some recent, others long-standing. The man's threadbare overcoat hung unbuttoned over his narrow shoulders – his shoes were down at heel and in sore need of polish; even to the unsophisticated Titch he was an uninspiring figure.

The boy studied the face opposite him as the

train rocked and rumbled over the rails – the lad was fascinated by a wart on the side of the man's hooked nose that had a long bristle right on the end; with every word the cleric uttered, this hair would wave. The holy man drew deep on his cigarette and exhaled a plume of smoke from nicotine-stained lips – his mouth opened to inhale and Titch saw tobacco-stained teeth that, even to the boy's inexperienced eyes had not felt the bristles of a brush for a very long time. The cleric drew again on his cigarette in a deep inhalation – the man's Adam's apple leapt in a convulsion as he swallowed the smoke. Titch watched fascinated – after what seemed an age, the parson's proboscis-like nose blew two plumes of smoke in the lad's direction. Titch watched – to the boy's imagination they appeared like tongues of flame emitted from the nostrils of a fiery dragon in one of the stories in his Boys Own Annual lying with his other small treasures and a change of underwear in a brown paper parcel on the seat beside him.

The deputy headmaster tossed his cigarette onto the already dirty floor and ground it to pulp with his foot – he leaned back in his corner seat with a sigh and folded his nicotine-stained hands on his lap. The man closed his eyes and Titch assumed, and he hoped, that he had finished his lecture and would perhaps sleep.

London astonished and revolted Titch. The cold dirty train with its overstuffed dusty seats, the filthy black of the sooty railway stations on the way to the city and the grey people who gazed indifferently with glazed eyes at life about them.

The traffic alarmed him as the pair emerged from the soot-ingrained dome of Victoria Station, and the people! Titch never knew there were so many human beings, and all seemed oblivious of his neighbour each intent only in their own affairs. For 10 years, other than his sojourn in Broadstairs, he had known only the confines of the orphanage – this was all another world, but he had long ago learned to suppress his emotions so had the look of equal indifference as the bustling crowd threatened to crush him with their very numbers and close proximity.

In the street the Reverend Jones enquired the whereabouts of Park Lane and, deciding the changes of buses was too complicated, hailed a taxi. What was said as the reverend bargained with the cabby Titch did not hear. Suddenly he and his brown paper parcel were bundled into the cab and they took off. Titch stared out of the window in awe, to the extent that he neither heard nor cared that the Reverend Jones was holding forth yet again on his good fortune at such a 'Heaven-sent opportunity... Do you hear me boy!' Titch faced the cleric with alarm – he was saved further admonition by the cab swinging into the curb before Park Lane Mansions. There was some altercation as the parson bargained again with the cabby.

'But you said one shilling and three pence not two shillings.' The cleric's voice had a whine of complaint.

'Ah... But I fer'got the nipper didn't I... An' the luggage.' The cabby nodded towards Titch's brown paper parcel.

'Sheer robbery.' The parson fumbled in a cheap

leather purse, extracted a florin and passed it to the cabby who eyed it with disgust. 'Wot' abart a tip y'grace.'

The Reverend Jones grinned through his yellow teeth. 'Have faith in God and pray for his mercy my son,' he swung on his heel as a splendid uniformed figure approached.

'Can I be of assistance y'worship?' Both Titch and his escort looked at the man that accosted them.

'Er, yes,' the reverend paused as the cab drove off with a roar and a cloud of blue exhaust. 'I have an appointment with Monsieur du Canne.'

'Ah... We've been h'expectin' you y'worship. Follow me, sir.' The smartly dressed man took Titch's parcel and headed up the steps followed closely by the Reverend Jones to the brass studded door of the apartments – Titch followed the pair and studied the back of the tall figure. He was indeed tall, and dressed in a royal blue uniform with gilt belt and epaulets – when he turned to open the door for them Titch saw the gleaming row of medals and brightly polished brass buttons. The man's face was clean shaven and a healthy pink – brown eyes under the peak of a military-type cap twinkled with amusement as he ushered the Reverend Jones through the door – he held the door for Titch to enter and the lad smiled as he saw the man wink and nod towards the back of the black coated parson.

Titch gazed in wonder at the splendour of the hallway they had entered and almost tiptoed across the polished marble floor to the door that bore the brass plate stating. 'OWNER MAN-

AGER.' Below 'MONSIEUR du CANNE' in even bolder letters.

Titch didn't like the look of Monsieur du Canne the moment he saw him. He was a small fat man. His belly bulged – it seemed to overhang his pelvis in a roll of flesh. Fat, smooth shaven jowls wobbled when he spoke – small very white teeth showed between full fed lips that glistened with moisture. The owner manager of Park Lane Mansions was dressed in a spotlessly clean silver-grey suit, he had a pale grey, almost white, waistcoat and a pale grey silver cravat fixed with a diamond pin that glittered as he moved. His patent leather pointed-toed boots with white spats reflected a distorted mirror image of the room's interior. A red carnation in his button hole completed the image of fastidious vanity. He reminded Titch of the picture of a fat penguin he had in his battered 'Boys Own Annual'.

The three sat in an over-furnished office that smelt of perfume and furniture polish – a single rose in a crystal vase was prominently displayed on the large mahogany desk that was otherwise bare. Monsieur du Canne lolled in a padded Moroccan leather swivel chair behind the desk – his little feet swinging an inch above the carpet; a carpet that was the softest Titch had ever walked on, the only one he had walked on except at Miss Cuthberson's house. The pile was thick – the deep burgundy colour made the room look rich; richer than Titch could imagine. Though it was cold outside the room was warm, too warm. Titch felt uncomfortable dressed in the oversize overcoat supplied by the home; he was too self-conscious to undo the buttons for more comfort.

Monsieur du Canne waved little pudgy ring-covered hands in front of him with every remark he made and continually touched Titch's knee as he sat beside his desk.

'Ah, dear boy. You are a treasure wee. So small and strong. So neat. The face of an angel with the body of an Apollo.' He looked at Titch with his little piggy eyes – Titch fidgeted; he wanted to run, but he needed the job.

'You are truly beautiful are you not. You will fit into my establishment perfectly. Such a pity that such a beautiful child should 'ave neither Papa or Mama. An orphan,' he looked at the gaunt figure of the cleric. 'Ze war was a terrible thing wee. I was myself… Ah… But you do not want to 'ear about me, no. This child is our concern wee?' He leaned forward and squeezed Titch's knee yet again.

The boy was at a loss to follow the man's conversation, what with the accent and his comments. Titch found it embarrassing, and the hand on his knee? But he needed the job and work was hard to find, especially in a 'live-in' situation. The Reverend Jones had made that very clear.

'You will like it 'ere, wee?' Titch's look was non-committal – he was anything but sure. The plump hand on Titch's knee gave another squeeze. There was more talk between the two adults and it was decided, by them. Titch took up his duties as Lift Boy Porter, Messenger, jack of all things, that very day.

The Reverend William Jones made a hurried departure without a farewell to his former charge. The tall commissionaire closed the door on the clergyman and raised his eyes to the heavens.

'Bloody parsons. Sod 'em all,' escaped from compressed lips.

The following day Titch was fitted with a smart uniform with 50 small silver buttons down the front. It had a military look with tight fitting trews and a pill box hat that Mr (he insisted on being Monsieur) du Canne adjusted to a jaunty angle. 'We must look... 'Ow do you say... Saucy. Wee. Saucy. I like that.' He patted Titch's buttocks as he turned away – the tall commissionaire doorman watched the little man as he went into his office. He turned to Titch.

'I'd watch yonder bugger if I were you, Titch. Don't ever turn yer back on 'im. And don't let 'im catch yer alone. All right?'

Titch was surprised, 'Yes. Thank you, sergeant.' But he didn't really know what he meant; he was soon to learn.

'Sergeant' Morgan and Titch were introduced the day the lad was engaged. He was a kind man, an ex-Grenadier Guardsman who had been invalided out of his regiment after the war with lung damage from mustard gas acquired in Flanders. It was he who showed Titch his duties that started at six in the morning with the polishing of all the brass in the foyer. The ex-soldier spent a patient half hour showing Titch how to get the best shine.'

'The secret is young 'un. A little polish. A lot'ter elbow grease and a clof' as soft as a baby's bum.' He laughed a pleasant laugh. 'You watch the old sergeant and you'll not go far wrong, Titch.'

The boy hung on his every word.

By the time the brasses were finished and the marble floor mopped and polished, 'The toffs', as the sergeant called the residents began to emerge and Titch was kept on his toes until nine at night operating the lift, running messages and walking pet dogs.

'Always talk proper to 'em Titch mate. Sir or Madam. Or if yer knows their names it's Mr this or Mrs that. If yer don't know their names call the blokes m'lud and the women m'lady. Don't matter if they ain't. They likes it and you could get a tip. Tickle their old vanity. Wot' the Irish calls Blarney. Know wot' I mean?' He laughed his pleasant laugh again. 'If they ain't a lord or lady, you can bet'cher bloody life they'd like ter be. A bunch 'er bloody snobs they are really. All of 'em.'

Titch followed his advice and on the first day received a sixpence for the effort – he was learning – by the end of the week he made over a pound in tips, in sixpences, shillings and florins; on one occasion half a crown for retrieving a lady's Poodle bitch that had got off its leash and ran across the road to the park opposite where a large Airedale was about to mount it.

'N' ruin more than its bloody pedigree,' was Sergeant Morgan's comment. 'Stoo'pid tart. Shouldn't take the bloody bitch out when its on 'eat.' The old guardsman muttered his disapproval of dogs and their stupid owners.

The second week Titch made thirty shillings and didn't mind when his employer gave him the princely sum of five shillings as his week's wage. Until then, Titch had not known that his wages were five shillings a week and his keep for a 12 hour day and on call all the time, but he had no need for money, then. He was getting nearly two pounds a week for working a lift, running a few errands, taking dogs for walks in the park and being pleasant to people – money for old rope; what else could he do with his time?

'You're lucky, Titch mate. The last little bleeder wot' was 'ere 'ad ter pay fer the job. 'Is dad paid 50 quid for the privilege of doffin' 'is lid to the gentry. 'Oped to get it back in tips 'e did. Lasted six months a'fore 'is nibs sacked 'im. Dun' know why, but I could make a guess or two.' He looked at Titch. 'Just you remember wot' I says. You watch that fat little bugger.' He tapped the side of his nose in a knowing way. Titch was puzzled – he didn't know the sergeant well enough to query the remark.

There was nearly three pounds in small change secreted in his little room in the basement flat that he shared with the sergeant and Mrs O'Brian the building's Irish laundress and charwoman. Mrs O'Brian was Irish and made this very clear to Titch the first time he met her – another of her duties was to cook the meals for the sergeant and himself; she spent her leisure-time, and most of her wages, in 'The Tyburn' Public House at Marble Arch. The sergeant was often called out of his own room along the passage to calm the old lady when she came home the worse for her many glasses of Guinness. At these times she cursed the English and the 'Black and Tans' and 'What they did to those lovely Irish lads.' It was all Greek to Titch – with memories of 'The Witches' and their debauching he steered a course well clear of the

Irish drunk – he enjoyed her cooking for when she was sober she was very kind; her pies and cakes were delicious.

It was late February and cold – a light snow lay in Hyde Park, but snowdrops were beginning to appear under the old plane trees. Titch had taken collection of dogs for a walk in the park and had delivered them safely to their owners – he hurried to his room to discard his coat and hopefully have a hot cup of Mrs O'Brian's cocoa and maybe one of her hard tasty rock cakes. With a run he burst into his room, his overcoat already off his shoulders – the door slammed shut behind. Titch spun around surprised at the sound and saw his fat employer standing with his back to the panels. The little man deftly turned the key in the lock and slipped it into his waistcoat pocket. The only window in the room was five feet from the floor and barred on the outside – Titch was trapped; he remembered Sergeant Morgan's warning that first day.

'Don't let 'im catch yer alone.' Titch didn't know what he meant then – he was beginning to understand. Memories of some of the dormitory scenes at Annerly came back to him. 'Was he like them? Would he try to....?'

Fear gripped Titch's bowels and his heart pounded – he thought all that sort of thing was behind him. The fat little dandy walked towards him with a twisted smile on his fat face – the diamond tie pin glittered like an evil third eye set below his throat.

'Come, Rupert my pigeon. Uncle Paul will not 'urt you. Not if you are good. See, I will give you a nice new one pound note.'

That accent – how Titch hated it; du Canne held out a green one pound note towards Titch. The fat man was close to the boy and put his hand on his shoulder and then his cheek – the note in the pudgy hand crackled as he crushed it in his fist. Titch was frozen with fear – his flesh cringed; fat fingers caressed him. Everything in the boy wanted to run, but the door was locked and his tormentor had the key.

Suddenly Titch's mind cleared of the mists of fear and shock – he was determined that he was not going to be humiliated; not again. He had fought against this, lived through it, and had suffered beatings for his struggles. He would fight it again – even if he had to suffer another beating; he would take any beating rather than submit.

The warm fat hand was on the side of his face in a downward movement – in a flash Titch caught it and fastened his teeth into the soft tissue; deep. There was a bellow of rage and pain – du Canne tried to pull away but Titch's teeth held fast. The fat little man struck Titch a blow on the side of his head, but the boy hung on; biting harder. Du Canne screamed a torrent of obscenities in the purest London East End cockney; vile abuse tumbled from those fat lips.

'You 'orrible little bleeder' screamed the irate aggressor. 'I'll skin you a-bloody-live fer that. I'll kill yer, yer little shit.' And more. The air was rent with his bellows. Titch cut off the man's tirade – his clenched fist with the knuckle of the second finger protruding sank hard into the fat stomach, right where it hurt, simultaneous to the youngster's teeth unclenching. In fluid motion born of fear and trained by experience, the boy's knee made contact with the man's soft crotch; hard. The pseudo Frenchman gasped – he groped his way to Titch's bed across the room; the lad helped him on his way with a hard shove. A brief search and Titch snatched the key out of the man's pocket – for moments he fumbled with the lock, stumbled through the door and ran blindly down the passage and into the kitchen to find the sergeant quietly smoking a cigarette.

'Tried it on did 'e, Titch mate? The fat little sod. I f'ought 'e would sooner or later. You all right?' Titch nodded for he was quite breathless. 'You get a cuppa cocoa and leave 'im ter me.' The sergeant stubbed out his cigarette and left the room – almost immediately Titch heard voices above the click of the latch as the door closed behind the sergeant's broad back.

'Why Monsieur du Canne! Wot 'appened?' There was a note of mock alarm in the sergeant's voice. 'Fall down the stairs, did yer? N'cut yer 'and 'ave yer? 'Ere, let me 'elp yer to yer office and put a bandage on it for yer. Nasty cut that. They go septic very quickly. Must look after yerself yer know.' They passed the closed kitchen door. 'Them stairs is dangerous. I was only a'saying ter Mrs O'Brian the 'uvver day. "Mrs O'Brian, I says..."' Titch heard their footsteps on the stairs going up – for the minute he was safe.

Mrs O'Brian poured boiling water onto the mixture of cocoa powder, sugar and condensed milk – she said not a word but her wink said more than a book. Titch finished the cocoa – it gave him time to think.

'I have to get away – du Canne, or whatever his real name is, is dangerous.' Titch was convinced the little fat man would seek an opportunity to revenge the humiliation of his defeat from such a small adversary. There seemed only one way, bolt.

Titch tidied himself and reported for work – he looked anxiously at the closed door of the office as he passed; the sergeant's eyes met his and at his saviour's silent nod Titch walked over to him.

'I knowed it would 'appen sooner or later, Titch mate. The fat little bastard. You ain't the first one yer know. No not by a long chalk. About five there've been ter my certin' knowledge.' The old soldier looked at Titch a little sheepishly. 'I don't let on that I knows a'course. Jobs is 'ard ter find these days. So keeps me eyes open and me mouth shut. Like the wise monkey. 'Ear all. See all, but say nuffin'. That's me.' He looked down at Titch from his six feet of height. 'But wot abart you, Titch boy. You 'ad better scarper. Yer know. Scarper Flow. Go. N'quick. A'fore the little bastard can 'fink up somefin' diabolical for yer.'

They were Titch's own thoughts – he decided to act on them at once.

'You're right, Serg. I think I will.' Though he had no idea where to.

'Then shove off now. While 'e's still sore. 'Ere.' He fumbled in his pocket and withdrew two halfcrowns. 'Take these, Titch. Call it a loan. Go an see a mate o'mine. Lives down Praed Street Paddington. Number five 'undred and fifty four. Tom Wilson's 'is name. Nice bloke. 'E lives wiv 'is missus n'kids above a pork butcher's shop. Yer can't miss it. It's on the right as yer go down.'

He cast an uneasy glance at the office door. 'Yeah. Tom'll look after yer. Fer a while anyway. We was in the trenches together. Tell 'im as 'ow I sent 'cher. All right? Now bugger off. Grab yer dunnage 'ngo.'

'Thanks Serg.' Titch was about to go – he turned. 'Serg … I won't forget cher'know. The five bob, I mean.'

'I knows that, mate. Now 'op it quick. I'll says as 'ow you are out wiv' some dogs. Now scarper.'

Titch gathered his few things – he left his uniform all folded and tidy on his bed. He put his three pounds fifteen shillings and ninepence in his pocket and looked into the kitchen to say 'Good Bye' to Mrs O'Brian.

'Oiy t'ought you'd be off, laddie. T'is a terrible little man he is for sure.' Her Dublin accent was thick and homely. 'Here, lad, take this. T'will keep the cold out'a you until the mornin'.' She thrust a small parcel of food at Titch. 'Now be off before himself recovers and t'inks up somethin' terrible for you.'

Titch thanked her and ran up the back stairs to the rear exit – something was missing; he remembered and hurried back to his room to retrieve his 'Boys Own Annual' he kept under his pillow. Grabbing it quickly, he was about to run when he saw du Canne's crumpled one pound note on the floor. A quick movement and he had scooped it up and left the room; he stretched his legs and took the stairs two at a time.

The door into the alley slammed after him and

he was legging it as fast as he could out onto Park Lane. Titch slowed to an anxious walk in the main thoroughfare and cast several glances over his shoulder fearing pursuit – the pound note felt hot in his hand; he was beginning to regret taking it. It somehow soiled him – he knew then that he had done the wrong thing.

'I should have left it there. I won't enjoy spending it.' Was his thought.

The sound of a trumpet and the beating of a drum reached Titch as he approached Marble Arch. The sight of a group of old wounded servicemen playing their instruments and walking through the people entering Hyde Park gave him an idea. The bent figure of an old wounded soldier was walking with a crutch; an empty trouser leg flapped in the breeze. As Titch approached he stooped awkwardly and picked up a cigarette end from the pavement and tucked it in the pocket of his tattered jacket. Titch looked at the cripple's medals twinkling in the pale February sunlight, and at the prematurely old face pinched with the cold and the need for a good feed. The old soldier coughed a deep hacking cough that wracked his thin shoulders. The battered hat he was holding out to the passing people shook with every heave of his chest. Very few of the crowd even looked at him – a middle-aged man dropped a coin into the maw of the hat as Titch got close enough to read the board around the old soldier's neck. 'I left my leg at Mons in 1914. Thank You.'

Titch didn't know where Mons was, but he knew about the 1914 war – he dropped the pound note into the old hat and hurried on.

'Hey!' There was a pause. 'S'truth. Tar mate. I mean sir.' The sir was long drawn out, and incredulous. Titch was in earshot so heard the exclamation to his companions blowing hard and beating the drum in the cold February noon; the music petered out in mid-tune.'

'Bli'me. Look wot I've got. A whole bloody quid.' The cry of joy reached Titch as he hurried along.

'Where from, Bert?' It was a tall man with one arm amputated at the elbow – he seemed to be their leader.

'That nipper wot's just leavin' the park.'

Titch looked around at that moment and caught their eyes – the six of them waved their thanks; he felt better as he ran through the traffic into the Edgware Road on his way to Paddington. The small band struck up again – the tune was ragged but loud; people looked in its direction as the march 'Pack up your Troubles' blared out above the noise of the traffic. Titch caught sight of himself in a shop window and saw he was smiling – he thought he looked taller too.

Spring had been quite mild so far, not that the weather inconveniences any of them on their graves. A sprinkling of rain fell during the night and made the haze of bluebells look even nicer in the April sun – there were daffodils still blooming profusely among the grass; primroses were withered flowerheads on lush crinkly green leaves.

Titch looked about him – the young girl near the grave of the tiny baby looked as if she was basking in the pale warmth of the sun. She had her head back and her eyes closed. Titch would love to talk with her but she was too far away. It seems they can only talk with those spirits close to their own graves. The old lady, Miss Burnett, that is, and Titch have had many a chat. What a life she has had – the stories she has told Titch of the goings on in Cape Town, and later with the gentry of Broadstairs would fill a book. She seems lost in her own thoughts now – Titch looked beyond the young policeman on the other side of the gravel path to the young woman; there was a soft laugh.

'Ain't no good a'hankering after her sergeant. She be beyond us both. By the way I be Constable 'iggins o'the Kent Constabulary. Or I were like.'

The accent was of the countryside of Kent, warm and friendly.

'Hallo. Nice to know you. I know she is not available. If you know what I mean. I'm just a little curious about her. She's so young. And that tiny baby. What happened to it, I wonder.'

'I don't know about the child but the girl committed suicide. In 1915 it were. Her young 'usband, a second lieutenant, got killed in France. Killed by German chlorine gas during the second battle of Ypres she told I. Her world did come to an end she did say. Wanted to be with him she did. Couldn't bear to think o' 'im a'drownin' in 'is own blood as 'is lungs filled with 'is own fluids from the effect of the poison gas. Knows all about it she does. Read it up in some h'encyclopaedia or somethin' she did.' He paused and looked across at the young woman who had opened her eyes

82

and was looking their way. 'Poor lass. He was killed in April, she died in May. She did cut her wrists and bled to death a'lyin' in a wood surrounded by bluebells. They were his favourite flowers she told I.' Both men looked at the young girl – she was truly beautiful with her face into the sun again. ''Er husband be probably on 'is grave in Belgium somewheres a'wondering about 'er, as she is about 'im. Do 'ee think she'll ever see 'im? Funny ol' thing, this afterlife business. Us a'bein' 'ere like this I do mean.'

Titch couldn't answer that question – this life after death was not a bit like the church talked about; he too worried how it would all end. Were they all in Purgatory? Titch remembered reading once of such a place though he could not quite imagine where, or what, it was. Some of the characters he could see, old Miss Burnett for example, had been here a long time. It didn't seem a temporary period of time. Titch wished he had found out more about it.

The young policeman seemed inclined to want to chat. He looked a bright young fellow about Titch's own age, but had died much earlier; Titch could tell that by the style of his uniform and the whiskers he sported. Coppers didn't look like that any more.

'What happened to you then? Hit on the head by a robber?' They laughed together; funny how they could enjoy a joke?

'No… It were nothin' like that. Nineteen hundred n'two it were. Some children got cut off by the tide below South Cliff. You know. Where all they rocks be. Children love to fossick over them

83

fer crabs n' winkles n'such like. You know?' Titch knew what he meant and said so – he remembered his own childhood forays. 'The tide comes in pretty fast, and it was th'Spring tide and they be faster and higher than th'ordinary tides. Anyways whey were trapped and I did volunteer to climb down on a rope and help 'em to th'top. A hundred feet or more it were.' He paused and looked at the girl in the next grave – he had somehow sensed that she was looking at them again; possibly trying to hear what they were saying. After a moment he continued. 'Th'folk at th'top pulled they children up, there were four on'em. They did lower the rope for I. I tied it around me-sel wi' a bowline and gave th'signal to 'aul away. They did. Too fast I do reckon. The darn rope broke just ten feet from the top. I went arse over kettle to the bottom. Cracked me skull, broke me back and goodness knows what. Then, to top it all, th'tide came in and carried I out to sea. Washed up down in Sussex three days later I were.' He sighed deeply. 'They gave I a wonderful funeral though. Just about th'whole of the County o' Kent Constabulary were 'ere. From the Chief Constable to Tom Hardcastle, our junior constable. He were a mate o' mine at th'station 'ere at Broadstairs. Enjoyed many a pint in the 'Lifeboat' Pub us did. Good bloke were Tom. Died in a traffic accident about 10 years ago. Just a year a'fore he were to retire. Made Station Sergeant 'e did. 'E's a'buried t'other side of th' church yard. 'Is funeral passed this very spot on th' road to 'is grave. 'Ad a quick word wi' Tom, I did. Nice to see him again.' He sighed again. ''Im

84

and me were a'walking out wi' two sisters. Lovely lasses they were. I were a'thinkin' of asking Jane, she were th'eldest. I were a'thinkin' of asking 'er to marry me. Then daft like I went and got me'self killed. 'He looked at Titch rather sadly. 'Pity, really. She'd've made a good wife for an ordinary copper. Had th'right attitude. About dooty n'that sort'a thin'.' He cheered up and looked straight at Titch. 'Yus, they do give us coppers a good funeral. Better than yours, if you don't mind I a'sayin' so.'

No Titch didn't mind him saying so. Wasn't there a war on now. 'Bomber' Harris could hardly send the whole of Bomber Command down to see Titch Wilkins buried. He had other things to do; so did they.

Titch found Tom Wilson's place – like the sergeant said. 'Over a pork butcher's shop.' Tom Wilson looked hard at Titch after he had told his story.

'I know'd Scrapper Morgan'll only send yer' to us if you was a good kid.'

He looked apprehensively across at his sturdy wife leaning on the kitchen sink looking hard at them both. 'I reckon as 'ow we c'n put up wiv yer fer a day or so. Until yer find yer self a ber'f of yer own...' He paused and looked questioningly at his spouse. 'Can't we muvver?' He added. Mrs Wilson grunted and looked directly at Titch.

'Not in trouble wiv' the coppers are yer young feller? We don't want yer a'bringin' trouble ter this 'ouse. A'bringin' trouble ter me n'mine.' Titch looked at the lady alarmed – he eyed apprehensively the wooden spoon she held in her right hand.

'No Madam,' he said, 'H'onest I 'aven't.'

'You c'n stop the Madam rubbish. Missus Wilson'll do fer starters n' you'd better be right ab'art them coppers. 'Cos if you ain't,' she looked at Titch aggressively 'You'll be out'a that door quick sharp wiv' a f'ick ear from me n'my Tom's boot up your little arse, right up to the last lace 'ole.'

'I 'aven't, Mrs Wilson... H'onest.' Titch took in every word of the cockney woman's dialogue – her accent, like her husband's was East End London and seemed to add weight to her threat. Mrs Wilson gave a snort and turned to stir a huge pot simmering on the black gas stove.

She was a large woman – big bones, wide of hip and full-breasted, with ample flesh elsewhere. Her exposed forearms were like legs of lamb ready for roasting; her hands were red and well-muscled with toil, but her face was kindly, try as she did to look severe – a wide mouth and full lips concealed a full set of very white and even teeth. Titch gazed at the handsome wife and mother with no little awe.

There was a clatter of feet and the sound of children's voices on the outside stairs in the yard at the back of the butcher's shop. Mrs Wilson slammed the lid on the pot.

'That'll be the kids 'ome from school, and ab'art time, too.' She wiped her hands on her apron. 'An' if young Billy 'as got 'is self messed up again, I'll tan his arse till 'e wets 'is self.' She sniffed and looked towards the door as she continued. 'The

86

bane of my life is that lad. Too much like 'is dad. Too full'a mischief fer 'is own good.' The door of the flat burst open and five children spilled into the room.

They were led by a girl of about 10 – she was followed by three urchin-looking little boys whose ages ranged from nine to six; lagging behind them was a pretty four or five year old girl. Titch first noticed her heart-shape face surmounted by a crop of unruly auburn curls that tumbled over her shoulders – as she cleared the door the youth noticed she had a severe limp; closer scrutiny revealed she had a club foot that dragged from the weight of the heavy surgical boot she wore. Titch eyed the foursome and though each had minor facial differences they all had in common the colour of their hair; they were all red-heads. Titch looked from the children to their mother – Mrs Wilson's hair was a deep auburn.

Five children stood motionless for a long moment and stared at Titch with the curiosity of their kind. Mrs Wilson burst into action.

'Come on in you lot. Get a move on, 'ain't cher never seen a young bloke a'fore.' She straightened her apron, ''N'close the door. It's too cold to 'ave it open all bloody day. N'say 'ello to yer 'farver. 'E's been a'workin' since a'fore you was up this mornin'.'

The eldest girl ran across to her father sitting in the only armchair in the room and gave him an affectionate hug – the younger limped painfully over to Tom Wilson and climbed awkwardly onto the big man's knee and placed a wet kiss on his cheek; there was a chorus of ''Ello, dad', from three childish throats as the boys made a rush for the door that led to the stairway and, Titch learned later, their communal bedroom. Mrs Wilson's cry followed them.

'Don't you little 'orrors make a din up there or I'll come up and larrup the lot a'yer.' The clatter on the wooden stair faltered, but only for a moment – as if at a signal the rumpus started up again. Titch looked at the father and the two daughters sitting near him in a tableaux of three.

Tom Wilson saw Titch's interest and spoke.

''Ere Judy. Meet a young mate o'mine. Rupert Wilkins, but he likes ter be called Titch.' The big ex-guardsman looked from his daughter to Titch. 'This 'ere is our eldest. Judy. 'N'this one,' he picked up the little girl and gave her a kiss. 'This 'ere is Molly, our youngest. Pretty ain't she?' Titch conceded to himself that she was, but he did not speak, he was looking at Judy. The older girl returned his look and smiled. Titch's heart leapt. If Molly was pretty Judy was beautiful, but the word only vaguely impinged on Titch's mind – his experience with girls of his own generation was minimal; he was just fascinated at the sight of such a wonderful creature.

The girl was as tall as he was, and had eyes as big as saucers and as blue as any sky Titch had ever seen. Like Molly, she had a heart-shaped face – when she smiled full red lips parted and showed small, even white teeth; there was the shadow of a dimple on her chin – a sprinkling of freckles on her small nose added to her charm, and her hair. It was straight and hung to her shoulders like a torrent of molten copper, reminding Titch of a picture in his 'Boys Own Annual'.

Titch's throat was dry but he managed a gasped, 'How do you do,' in the manner of Miss Cuthberson. Judy smiled a greeting – little Molly just sat on her father's knee and looked at the youth standing tongue-tied. Mrs Wilson broke the spell.

'Don't just stand there a'gawkin, Judy. Show 'im where the lav is n'where ter wash 'is 'ands.' Judy moved to obey – her mother continued. 'N' tell them bruv'vers o'yours that if they ain't down 'ere wiv' clean 'ands in two minutes I'll belt the lot o'them.' The good woman turned to the pot simmering on the stove – she turned her head and addressed Judy making for the outside door. 'Then get back 'ere n'set a place fer Rupert.' She looked at Titch, 'Or does I calls yer Titch?'

Titch found his tongue. 'Everyone calls me Titch, Mrs Wilson.'

'Okay. Then Titch it is… Now off wiv' yer.' She began to stir the pot.

Judy led the way through the exterior door to a small room on the concrete landing.

'This is the wash house where we wash our hands.' She pointed to an earthenware sink with a solitary cold water tap over it. 'The lav is down in the yard. The boys use a bucket at night. They'll show you. They take turns to empty it.' She laughed a bell-like laugh. 'They always fight over it.' She hesitated, then shyly. 'Who empties it, I mean.' She made to leave, and paused.

'Friday is bath night. We bath in that.' She nodded towards a full length tin bath hanging on a nail. 'Molly n'me go first. Then mum. Dad n'the boys have fresh water and come after us. I suppose you'll fit in there somewhere.' Titch laughed nervously and said he didn't mind – she left him to wash his hands.

There then began Titch's first experience of a family. It was chaos, but a chaos that was in the control of strict and loving parents. The Wilsons were poor but had a roof over their heads, food of a sort on the table every day, and clothes on their backs, albeit that they were home made hand-me-downs from older children. They were poor but not impoverished – they had a dignity; they were respected in the community and walked tall among their neighbours.

Their food was simple and wholesome with lots of filling bread and dripping – butter was served on a Sunday and special days like birthdays and Christmas. Potatoes were plentiful, but meat was served only occasionally – then only the cheaper cuts. Herrings were frequent as were rice puddings and heavy slabs of bread pudding eaten hot or cold. Pease pudding and faggots was a favourite meal, but pease pudding like Titch had never tasted before and faggots that melted in his mouth.

Chapter Four

The day began early in the Wilson household. A born cockney, Tom Wilson had a dual employment – his secondary source of income was that of professional 'Knocker Upper'. Rising before five Tom would drink a cup of tea – leap on his bicycle and do a round of waking a hundred or more working people by knocking on their bedroom windows until they appeared as evidence that they were at least out of bed. Not until he saw a face did Tom go on to the next house. He would cycle along the long rows of terraced houses that had their front doors opening onto the street knocking as he went. He carried a long cane with a bent piece of brass tubing covered at the end with a rubber pad. With this he would reach up from the saddle on his bicycle and tap on the client's upstairs window. For this service each of them paid him sixpence a week. With over 100 clients it brought the family an extra 50 shillings a week into the family budget; no mean sum in 1931.

'Some folks can't trust their self's ter wake up in the mornin',' he confided to Titch. 'Mind you. It would be easier for 'em if they drank less the night before.' He laughed. 'But I ain't a'goin' to tell 'em am I? Ruin me wouldn't it? If they took notice of me that is.'

It was Mrs Wilson who woke Tom – Titch never discovered who woke Mrs Wilson.

Tom would be home again about 6.30 for a quick breakfast and off again on his bicycle the two miles to the Borough of Paddington Council Yard where he worked from eight until five as a road maintenance man. The cycle ride home was direct, except on Friday nights when he was 'delayed' at the Lord Nelson public house.

'A bloke's got'ter wash the tar out'er his guts Titch. Chokes 'im else. T'say nuffin' of wot' it

91

might do to 'is underpants.' He laughed a tipsy laugh and hiccupped. 'Besides, 'ow else could I bring 'ome a bottle a'brown ale fer the best missus any bloke ever 'ad.'

His weekly gift for his buxom spouse never diminished the tirade of language she poured on his broad shoulders. He would shrug like a bear and gather the lady in his arms and hug her to silence.

After work on Saturday afternoons Tom and Judy would make the round of clients to collect their sixpences. There would be a brief stop for Judy at the local sweet shop where she would spend the whole of a client's sixpence on sweets for herself and her siblings – another stop for Tom at the Lord Nelson that never received a rebuke; provided he was at home for the Saturday evening high tea. Saturday's high tea was invariably fish and chips with black beans bought from the travelling 'Chipman's' noisy, savoury smelling lorry.

Titch ate, slept and laughed with this family – there were never tears unless one or the other of the boys caught an extra hard 'back hander' from one of their parents. Titch squabbled with the boys and played and read to little Molly. Judy and the youth said little to each other – silence seemed more companionable, but Titch would meet her eyes sometimes as he was reading to her sister. On those occasions she would smile – each time his heart would leap; she was surely the loveliest creature God ever made.

If this was family living then Titch Wilkins knew he had missed a lot. The adults' lives revolved around their children – in turn the children doted on their parents, in spite of the bellows of rage and many not too gentle whacks on the rumps of the three boys from both parents; Mrs Wilson was especially handy with her large wooden spoon.

That first day began for Titch by rising at six thirty from his bed on the floor in the boy's small bedroom – it contained a large double bed in which all three brothers slept in a tangle of limbs – a quick breakfast of bread and dripping washed down with a mug of strong sweet tea; he was out of the house to look for work before eight o'clock.

He had no idea how to begin – he didn't know even what he wanted to do for a living. Tom Wilson had made several suggestions the night before – choices ranging from delivery boy in the pork butchers downstairs, to a Post Office telegraph boy and several in between; all of them seemed impossible goals.

'I don't want ter be a wet blanket Titch, but yer ain't much ter look at. I mean. You're no Goliath are yer?' He looked at Titch sadly. The boy saw Mrs Wilson wince at her husband's frankness; she wisely said nothing and became engrossed in her sewing.

'You're a nice-lookin' kid all right, but there ain't much of yer. Know wot' I mean?'

Titch knew too well what he meant. Miss Cuthberson's words about being big inside seemed empty.

It was with considerable trepidation that Titch launched himself onto the labour market. He knocked on doors – he walked miles and was asked all manner of questions. He received many emphatic no's, and some sad shakes of the head;

they all amounted to failure.

The second day Titch cast his net wider – he walked along Oxford Street and tried the big shops along that busy road thinking he could be a uniformed messenger boy or the like. It was nearly ten in the morning and he was thirsty, tired and discouraged after about a dozen 'Sorry lad. Try...' To 'Bugger off yer little squirt', from an uncouth shopkeeper in Oxford Circus.

He saw a lorry coming out of a building site and stopped as it made its way into the busy traffic. He waited and looked about and saw a large man with a bowler hat on the back of his head and a pencil behind his ear. He was tall and heavily built and wore a navy blue serge suit that was tight around the middle; a heavy gold watch chain stretched across his broad waist and he wore a collar and a tie. The sheaf of papers in his hand and the roll of drawings under his arm impressed Titch that he was a boss of some sort; on an impulse the lad approached him. The man was indeed the boss, with the title of General Foreman.

'Excuse me, sir,' the boy said in his best Miss Cuthberson manner. 'Can you give me a job please?'

The man stopped in mid-stride and pushed his hat further back on his head. A yellow pencil from behind his ear fell to the ground – Titch stooped and retrieved it. The boy wiped the mud off it by passing it under his armpit and offered it to the figure towering above him – before he could be thanked Titch blurted out.

'Are you left handed, sir?'

'Yes, I am, you young bugger. But how the hell did you know?'

'You had the pencil on your left ear. I thought you might be.'

The figure in the blue suit looked down at Titch and thought for a full 30 seconds – it seemed an hour.

'Well, you're bright enough but I really can't use you. How old are you?'

'Fourteen, sir. But I'll be fifteen soon.' The words burst from Titch's lips.'

'How soon?' There was a hint of suspicion in the man's voice.

Titch looked up at him and trembled inside himself. He was so big – Titch felt he could swallow him whole; especially if he lied.

'Not until Christmas.' Titch confessed. The big man laughed a hearty laugh.

'By Christ, you deserve a job.' He thought again. 'Can you make tea?'

In all honesty Titch could answer yes – he had made a pot of tea many times for Miss Cuthberson; he remembered her instructions. 'One teaspoon for each person and one for the pot.' It was all so simple.

'Yes, sir.'

'Then you've got yourself a job. You've got an hour to make two buckets of tea fer all the blokes here. Forty-eight of the buggers. Bert!'

A short stocky middle aged man appeared from behind a shed brushing brick dust off his clothes.

'What is it, Mr Whittaker?' The general foreman looked down at Titch.

'What's your name, son?'

'Rupert, sir. Rupert Wilkins, but they all call me Titch.'

'Then Titch it is. Titch Wilkins?'

'Yes sir.' The middle aged man was at Titch's side.

'Here, Bert. Show Titch here where he has to make the tea. You'll have to hurry, I'll be blowing up fer dinner at twelve.' He looked again at Titch. 'All right, son? I mean Titch. Five bob a week n'all the tea money's yours.' He laughed again. 'And remember this. I like my tea hot, strong, sweet n'lightly tanned. Like I like my ladies.' He laughed again and gave the man he called Bert a playful nudge, put the pencil behind his ear and strode off laughing at his own joke.

Titch Wilkins looked at the man standing beside him – he was taller than he was, but not by much, and muscular. He had a grey moustache and a cloth peaked cap on his head that had once been grey. His face was ruddy both from working out of doors and the red brickdust that was sprinkled liberally on it; laughing blue eyes glittered under thick dust-covered eyebrows and he had a ready smile. His clothes were rough and covered with deep-seated red brick dust that made it difficult to see the original colouring – his boots were impregnated with red dust.

'Come on then, Titch. I'll show yer where ter light a fire and get the water. Yer know 'ow ter make tea, do yer?'

Titch recognised the accent – he was a Londoner, like the Wilsons – probably from within the 'Sound of Bow Bells'.

'Oh, yes,' he said. Well he did – many times he

had made it at school for the House Master and for Miss Cuthberson; he remembered again the recipe. A teaspoonful for each person, and one for the pot. It was easy. Titch followed behind his guide to the mess hut.

'There y'are Titch. There's the wood. The water is at the tap by the cement mixer.' Then almost as an afterthought. 'And 'ere's the buckets.' He pulled two iron buckets from nails that were driven into a roof beam of the mess hut. Titch looked at the two black vessels the man was holding. There were soot black on the outside and stained a deep brown on the insides. They looked heavy, filthy and huge. Titch was completely at loss – he had expected a tea pot; a larger tea pot no doubt, but a tea pot. How could he make tea in a bucket? His guide saw his bewilderment.

'Ain't never done this a'fore 'ave yer, son.' It was a statement rather than a question.

'Not in a bucket, sir.'

''Ere. Cut out the sir. I ain't no boss. Just a bricklayer. Mind you. The best bricklayer 'ere but a bricklayer all the same. Bert James is me name. Alright?' He tipped the bucket upside-down and shook out some dust. 'Now, wot' about this 'ere tea. Got any money?'

'Yes, Mr James.'

''Ow much?'

'Five bob, but I have more at home. I mean in Mr Wilson's house.'

'Five bob'll do fer now. Get yerself down to the shop on the corner and buy two quarter a'pound packets a'tea. Two two pound packets a'sugar and two tins a'condensed milk. The 'ole lot

97

shouldn't come ter more than 'alf a crown so don't let that Greek bloke rob yer. Tell 'im as 'ow Bert James a'knows the price a'fings. All right? Then buzz off while I lights yer fire.'

Titch was back in less than ten minutes and found the fire lit and the two buckets on the flames, but no Bert. The noise of sawing came from behind the mess hut – Titch went around to investigate and saw his helper and guide sawing a large lump of soft red brick with a bow saw. The red dust flew with each stroke; as Titch watched a wedge-shaped brick grow before his eyes.

The bricklayer straightened his back, looked at Titch and grinned.

'Easy ain't it. But you'd better be a'getting' back to that fire o'yours. It'll need more wood or my name ain't Bert James.'

Titch hurried back to the fire. The man was right – it was low. Titch laid more wood around the buckets and soon had a blaze going again. He stood and saw that each of the buckets had a spent match floating in the water; he reached to take them out.

'No!... Always put a dead match in'ter water. It takes the taste of the smoke away. Learned that trick in the army I did.' Bert James had followed Titch into the hut. He looked at the water beginning to boil.

'Now, young Titch. Get yer packets a'tea and pour one 'ole packet in'ter each bucket.' Surprised, Titch did as he was told. 'Now a packet a'sugar in'ter each bucket. That's my boy,' he said encouragingly as two pounds of white sugar disappeared into each bucket of boiling water.

'Now…' The teacher extracted from his pocket an old army pocket knife that had a vicious looking spike folded on the side. He opened the spike and plunged the point into the top of one of the tins of condensed milk. He repeated it on the opposite side and held the punctured tin out to Titch.

'Take it. 'Old it over the bucket and blow f'rough one of the 'oles.'

Titch did – he was rewarded by seeing a thick jet of sweet milk, poured into the bucket – it took a minute before bubbles, and then just air came out. He repeated it with the second bucket and was given a piece of batten and told to stir. Titch did as he was told and was delighted to see the black water change into a deep tan, and not a tea leaf floating. He kept stirring until he and his instructor were sure the sugar had dissolved. Bert James helped Titch to lift the buckets off the fire and arrange a row of filthy mugs in a line. From another nail in the roof beam he took a mug nailed to the end of a stick.

'This 'ere's fer dippin' in the buckets. Don't let them blokes dip their dirty mugs in it or it'll finish up filthy and not fit fer drinkin'. All right?'

Titch nodded – he was wondering what happened next when Mr Whittaker's whistle blew for the dinner break. There was no time for further thought as 40 or 50 hungry building workers descended on the buckets – in 20 minutes only sloppy tea leaves were left to show for his labours.

In all the rush Titch and forgotten to take Mr Whittaker's tea to his hut, but his benefactor was a genial man and forgave his oversight. It never happened again.

The weather became fine after a series of storms – little white clouds scudded across a blue sky making everything bright and sunny. A gentle breeze blew off the English Channel – Broadstairs was enjoying the kind of day peace time holiday makers loved.

Titch had seen what he thought were a line of five fishermen all dressed in oilskins and bulbous life jackets. All but the nearest had sou'westers almost covering their faces. The nearest was a giant of a man, he was bareheaded – a mane of white hair flowed to his shoulders. His tanned face had a three day growth of silver-white whiskers – his face looked like a wrinkled sugar doughnut. Sea blue eyes looked from beneath white bushy eyebrows – when he spoke his voice was like a fresh wind; a wind with the deep accent of the hop fields of Kent.

'Knows the Lifeboat 'Ouse do 'e lad? And the Pub across the road no doubt.'

He laughed a short bark of a laugh. 'You young buggers is all the same.'

He was older than middle aged and his laugh was dry but merry; the monstrous life jacket over the yellow oilskins shook with his laughter.

'T'were t'same wi' I when I were your age. A'drinkin' and a'wenchin'. 'Cept when we be fishin' a'course. Ah... What it be ter be a young'un.'

There was a remark from an oilskin clad man hovering on the next grave; Titch could not hear – his white haired neighbour laughed again and looked at the young rear gunner.

'Young Charley 'ere was a'wonderin' as 'ow it be difficult f'yee t'fish in the clobber yee be a'wearin'.'

'This.' Titch looked down at his body dressed in flying clothing. His flying helmet was still on his head and the goggles were over his eyes; just as they were when he died. Titch looked across at the young man in the oilskins who his neighbour called Charley.

'I'm no fisherman! I was flying in a Lancaster! I crashed!' Titch found himself shouting until he remembered their voices didn't carry beyond their immediate neighbours. Titch addressed the older man. 'Tell him I was a gunner in a Lancaster that crashed into the sea.'

The white haired gent passed on the information but Titch could see that neither of them understood. It took some minutes to fill in the gap of years between their burials and his own.

'Th'Royal Air Force, you do say. Do Queen Victoria 'ave an air force then? I did never 'ear of it a'fore.'

Titch explained the lapse of years and the death of the old Queen and her son King Edward, and that her Great Grandson George was now the King of England.

'Be that true then? It do explain a lot I reckon. They fancy blue uniforms o'they chaps as buried yee. And they fangled machine birds that created such a rumpus a'swoopin' over us 'ere a couple a'years back. Made 'ell of a din they did. And they h'explosions we did 'ear. Be they life boat maroons a'callin' th'lifeboat crew out?'

Titch explained an aeroplane and bombs, and

the Battle of Britain that had been fought over their heads in 1940 – his explanations were interrupted repeatedly as the information was passed along the line of men. It took some minutes; with all the wonderment on their faces it was hard for them to comprehend modern life.

'Bit different from the ol' "Pride o'Kent". Though she were a beauty and no mistake.' The white haired old gent received a nod of agreement from his neighbour.

'What was "The Pride of Kent"?' It was Titch's turn to be curious.

'She were the Broadstairs Life Boat. Lost 'er in a March gale in '74, us did. 'N'us five w'it. Terrible night that were I do tell 'ee.' He shook his head – the mane of white hair shone in the sunlight. He looked at Titch and continued.

'A schooner got caught on th'Goodwin Sands. A'flounderin' she were. It were that bad the Ramsgate boat couldn't be launched. It were up to us. We got to her as she broke up. Took off four o'the crew. Th'old Captin and t'others were lost.' The old man paused as he remembered. 'Ah... Terrible night it were. The worst as I remember and I were wi' the lifeboat fer 40 year. T'last 20 as coxswain. Ah... Real terrible. They waves were a'comin' at us like great cliffs a'water. Like great lines o'grey 'ouses they were. Dirty grey 'ouses wi'white roofs as th' crests broke off th'waves. Tall an'steep as Dover's cliffs they were. Terrible. A'takin' water the 'ole time us were. A'pumpin' and a'bailin' fer our lives the 'ole time. Us made it to the foot o'the cliffs when a real whopper o' a wave caught us a'midships. I see'de it a'comin' and hauled the helm over but the old Pride couldn't meet it fast enough and it caught us beam on. Arse over beam us went. Th'coves as us 'ad a'rescued were thrown clear, as was t'other five o'me crew. Us five got trapped under th'ull. Couldn't get out us couldn't. Us got battered t'death on the rocks below South Cliff n'got washed ashore ter finish up 'ere.' Titch saw all the other four were remembering. They hovered over their graves with a look of sadness. He looked along at them – they were all young, one a mere youth. Titch sighed.

'Makes flying over the Rhur in 1943 hardly dangerous at all.' But the old man failed to understand.

A month passed – Titch developed a technique for making tea and could do it without bother though he always found the buckets heavy. He had scoured the buckets to a brilliant shine – cleaned the men's mugs; so clean they hardly recognised their own. It was much appreciated by them all – each man paid Titch one shilling and three pence a week for the service. It gave the lad a profit of one pound fifteen shillings a week after buying the tea and sugar. Titch cleaned Mr Whittaker's office each morning for another two shillings – by running errands, buying cigarettes, cakes, pies etc at the little Greek shop at the corner he averaged another seven shillings a week in tips from the men; a total of around two pounds seven shillings a week. Quite a sum for a boy of 14.

Titch looked at the sky above the trees of the church yard – he smiled as he remembered – a packet of five 'Woodbines' cigarettes cost two pence and a box of matches a halfpenny. He recalled the men gave him a silver three penny piece and gave him the change for going. Not much? It wasn't, but it mounted up. After he paid Mrs Wilson twenty five shillings for board, he was left with a little over one pound for pocket money.

Weeks went by and clothes became a worry – Mrs Wilson did her best patching his old Annerly clothes and Tom had supplied a jacket for work that his wife had cut and sewn to fit him, almost. He was growing too – not much, but his trouser bottoms were above his ankles.

Titch had five pounds saved – accompanied by the whole Wilson family he went shopping for a new suit. He had his eye on one in 'Burton's Tailors' for seventy five shillings. It was a dark blue with a deep red stripe through it. The lad showed it to the family – they all stood outside looking at it on a dummy in the window. Titch thought he would look good in it; Judy agreed. 'You've got good taste, young Titch. I admit that. They stripes'll make you look taller. But you'll never wear it out mate. Waste a'good money if yer ask me' Mrs Wilson agreed with Tom

'You'll be too tall fer it in a few mum'fs Titch. Let's 'ave a look at the 'Fifty Bob' tailors in the 'Igh Street.'

Titch was disappointed but gave in to adult pressure. Judy and he trailed a little behind the other five. The three boys scampered about in and out of the shops and stalls that lined the street. Neither said a word when they saw the boys eating applies that they had obviously 'pinched' from one of the many coster barrows along the way.

Mrs Wilson was right – Titch forgot his disappointment about Burtons – paid fifty shillings and was the proud owner of a grey flannel double-breasted suit. It had a thin paler grey stripe through it – to make him look taller.

'Now you c'n buy a shirt 'n' a tie t'go wiv'it.'

Practical Mrs Wilson was a fund of help and advice. The good lady hovered in the background as the younger children delved into ties and shirts, and later socks and shoes; she was wise enough to allow the young people to indulge themselves in terms of colour for the ties. The result – Titch finished paying two shillings for a garish red and blue combination he seldom wore. Mrs Wilson's own little gift of a more subdued tie he wore for years.

Tom Wilson thought it outrageous to pay fifteen shillings for a pair of shoes, but Titch liked them; so did everyone else. The kindly ex-guardsman was outnumbered and gave in with a good humoured snort – Mrs Wilson raised her eyebrows to the sky in resignation.

'More money n'bloody sense if y'ask me.' Was her comment then and later.

The group could not get home fast enough to see the purchases unwrapped and for Titch to try them on; they waited impatiently while Mrs Wilson bought kippers for their Saturday tea. There was a party mood in the house when Titch entered the living room in all his finery. The suit needed a little alteration and the shirt was too big. The shoes fitted perfectly and Titch's choice of tie matched nothing – it was like a gash of a wound down his shirt front. Mrs Wilson's gift was well received by all of them.

'Don't worry about the shirt Titch. You'll grow in'ter it soon enough. Won't 'e luv.' Mrs Wilson had a mouth full of pins and was on her knees shortening the new trousers so made no reply to her husband.

Meg Wilson must have stayed up late that Saturday because everything was ready in the morning. Titch was dressed and ready for the day by eight o'clock – Judy came down shortly afterwards looking as pretty as a picture. Titch suggested they went for a walk to Hyde Park – the four younger Wilsons insisted on joining them – not the day Titch had expected; he had five shillings and planned to spend it on Judy for a swanky tea at a Lyons tea shop. They settled for ice creams, lemonade and a bar of Sharps Toffee each. The six children arrived home in the late afternoon tired and hungry with the younger children squabbling as to who should give their mother the six irises Titch had bought with his last shilling.

Months passed in a whirl of laughter and happiness for Titch, but he could see there would come a time when he would have to find another place; the little flat above the pork butchers was crowded even without him. With him there squabbles developed for no other reason than the overcrowded conditions. It made Titch sad – he could see it was up to him to make the decision; the Wilsons could not bring themselves to tell him.

It was a Monday morning – Titch had finished cleaning up after the morning tea break; the mugs had been washed and all was ready for the dinner break at noon. The lad had made a habit of helping Bert James cutting his bricks for the many arches in the new building. He taught Titch how to mark the blocks of soft brick and how to cut them out. Titch had even worked with Bert setting the arches left by the team of bricklayers working on the scaffolds.

'Sort of a special job Titch. Not every body 'as the patience ter cut n'mould the bricks in'ter place. Then you've got'ter grout 'em in so'se they sets 'ard an' don't move when the brickies build a'top o'them. I likes ter put a bit'ter steel rod fr'ough 'em. Gives 'em a bit more strength like. Know wot' I mean?' Titch didn't and Bert had the patience to show him.

'You've got'ter remember. These 'ere is 'ere fer ever. They can't knock it down. There ain't nuffin' big enough in this world ter do it. 'Ceptin' an earthquake a'course.'

Bert James never stopped work to talk. Things grew with every word he uttered, he seemed tireless. He never stopped for a cigarette, and always had a tool of some sort in his hand. Bert James could work without thinking – or so it seemed; he would philosophise.

'Just f'ink a'this 'ere buildin' a'standin' 'ere in a 'undred years from now. A f'ousand may be. Marvellous, ain't it. A'leavin' a bit of 'istory like. Like Windsor Castle or Westminster Abbey maybe.'

A wind ruffled the trees in the church yard. Titch smiled grimly as he recalled Bert James' confidence in the future. Hitler's bombs had shattered his belief, and the work of generations of bricklayers like his old friend. Perhaps it was as well that old man had never known.

A Monday morning – the bricklayer was working marking out the bricks for a new arch when Titch walked around the shed to his corner. The lad picked up the bow saw and examined the blade as he had been taught.

'Sharp enough is it, Titch?' Titch ran his fingers over the blade again.

'I reckon so, Mr Bert.'

'Good.' He was standing in front of Titch – something in the boy's voice sounded different.

'Wot's the trouble young'un? Upset some one? Get yer'self in'ter strife?'

'No, not really Mr Bert. It's just that...' Titch hesitated – it didn't seem right to involve him in his troubles.

'Yer don't 'ave ter tell me if yer don't want to. But I c'n listen if yer do. Though 'ow I c'n 'elp I dun' know.'

'Well Mr Bert, it's where I live...' And Titch told him how he thought he ought to move. The man heard the boy through without an interruption except to put another brick onto the block while Titch placed the brick he had marked for cutting.

'Don't sound too bad ter me young Titch. Nuffin' there wot' can't be a'sorted out wiv' a bit'ter good will if yer know wot' I mean.'

Titch didn't, but he didn't say so – it did not seem an answer to him. Nothing else was said and the day finished with Titch even more worried than when he started. It seemed a waste of time talking to the old bricklayer. Like he had said on one occasion.

'The Lord above 'as made all our little troubles ter fit us. Sort of personal like. They don't fit no one else. Just us. Your troubles fits only Titch Wilkins. Mine fits only ol' Bert James. If them troubles looks too big fer us, it ain't really that they is too big. It's that us is too small for 'em. We've gotta grow like n'elp ourselves. If I takes on your troubles Titch I wouldn't be a'elpin you much. Just a'listenin' maybe. Likewise if you a'took on my strife. All we would be doin' would be a'wastin' time wiv' each other instead'er workin' at the problem. 'S'logical really, an' it?'

Titch wasn't at all sure that it was – he wasn't sure what logic was even.

'But what do we do about it if our troubles really are too big for us?'

'But they ain't Titch. That's wot' I'm a'sayin' of. They ain't too big. We is too small yer see. So we 'ave ter grow.' He slapped himself in the chest. 'Inside I mean. In our 'earts n'minds. In our guts if yer like.' He gave his flat stomach a hard slap. 'Grow big enough inside ter carry our own problems. An' solve 'em.'

'Can we do that, Mr Bert?'

'A'course we can Titch boy. Christians do it wiv prayer. 'Eathens through their idols and such. It's easy when yer know 'ow.'

'How do you do it, Mr James?'

'Well, Titch.' Titch remembered he straightened his old back and looked into the distance with a far away look. 'I think of all the 'ard times I 'ave lived fr'ough. Four years in the trenches in Belgium. All the mud n'the death n'the 'orror of it. I f'inks of all me mates as never came 'ome from the war. And the time I nealy lost me missus when our young'un died. When I was out'er work, and no 'ope of a job and nuffin' to eat in the 'ouse. 'Ard times were them. All of 'em. I thinks of 'em and I says to me'self. Bert, I says. Nuffin' could 'appen ter you t'day as was as bad as wot' 'appened in them days. 'Cept dyin' a'course.' He looked hard at Titch. 'That gives me a sorter' streng'f. The sorter' streng'f I must 'ave 'ad in them times and didn't know I 'ad it. I finds that streng'f again like. I digs down in'ter me guts if I 'ave to. But I finds it.' He stopped and looked into the distance again for a moment – he looked at the young boy hanging on every word he uttered.

'Some'ow Titch I finds it, n'I carries on sorter f'ing. I sort out me problem like. Know wot, I mean?' He looked at Titch yet again as he continued.

'Yer see Titch matey. Most of us is little people. Little inside, and little outside. You n'me. We're little blokes outside so we must work on bein' big inside. Bigger than 'uvver people. Know wot' I mean ol' son?' Titch did. It was like Miss Cuthberson had told him those years ago in Broadstairs.

Titch was back with him again after the morning tea and following day. They were up on the scaffold building an arch. Bert 'buttered' a key brick with mortar and invited Titch to lay it in place.

'The most h'important brick in the arch Titch. It's the one wot' 'olds it all together. The key brick we calls it. It's a bit like some one yer loves. Take them away and yer life could fall apart. Take my ol' missus now. If any'fing 'appened to 'er I

110

reckon as 'ow I would fall to pieces. Fer a while anyway.' He looked at Titch and their hands touched as he guided the brick into place. Together they slid the brick into the gap. It needed a slight tap to firm it home.

'Take that there key brick away and the arch falls down. As simple as that Titch.'

Titch took up the heavy club hammer to drive the brick home.

'No, not wiv' that matey.' He handed the boy a wooden maul. 'Gentle with it lad. Two soft'uns is better than one 'ard 'un.'

Titch tapped the brick gently with the large maul until it sat firmly into place. Bert passed the boy a trowel to wipe the joint.

'Well done. I'll make a bricklayer of yer yet.' He laughed and bent and gathered the mortar on the mortar board into a neat pile; Titch saw him wink at Mr Whittaker who stood quietly watching.

The two spent a few minutes cleaning up – they gathered their tools and walked the length of the scaffold to the ladder. Bert James stopped with his foot on the first rung. He turned and looked at Titch.

'Hey! I almost fer'got. 'Ow would yer like ter come n'live wiv me n'the missus?' Titch almost dropped the bag of tools in his surprise.

'Yer mean in your 'ouse?... As a lodger?'

'A'course. But like the toffs... More like a guest as they say... But you'll 'ave ter pay muvver board.' He said as an afterthought. He began to descend. 'F'ink abart it, lad.' His foot was on the second rung.

Titch didn't hesitate.

'I don't 'ave to, Mr Bert. I'd love ter come. H'onest. And Mrs Wilson'll be glad.'

She was – and Tom – the children were sad, especially Judy, but she never mentioned it.

Titch moved in the following Saturday after work – all the Wilsons helping, even coming on the underground train and the trolley bus to the James' little terraced house in East Acton. The family paraded down the narrow street carrying between them Titch's meagre possessions; even Molly carrying a small parcel of handkerchiefs Titch had purchased for the occasion.

Mrs James wondered what had hit her when the group arrived – after a cup of tea and the Wilsons looking at the bedroom where Titch was to sleep they left, but only after extracting a promise from the boy that he would visit them at weekends. Titch promised – intending to keep his word – he had grown fond of the family, especially Judy; she occupied a great deal of his thoughts as he worked. He began to see her as the sister he imagined he might have had if his life had been different. How very young he was – how little he understood his own growing feelings.

Chapter Five

The summer of 1931 passed through the seasons to the autumn of 1932 – an eventful year, though not good for many of the world population. Thousands were being killed or banished to Siberia in the new USSR. Joseph Stalin was 'cleansing' his Soviet Republics of opposition. People died of starvation and disaster in remote parts of the globe while food surpluses were dumped in the sea by more affluent countries.

Britain and the world were emerging from the depression with governments giving a 'New Deal' to their countries. Work was easier to find; there was an air of optimism abroad.

A bridge in Sydney, Australia, was opened by an Irish Nationalist charging through the official party on a horse. Amelia Earhart, the celebrated aviatrix, flew the Atlantic on a solo flight in 15 hours. The Olympic Games had been held in Los Angeles, USA. A man called Adolf Hitler was making headlines in Germany, and the US gangster Al Capone was jailed for income tax evasion. The same year Franklin Delano Roosevelt was elected the 32nd President of the United States of America. More importantly for Titch, he was given a pay rise to nine pence an hour.

For over a year he had been apprenticed as a bricklayer with Messrs Waller and Franklin & Company, Building Contractors of Ealing, London SW5. It was a prosperous small firm employing permanent artisans plus a floating number of temporary tradesmen and labourers, depending on what contracts they had. Mr Whittaker was Titch's boss – Bert James his instructor and mentor.

The job in Oxford Street was behind them and they were working building a block of flats in Kensington. Bert James and Titch had been the first on the job with Mr Whittaker – setting out the site and preparing the foundations for the gang of bricklayers that would be needed.

Titch learned later that it was on Bert James' suggestion to the General Foreman that he be apprenticed. Mr Whittaker had seen to all the paperwork and read out to Titch all the conditions – now he was in his second year; though he still made the tea for the men and made a little money on the side.

Life had been good to the orphaned boy – he was living with Bert James and his wife who he called Ma; a lovely lady. Kind and gentle – a tiny person, smaller even than Titch, but with a heart as big as a house. She and Bert James were devoted to each other. They were childless having lost a son at birth when Mrs James nearly died; it was all Bert James ever said on the subject

Bert, or Mr Bert, as Titch called him out of respect, had a wooden shed at the end of their tiny garden.

'Me workshop, I calls it. I'd like ter call it me study but that's too swanky.' Bert explained apologetically.

It was nothing like a workshop – one wall was lined with books of all sizes and colours all bought secondhand – there was an old office desk under the only window, and a small pot-belly stove, the kind that gypsies have in their vardos, was against one wall with a steep pipe chimney going through the roof.

'Bought the stove in the lane, I did. Petticoat Lane, that is. Same as most of me books.' Bert James paused and fumbled in his pocket for his pipe. ''Erd of it Titch? The Lane I mean?'

Titch hadn't, so Bert and Ma took him there one Sunday morning; they were people like that. There were two battered armchairs each side of the stove, and a worn rug on the concrete floor. It was a cosy den.

'Just the f'ing fer a couple o'gents like us. We c'n get out'er Ma's way and I c'n 'ave a smoke.' Bert James laughed. 'Know wot' I mean?'

In Cockney fashion, Bert ended a sentence with a question that needed no answer.

Mrs James did not allow her husband to smoke his pipe in the house.

'Disgustin' 'abit. I calls it. If Gawd 'ad meant us t'smoke, 'E'de 'ave stuck a chimney in our 'eads.' Was the way she voiced her disapproval; Bert James smoked his pipe in 'The Workshop'. As far as Titch could see it was his only vice, and that indulged in only at home, and only in the short time he spent in the workshop each evening. The old bricklayer would sit with a pair of steel rimmed spectacles on the end of his nose – when necessary with an oil lamp burning on his desk for illumination, and read. Titch could hardly believe a man could get so much out of books – Bert James did; so did Titch later.

The boy was allowed into the sanctuary a few days after he moved in. It was summer – there was no need for a fire and daylight lasted until 10 o'clock at night. Titch sat night after night with the old bricklayer and absorbed all that he had to teach him – from bricklaying and homely philosophy to sailing; yes sailing.

Bert James had never been to sea – the only time he ever saw it was when he went to Brighton for a weekend one year; and crossing to France during the War. But his knowledge of sailing, small ship navigation, seamanship and sailors was wide; especially those brave enough to sail single-handed on long voyages in small yachts. The American Joshua Slocum was his hero.

'Yer know Titch. That there bloke was out'er work. A h'unemployed sailin' ship captain, 'e was. Ab'art 60 years ago it were. Anyway 'e was a'talkin' to a mate as 'ow 'e couldn't get a ship no 'ow. 'Is mate must've been a bit of a stinker 'cos 'e said, "I've got 'er ship fer yer, Josh." N'e took 'im 'ome and showed 'im this 'ere wreck of a oyster boat in 'is cherry orchard. Rotten as a pear it was by all accounts. "'Ere," 'e said. "You c'n 'ave it," 'e says. An' 'e gives it to ol' Josh 'e does. 'Bloody cheek I would'a called it. Well Joshua Slocum wasn't put out. 'E rebuilds that there boat wiv' 'is own 'ands and sails it around the world by 'is self. The first bloke wot' ever done it, 'e was.' The old bricklayer rose from his chair and went to the book case – after a minute he returned with a book.

''Ere it is, Titch. 'E called 'is ship The Spray.' The old man paused – raised his eyes and looked into the distance. 'I use'ter f'ink that one day I would do that. Sail round the world by meself.' He had a far away look for a moment. 'I would 'ave called me boat Spray, jus' like ol' Josh.' He pulled himself together with a jerk. Almost gruffly he thrust the book at Titch ''Ere, read it. Read about the first bloke as done it. In a boat only f'irty five feet long n'an alarm clock 'e bought fer a dollar fer 'is chronometer.' Titch took the book and read it – twice. It was his initiation to sailing.

116

Titch never set foot on a sailing boat either, but between them they sailed to far off places. Fought storms and savages and basked on sunny sandy beaches and spoke to strange people as they ate coconuts, paw-paws, custard apples and mangoes; all the time they never left those two armchairs in the workshop at East Acton. Many an evening they sat and read, or talked sailing. The stove would be warm and Bert James smoking his pipe. Often Ma would come out to get them to bed.

Nineteen thirty three and Adolf Hitler became Chancellor of Germany – Prohibition ended in the USA – gangsters were being killed by 'G' men; and people were still being sent to Siberia by Stalin.

Prime Minister Ramsey MacDonald headed a Coalition government in Britain and was leading the country out of 'The Great Depression'. Bert James and Titch were working in Chelsea, and the youth bought his first bicycle.

It was a 'Rudge Supreme' – painted a brilliant blue with red facings and lots of chrome. It had drop handlebars, calliper brakes and a Sturmey Archer three speed. Titch now cycled everywhere. To work, to night school, and often to see the Wilsons; more especially to see Judy.

Judy Wilson was 13 and lovelier than ever – very grown-up, Titch thought her – she could talk about politics and religion, and people; the lad was convinced she was very clever.

'A sensible young gell that. Comes from bein' the eldest in the family I suppose. Emotionally

117

mature. That wot' she is,' was the way Bert James described her on one occasion. Sometimes Titch would spend the night at the Wilson's flat and the two would walk around Hyde Park on the Sunday morning, but always accompanied by the younger Wilsons. The young apprentice would allow the three boys to ride his bicycle so they left Judy and him alone with little Molly who couldn't play like other children. She contented herself with the new doll Titch had bought her for her birthday.

They were happy times – the two of them would walk and talk – or just sit and take care of the little girl. Titch would tell Judy about the books he was reading, where he was working, and what Bert James and he talked about. Judy laughed with him when he told her of Bert James' and his own mental adventures to far away places. The laugh changed to a smile.

'It sounds wonderful, Rupert.' She had asked Titch a long time before if she could call him Rupert – he had said yes.

'But only when we are alone.' That is how it has been.

Judy smiled again and touched Titch's hand.

'I would love to go to Australia Rupert. All that sun and blue sky. I read about it in a book from the library.' Her eyes were alight as she told Titch about kangaroos, gold mines and sheep farms. 'They are so big they measure them in square miles, not acres. Stations they call them. Sheep stations. Not farms. And there are cattle stations where they have cows and the men ride horses.'

'Like they do in America? I didn't know that.' Again Titch marvelled at her knowledge.

'Yes Rupert. And the cattle stations are even bigger than where they have the sheep.'

It sounded exciting. Titch remembered how impressed he was – by what she had told him, and the fact that she knew so much.

'Let's go to Australia when we grow up, Judy. Just you and me.'

Judy was silent. Titch thought he had said something terrible and looked at her. Judy looked away, then back to him – their eyes met; she spoke.

'That means we will have to get married, doesn't it?'

'Does it? Do you have to be married to go to Australia then?'

'I don't think so, but if we are going together we ought, don't you think?' Titch was not sure, he had never thought of it; not marriage or anything like that – he almost stammered as he said,

'Would you… Would you like that Judy?'

It was a question that he never dreamed he would ask – with more courage he continued. 'I mean. I wouldn't want you to marry me if you didn't want to really. But I think I would like to marry you.'

Molly came over at that point and asked her sister to tie her doll's hat on. The little girl walked back to the seat. It had given them both a moment to think – a moment when Titch thrilled at the thought of having Judy forever. The youth looked at her – their eyes met again.

'I think I would like to marry you too Rupert. But not yet.' She added the last hurriedly.

'Then let us. Just before we go to Australia.'

'Yes, let's.' She paused and Titch heard her

catch her breath. 'That means we are engaged.'

'Does it? What does that mean?'

'It means we are promised to each other and I mustn't go with another boy, and you mustn't go with another girl... and we can kiss.' Titch could see she was embarrassed, but no more than he was.

'What? Like they do on the pictures?'

It had Titch puzzled. He knew fellows did things like kissing girls and other things. He heard a lot about it at work among the men and intended to ask Bert James what it was all about – so far the opportunity had not arisen. Titch made up his mind to ask the old fellow as soon as possible. He looked at Judy again.

'I don't think we ought to kiss, though.' It seemed a way for Titch to buy time. 'Not yet. Not until we are grown up. And perhaps your Mum and Dad won't like us being,' the boy's tongue stumbled on the word. 'Engaged.' Titch blurted the word out. The lad was sure he saw relief in Judy's eyes.

'Perhaps you are right. And perhaps we ought to keep it a secret for the time being.'

'Until we are grown up you mean.'

'Yes, Rupert. Then we won't have to kiss.'

Titch could see her point and agreed – it would make things a lot simpler, he could see that. The thought of kissing Judy like film stars did in the pictures alarmed yet excited him.

With the spring of 1933 Titch began to extend his cycling range. He ventured into the countryside of Middlesex and Hertfordshire; even into Surrey – sometimes a 100 mile round trip on a

Sunday. It was a long way but he was fit and enjoyed it. His journeys took him as far as Harrow-on-the-Hill to see the famous Harrow school. The boy was tickled at the sight of the Harrow Boys walking around in their small peaked caps. They were boys just a little younger than he was. There was nothing for it but that he had to go to that other famous school, Eton, and was equally tickled at the short jackets and straw hats of their uniforms. 'Boaters' they called the hats. Dozens of boys, all shapes and sizes promenaded along the banks of the River Thames. Titch saw the famous playing fields and remembered reading that battles were won on them; he couldn't see how, though they were big enough.

On the way home, he looked at Windsor Castle and recalled Bert James' comment about his work lasting forever. 'Like Windsor Castle.' Titch looked at the huge grey walls and imagined a boy in the year 2033 looking at his own work and perhaps marvelling.

Runnymede was on the way home and he stopped for a lemonade at the roadside kiosk and walked to the site of where the Magna Carta was signed in 1215 by King John of England. Titch closed his eyes on the spot to 'see' the pavilions of the knights. He 'heard' the braying trumpets and the clashing of armour. Ranks of English longbowmen and helmeted pikemen stood before the king and his nobles. It all became real for the boy better than what he had read.

It was a cold November night – there was a thick 'London Pea Souper' of a fog so Titch had not gone to night school. Bert James and he were sitting close to the stove. Bert was puffing away on the second pipe of the evening and reading; Titch was leaning back in his chair thinking with his eyes closed.

The boy heard Bert knocking his pipe out on the lid of the stove, but did not move.

'I wouldn't give yer a bob fer yer f'oughts Titch. Tuppence, maybe.'

'Nothing really, Mr Bert. I was just wondering about my mum. I never had a dad, but I often wonder what he was like. Who he was. You know what I mean. My mum never told me about him, or if she did I can't remember.'

Titch opened his eyes and looked at the old bricklayer. Bert peered at the lad over the tops of his glasses.

'Don't reckon as 'ow that's too 'ard ter find out Titch.' He thought for a moment and reached for the battered tin that contained his tobacco.

'Somerset 'Ouse.' He said after a moment of thought. 'They'll know. Go there n'ask fer yer birf' certificate. That'll tell yer where you was born and yer Dad's name n'f'ings.' The pair talked more on the subject before they went in for the night.

The next day Titch asked Mr Whittaker if he could leave work an hour early and cycled all the way to the large black stone building that housed all the Birth, Death and Marriage Certificates of just about all the people of Britain. Titch paid his 2/6d for the document and cycled home in the dark with another pea souper threatening. That evening, Bert James and the boy examined the birth certificate.

'Well,' said Bert after he had examined it. 'You

was born in Wandsworth, but yer mum was a spinster. Gave 'er address as in St Albans. That's in Hertfordshire.' He looked at Titch over the tops of his glasses. 'It says 'ere "Father Unknown". And you as h'illegitimate.'

They were silent – Bert scraped a match and relit his pipe – Titch found that tears were forming in his eyes. His mother was not a war widow as he believed, and he was a bastard. Something you called someone you don't like – a swear word. It was all a shock. Bert James sensed the boy's distress.

'Don't let it get cher down, Titch. Some'a the greatest men in 'istory were bastards. S'nuffin ter be ashamed of. S'not your fault. You didn't ask ter be born, did yer?' He laughed his short laugh. 'Ma always says as 'ow a person's lucky if they're sure who their dad is.'

Titch laughed too – it was alright after that. Five minutes later and the boy could not concentrate on the book of Building Construction he was reading. He put it down at last and looked across at his old friend.

'If the weather is OK on Sunday, I'm going to St Albans to that address. Perhaps there is someone there who remembers my mum.'

Bert James studied the youth.

'S'a long way, Titch. It'll be dark a'fore you gets 'ome. Ma'll worry yer know.'

'I'll be alright Mr Bert. I'll buy new batteries for my lamps and carry a spare one in case. If I'm going to be late I will phone Mrs Jenkins in the newsagents and ask her to tell Ma.'

'Good idea.' He lit his pipe again and took up

his book. Titch managed to finish the chapter he had as an assignment from night school before Ma came to tell them that it was time for bed and their cocoa was on the table.

St Albans was a long way – 50 miles? The cold ate into Titch – the wind cut through his clothing and in no time his feet were like ice. He had his head down and his bum up and he went – pedalling as hard as he could to get warm. The lad soon warmed up – except his hands; two pairs of gloves didn't seem to help. It was a bitterly cold day in early December – the skies were clear and there was a frost when he left home before it was light.

It was still dark – street lights had been turned off; stars shone above roofs of the sordid London buildings unseen by the youth as he sped by. There was light enough to steer by; his lamp cut a swath through the darkness at gutter level. The suburbs of North London seemed endless; dawn was a wonderful experience as it came up on his right hand side. Each of the few open spaces revealed the promise of a fine day. It was – the sun came out and warmed him a little as he left the houses and streets behind and found himself in Hertfordshire.

The trees were bare of leaves – it was hardly the 'Leafy Hertfordshire' of the glossy brochures; green fields stretched away over the hills. There was little traffic so he made good time – sweat was beginning to form on his brow as the morning progressed. Titch put the woolly hat Judy had knitted for him in his pocket – his hands were warmer though he still wore two pairs of gloves, but his nose continued to run. His handkerchief was beneath his hat stuffed firmly in his pocket so he just sniffed as his legs pumped the pedals; miles slipped away beneath the wheels of his Rudge.

Titch saw the spire of St Albans' Cathedral miles away; he hurried towards it. He stood on the pedals and pushed and puffed his way up the hill; too proud to get off and walk.

The congregation were leaving as Titch got to the ancient doors of the Cathedral – he relaxed and free-wheeled past and was able to take a breather and look about him. The devout burghers of the Cathedral City did not notice the youth sitting up on his bicycle saddle studying them.

St Albans was a sleepy little town that Sunday morning. The main street was lined with old fashioned looking shops – bow windows reminded Titch of a book from Mr Bert's book shelf. There was a little café on a corner – more of a tea shop really; the sort of place lorry drivers stop. Titch stopped for a cup of tea, and the hope that someone could guide him to his destination.

He had finished his tea and an Eccles cake when the old man came in and spoke to the lady proprietor. The old gent sat down at a table close to Titch. He was old, stooped and poorly dressed; a battered trilby hat still on his head had a wide band of grease around the trim. The lady brought him a cup of tea and he delved into his pocket with a hand covered with tattered, moth-eaten mittens. Carefully, he extracted some small change and passed it with nothing more than a sniff. Straight away he dived his nose into the drink and drank deep. His cup hit the saucer rather noisily – looked at Titch as if to apologise; the lad took his cue.

'Would you know where Bethesda Crescent is, please?'

Old eyes looked at Titch – they were almost black, and he had deep shadows beneath them.

'A'course. It's just down the street on y'right.' He dived into the cup and drained it.

'Thank you. Will you join me in another cup of tea.'

'Ta. Don't mind if I do,' He looked hard at Titch with rheumy eyes. 'You 'avin' one?' he snapped.

'Of course, and another cake. Will you join me?'

'Yeh...' then, as an afterthought 'Ta.'

Titch didn't know why he made the gesture – the man didn't look a very nice sort of person. Thinking about it afterwards, Titch thought he felt sorry for him. He looked so cold and hungry – the boy supposed he was for he swallowed the cake in two bites, then picked up the crumbs from his coat; the cup of tea disappeared in much the same way as his first. He would have bought him another but he couldn't afford it. Titch said a polite 'Good Morning' and left him picking the crumbs from his plate – Titch remembered, smiling at how Miss Cuthberson would have disapproved of him. He could hear her say. 'He did not even say thank you, Rupert. A really terrible man.' And she would have been right.

Bethesda Crescent, when Titch found it, was a bow shaped road of tall, narrow Victorian terraced houses. Tall pointed gables reached into the blue December sky. Narrow unpainted windows peered out of dirty brick walls that showed where ivy had once climbed. The garden plots were

126

littered with debris of leaves and twigs blown off the roadside lime trees during the winter gales; several of the gates swung askew on broken hinges.

Number eleven was different – it had neat floral curtains hanging over recently painted window frames. A neat plot of garden was bare of growth other than a small square of close cropped grass that reached along the narrow frontage. As Titch opened the iron gate a large black cat ran from beneath a solitary rhododendron bush in a neighbour's plot. A short path led up to five steps that were a clean sandy colour. On a small landing as a brightly varnished, heavy wooden door – a polished brass knocker in the shape of a fox's head was in the centre at eye level. Titch knocked – the sound echoed through the house – it sounded empty, yet he was sure he saw movement at the curtain. The whole thing terrified the boy – he wanted to run; he was about to, when the door opened and an elderly gent peered at him.

'Yes?' It was a kindly question – one that Titch was not sure he could answer; his tongue seemed glued to the roof of his mouth. The youth hesitated long enough to arouse some suspicion in the man's mind.

'What do you want?' His voice took on a harsh tone – with a struggle, Titch controlled his vocal cords.

'Excuse me, sir. I am looking for the house of Miss Dorothy Wilkins.'

It was Titch's mother's name, the lad could think of no other way to broach the subject.

The man visibly paled. He clutched the door with a gnarled hand. Blue veins appeared in his neck and face. It was over in a minute – he seemed to recover and was about to open the door when a voice checked him.

'What is it Charles? Who is at the door?'

It was a woman's voice – before the man could answer a small neat elderly lady appeared at his side. She wore a long very dark, rather severe, green dress and black woollen shawl over her narrow shoulders. She had a pleasant enough face – hardly pretty for she was very pale and quite old – her mouth was a thin line of un-rouged lips. When Titch told Bert James about it later, he called it a neat face – a rather hard face, and it was. It was long with a pointed chin. Her eyes were brown and very clear. Titch recalled that at the time he was surprised how white the whites of her eyes were. The orphaned youth managed to look into those eyes and repeated the question he had put to the man.

'I am sorry to bother you, Madam but I am looking for the house of Miss Dorothy Wilkins.'

The woman hesitated, for just a moment – her hand went to the door as if to close it; she seemed to grow in stature as she drew in a deep breath.

'You had better come in young man.'

The man just stood. The old lady opened the door wider and allowed Titch to enter – he heard the door close behind him; the man's footsteps were muffled as they followed the old woman. She led them through a door and into a neat room that had a coal fire burning in a small tiled fireplace. The room looked comfortable and felt warm. The lady sat herself down on a well-padded armchair – the man closed the door and

128

went over to the fireplace; he stood with his back to the blaze. The silence was electric and seemed endless – Titch had a feeling he was trapped; he was beginning to regret ever coming and would have panicked if she had not spoken.

'Now young man. Who are you,' she hesitated as if trying to find the right words. 'And who is Dorothy Wilkins?'

Titch heard a gasp from the man – the boy was sure he was about to say something but she cut him off sharply.

'Be quiet Charles! I'll handle this.' She looked at Titch out of those brown eyes with the white whites. 'Well?'

Titch gulped, words tumbled from his mouth.

'Dorothy Wilkins was my mother. I am trying to find out where she lived. Do you, I mean, did you know her?' Titch began to sense that something was wrong – he added an afterthought. 'Please. That's all I want to know. I don't want to cause any bother.'

There was silence again – Titch heard the man's breathing coming in gasps. A coal shifted in the fire; the old lady's hands rustled as she dry washed them on her lap.

'I'm sorry to have troubled you. I'd best go.' Titch turned to leave but the old lady's hand shot out and caught him by the front of his jacket.

'No! Wait. Don't go. Charles.' She looked towards her husband. 'Bring a chair. Don't just stand there like a fool.' Her voice was harsh and the man obeyed.

Titch couldn't tear his eyes away from the top of the old lady's head as she held him. Her hair was combed back tight against her skull – it was grey, almost white, and thin; Titch saw pink flesh through the hair. He remembered thinking how small her head was – no bigger than a child's football. The man brought a straight back chair; when the woman's hand released him, the boy sat. Their eyes were level now and she looked deep into his. Young as he was, somehow Titch was able to meet them. The woman seemed to want to strip Titch with her eyes – not his clothes, but strip him to his soul. When she spoke her voice had a rasp in it. It was soft – soft yet it had a sharp edge to it. Sharp and jagged – like Bert James' bow saw. It cut through the atmosphere of the room like old Bert James' saw cut through those soft red bricks.

'We never mention that name in this house young man. I don't doubt that you are her son but we want nothing to do with you or anything that is hers. She disgraced us. It was sinful what she did. Quite unforgivable. By me, or by God.'

'But she is dead. She died a long time ago.' Titch's voice was almost a cry. Where was the forgiving Christ he was taught to believe in. He looked at the face close to his. A hardness, a resolve, had come over it.

'But Jane…' It was the voice of the man.

'No, Charles. Don't ask me to weaken. Don't ask me to forgive. This young fellow is her bastard and I want nothing to do with him.' She rolled her eyes upwards in desperation or frustration, Titch couldn't tell which.

'To think a daughter of ours could do such a thing as an unmarried woman. She was nothing but a slut. A whore. And after all we did for her.'

Her hands were working as she dry washed them. 'If she suffered for her looseness, it is no more than she deserved. To be truthful.' She hesitated, and drew a deep breath. 'I am glad she is dead.'

There was a groan from the man now sitting in another chair close to the door. Titch's mind was a blur – he didn't know what his mother had been but he was sure she had not been a whore. The boy heard men at work talking about whores and what they did. Titch didn't fully understand what it all meant but he knew instinctively that his mother was not like that.

Titch stood – he wanted to get out of the house into the fresh air. The hand stopped him again; he snatched himself away. The words came as a sob 'You must be my Grandma. I always wanted a Grandma but if they are all like you I am glad I haven't. 'Cos I don't want you! You lady are a bitch. An un-forgiving bitch.'

Bitch? It was a word he heard his workmates use for women that were not very nice. Tears welled up in Titch's eyes. He staggered to the door and by mistake turned the wrong way and stumbled into a kitchen-like room before realising his error. He turned and collided with the man just leaving the room where the old lady still sat in the arm-chair.

Titch barged past him not caring that he was ill-mannered or that the man was his grand-father; the boy just wanted to get out.

'Wait a moment, please. Don't go like that. Please.' It was a plea – a plea that made Titch pause in his rush for the door – tears were running down the boy's face; he hesitated. An old

131

hand clutched his arm hard – young eyes looked into a pair of ancient blue eyes that were brimming with tears.

'What is your name, son?'

'Rupert.' Titch said without thinking.

'Rupert? That was his name. She told me all about him.'

'Whose name?

'Your father's, lad. He was killed in the Battle of Jutland. They were to be married, but he got killed. It wasn't her fault. She wasn't a whore. It was the war and they were in love.'

Titch didn't understand – he was hurt; he was afraid. For him it was like being back in the orphanage and the workhouse with people hurting him. He fought them, but he couldn't fight these people – they were old and this hurt was different, almost more. It pained him where he had never had a pain before – deep down inside him. He couldn't fight so he wanted to run; like a wild animal he wanted to run and hide; run to his own lair. Titch wanted Bert and Ma – he saw them and their little terraced house as a sanctuary.

The old man's grip tightened on the youth's arm.

'Wait a moment. Please. I have something for you.'

Titch made to jerk his arm free – the old man tightened his grip.

'Please Rupert.' It was a croak – a plea.

Titch relaxed – the old grandfather released his hold and scurried back to the room where his wife still sat over the fire – head lowered; hands washing dryly. Titch heard voices raised in anger

– he couldn't make out what was said. The door burst open and the grandfather was at his side.

'Here, Rupert lad. Take these. They were hers. Your mother's.'

He handed Titch a photograph of a young officer in uniform, and a gold ring.

'And this was your mother.'

Titch looked through his tears – all was a blur. He took the ring and the photographs and stuffed them in his pocket and turned to go. He paused.

'If you knew who my father was, why is he marked as unknown on my birth certificate?'

'She didn't want his family to know. They are gentry I believe. She was adamant about that. I will carry his baby by myself she said. And she did, poor girl. She bore it alone. Much to my shame.'

The old man sniffed back a tear – Titch walked to the door; opened it and left the house. A voice came to him through the door panels. It was a cry of anguish.

'Good bye, Rupert! Gold bless you! Forgive us if you can!'

Titch ran – he fell down the steps in his hurry to leave. He mounted his bicycle and sped away with tears horizontal streaks across his face; it was like being four years old again. Workhouse memories flooded his mind – the hurt – the loneliness. Titch was not able to express it all as a child, but the indignity of it all struck him as he cycled towards the city and home.

Had there ever been such pain? Titch remembered what Bert James had told him about his own life – of his suffering, not that he ever called it that.

The time when Ma had nearly died, and all his mates dead in the mud and filth of the trenches in France; his un-employment and the empty larder. Things had been grim for the old bricklayer but he had survived.

Titch's sight and mind cleared – he descended the hill outside the old Cathedral City and the Hertfordshire countryside opened up before him. His tears dried in the cold December wind and he felt better – he put weight on the pedals and concentrated on the road ahead, but thoughts came.

'Old Mister Bert is right. A bloke's troubles are exclusively his own and only he can sort them out.' The lad sniffed back a tear that threatened. 'I am a bastard and must learn to live with that. Nobody else cares. I have no family so I must lump it n'like it.' He smiled grimly at the thought.

The miles sped under the wheels of the Rudge – Titch's mind would not release the events of the morning. The pain refused to go away. The lad thought of what he had been taught as a school boy of the first Easter – the story of Christ carrying his cross to Calvary. 'Being a bastard is my cross and I've got to carry it. It hurts but I'll do it.' As the decision cemented in his mind the weight of sorrow and loneliness lifted.

Street lights shone wanly through the city's frosty haze – a night's chill began to freeze Titch's hands, feet and face. The vision of Ma's warm fire and a hot drink comforted the youth as he pushed hard on the pedals of the Rudge. Soon the sparse traffic of outer suburbs gave way to the congestion of the city and he was rattling over the cobbles and weaving through the tram lines in East Acton High Street. Not until he was free-wheeling down the last downhill stretch did he relax and think of the future.

Chapter Six

The two men Titch saw on neighbouring graves were concerned more with their own discussions than with their neighbours. The aged military gent was too far away for Titch to speak to, but his direct neighbour, a younger rotund gent, monopolised the older man's attention. He was close to Titch so was able to talk, according to the 'rules' applying to this macabre situation.

He was portly; very like the picture of Mr Pickwick Titch had seen in one of Bert James' books by Charles Dickens. His belly bulged; it was as if he had a bladder of some sort concealed under his tight fitting pearl grey waistcoat that sported a gold watch chain and heavy gold fob. He was a little under medium height, quite bald with strands of hair that he endeavoured to 'stretch' across his pate hoping perhaps to give the impression that he was not completely without hair. A ruddy complexion told of more than a liking for the good life and the habitual use of a corkscrew. He was dressed well in a suit of charcoal grey material. His white shirt was clean; the tie around his neck was old school vintage. Expensive shoes were polished to a bright shine. A red carnation was conspicuous in his lapel. If Titch was asked to guess his line of work he would probably have said a publisher, a solicitor perhaps, or a bank manager. In point of fact the man was a doctor, or had been. And probably a good one; certainly a talkative one the way Titch saw him and the old soldier talking.

Titch had spent fruitless hours trying to make visual contact – just to be friendly, you understand. Death does not seem to alter basic personalities. Titch had always been a friendly cove though he would have confessed that at times he wished he hadn't been. Got him into a lot of trouble from time to time.

Bert James encouraged Titch in his friendly advances towards people – it had not always been so; Titch's experience with adults had not encouraged hasty communication. It was with Bert's cheerful help that he overcame this reticence and allowed what Titch believed was his natural friendliness to emerge. Bert asked him once why he was so shy with some people; strangers that is.

'Yer don't say much, Titch. Seems like you're unfriendly like. I knows you're ain't, but 'uvvers don't. They f'inks as 'ow maybe you're a'sulkin'. Got sum'fink to 'ide, maybe.' They were working together on an arch 50 feet above the London traffic at the time.

'You know I've got nothing to hide, Mr Bert. Except, well you know. I keep quiet because then I can't say the wrong thing if I say nothing, can I?' Titch remembered Bert looking at him closely.

'Can't say the right f'ing either, can yer Titch.

Know wot' I mean?' His little philosophical quips always set Titch thinking.

They were working building a new block of offices in the City at the time. High over the London streets – in sight of St Paul's. Bert laughed and straightened his back with a trowel-ful of mortar in his hand. He spread the soft compound along the apex of the arch, then looked at Titch as he stooped to take a brick from the pile. Like he said 'Bert never stopped work to talk.' 'Whistle n'ride, I says,' was the way he described it. 'You're paid fer workin' not a'yappin'.'

Bert James laid another brick, 'Anyways,' he continued. He looked at Titch again, his eyes twinkling with a secret joke.

'I remember,' he says. 'I were a young'un. A bit older than you. A'fore I met Ma, that is. I were at a local 'op. A dance. Know wot' I mean? I'd 'ad a beer or two so was feelin' a bit cocky like. Anyway, I sees this 'ere girl a'standin' on the side o'the dance floor. Quite a nice looker she was.' Bert tapped the brick into place with the edge of his trowel and scraped the overflowing mortar away. He threw the scraping on to the mortar board and rolled another trowel-ful of mortar ready to spread.

'Can I 'ave this dance, I says. Didn't say nuffin', she did. Just looked at me and we starts a'dancin' One o'they new quicksteps it were. Got 'alf way round the floor a'fore I looks at 'er n'says. "Comin' down the alley fer a cuddle after?"' He laughed again. 'Well, Titch. She steps back a pace and lands me a wallop right round the chops. Fair stung it did. I takes no notice and we dances a bit.' Another brick was laid and he reached for the spirit level.

'Just about all the way around the floor we was. She looks me straight in the eye n'says. "Does you always ask a girl that when yer first meets 'em then?" "Every time," says I. "You must get a lot a'slaps in the face," she says. "I do," I says. "But I gets a lot a'cuddles, too."'

They were both laughing; so was Paddy McCoy their hod carrier who had stopped to listen. Bert continued more seriously.

'So yer sees, Titch mate. It pays ter say sumfin'. Ter pass the time'a day so ter speak. Oh I know we all says the wrong 'fings sometimes. But as we learn, we say more o'the right f'ings. Know wot' I mean then?'

Titch did, and began to venture into more friendly communication with strangers after that, to the extent that he was generally the one to open a conversation.

The stout gent across the grave from Titch refused to give him the time of day and never even looked his way, always engrossed with the military gent. That was until the other day. A beautiful day it was – the sort of day it was good to be alive; a stupid thing to say when Titch knew he was dead, but you know what I mean. Titch looked across at the well-dressed gent – he was just hovering and not talking to his neighbour.

'Lovely day,' Titch said. Not that they can appreciate it totally. The can't feel anything, really. Not the warmth of the sun, or the rain or cold – just nice things – things that give them nice sort of feelings, and Titch supposed, nasty things too. He wasn't sure about that though; nothing nasty had happened so far, but they all seem to enjoy beauty. Like that day – it was beautiful; the sun shone and the sky was blue.'

'Yes. You are right. It is a lovely day.' The older man looked directly at Titch. Titch saw his neighbour, the military gent in the cream shade cord breeches and an oatmeal coloured tweed Norfolk jacket looking across the narrow footpath to his other neighbour. He doffed his old tweed hat and turned to a lady on a grave to his right and presumably began talking.

The stout man and Titch introduced themselves. He impressed Titch as a fellow who liked to do the talking.

'I've heard about you chaps. Formed the Royal Air Force in 1918, I remember. I was in France then. Royal Army Medical Corps. Heck of a life it was. Terrible time. Patched up some of you flying chaps. Ghastly burns some of them had.'

The conversation went on. He was a former Major in the RAMC. Served in France and Egypt until in 1918 when he returned to his practice in Broadstairs.

'Was here until I popped me clogs in thirty four. Just six months after the Colonel. Bit of a surprise when I found I was buried next to him. Rather nice though. I mean. If a chap has to go. Heart attack it was. Clean bowled me it did. Went into a coma and never woke up. I should have known better. Been telling people for years not to smoke or drink too much but never stopped either me'self. Liked me food too.' He patted his ample stomach. 'Really should have known better.' He looked across at his neighbour.

'The old Colonel there listened to me. Cut out smoking and sold a fine cellar of port thirty years before when I first told him. The old bounder lived to be ninety-eight. Then had to fall and break his neck watching the hunt. Had to go following the hounds. Never missed a meet. Was the Master until he had to give up riding.' He gave a short laugh. 'Climbed a wall and stood on the top for a better view. "Tally Ho'ing" like a young buck he was. Told him not to be an old fool but he is a stubborn old devil. Fell off the top he did. Only four feet but enough. His neck snapped like a carrot. Killed him instantly. Nice way for the old chap to go I suppose. He was getting cranky the last year or two. Going deaf he was too, but he denied it. Complained people mumbled all the time. Still is you know. Cranky I mean. Swears I should have treated him better and that I charged him too much. Even says I pushed him off the wall. I was trying to help the old devil. Always arguing he is. Cranky as ever. A damned good sort all the same.'

Titch felt compelled to comment. 'Well, you kept him going. Ninety-eight. Wonderful. Pity he didn't make a century. A Colonel you say he was. What regiment?' The doctor's information had Titch fascinated – he wanted to hear more; he soon learned. There was no need for Titch to say another word.

'Royal Kent Hussars I think,' the doctor had the bit between his teeth. 'Got swords and trophies and things dating back to the Crimea. He was an Ensign with the Light Brigade at Balaclava.

140

Carried the Regimental Colour in the charge. Only seventeen years old. Probably the youngest man there. Got his mount shot from under him in front of the Russian guns.'

'That must have been something.' Titch was thrilled to be able to see a member of that charge. Alfred Lord Tennyson's poem was learned off by heart by the lads at Swaffield Boys' School; Titch could hear them now.

'Half a League. Half a League. Half a League
    Onwards.
Into the Valley of Death rode the Six Hundred.'

Titch remembered it well – most boys had to learn it in his day. There was a four foot long print of a famous painting of the charge hanging in the dining hall of the school. Horses galloping – men screaming and waving sabres. Many a dream Titch had of that; saw himself leading it on a big black horse. 'It really must have been something.' Titch looked at the doctor and sighed. The medico disagreed.

'Bloody murder the old man says. The most stupid thing in the whole stupid war he says and he has seen a few. Quite vocal about it he is. Didn't like that chap Tennyson. Thought he romanticised a debacle instead of telling the sheer bloody insanity of it. Gets quite worked up about it he does. Mind you. The old fellow didn't see the last show. Too old, but he tells me he tried to enlist. If the Crimea was stupid. The Great War was utter madness. A different war altogether really. From the Colonel's wars I mean. The old man fought from the Crimea to the South African War in 1899. Over sixty he was yet he was wounded by

141

the Boers. Fought in Egypt and the Sudan too. In the battle of Omdurman in '98 I think it was. Was on Kitchener's staff but attached himself to the Lancers for the battle. Was wounded there, too. Got one of the fanatical Dervish chap's spears in his leg. One of those barbed things. Vicious weapons. They go in easy enough but they are the very devil to get out. His batman had to break off the shaft of the spear to get him back. Had the blade in his leg for hours he told me. Must have hurt like the blazes. One has to cut away great lumps of flesh to remove the barb.' He paused and looked across at the old cavalryman – admiration written all over his face. The doctor continued.

'The old chap was nearly 60 then. He was in the same charge as Winston Churchill. The last cavalry charge in history they tell me.' He paused again to cast another glance at the old man talking to his genteel lady neighbour. He turned and looked at Titch again.

'He's making a name for himself again, the last I heard in '34. Churchill I mean. Stirring up the government to arm against this Hitler fellow in Germany. Nasty piece of goods if you ask me. Going to cause a heap of trouble, you'll see. I agree with Churchill. If Germany starts another war, Britain may not be so lucky. It was a close thing last time, you know.' There was another pause as the doctor considered.

'Yes. He should be back in government. He'll make it to Number 10 if he doesn't smoke himself to death with those wretched cigars of his. I hear he drinks like a fish too. Idiot. I hope he stops in time.' He looked across at the old

Colonel again, then back to Titch.

'Terrible weed, tobacco. Killed more people than guns since that fool Raleigh brought it here from America.'

He prattled on for some minutes regarding the stupidity of man.

'They eat too much. Drink too much and smoke that terrible stuff. It'll kill 'em all before their time.' He laughed an almost merry laugh. 'I should talk. A case of do as I say, not what I do wouldn't you say?'

He laughed again and looked back at the old man, he seemed more anxious to talk with him than he was with Titch so the younger man let him go. The two were very obviously old friends.

The Cunard Liner *'QUEEN MARY'* made her maiden voyage in 1935. Britain, France and Germany had begun an armaments race. The Royal Navy launched the first of its new class battleships, *HMS King George V.* To be known affectionately as KG5. New Hawker Hurricane fighter aircraft were seen over English skies, and more ugly rumours reached world newspapers of atrocities in the USSR and now Germany.

Benito Mussolini's armies invaded Abyssinia – the world stood by and watched native peoples suppressed with modern weapons including poison gas; they did nothing but make feeble protests at The League of Nations in Geneva. Bert James and Titch were working in Whitehall, building air raid shelters under the government offices and Titch continued to worry and wonder about his parentage.

143

Bert James and Titch spent a spring evening recalling his experience in St Albans. They examined again the picture of Titch's father and that of his mother.

'C'n see where you get'cher good looks Titch. Yer mum and dad are good lookers n'no mistake. Always thought that maybe yer 'ad a bit'ter gentry about yer too. Breedin' they calls it. Know wot' I mean? N'you is the spittin' image of this 'ere photo. If 'e ain't yer dad then my name ain't Bert James.'

Titch wasn't sure what he meant about breeding. It must have shown on his face, for Bert continued.

'Breedin'? It shows in wot' they calls bone structure. Yer face, I mean. Take yer nose. Straight and clean lookin'. Now look at mine. All fat and pudgy. See.' he turned his head and showed Titch his profile. His nose was short and pudgy – fat if one chose to be unkind. 'Yours is wot' they calls classical. And me chin. Look at it now. No real shape to it. And if I didn't work so 'ard I would be rounder than one of Ma's suet puddin's. Yer see, Titch. I ain't gentry. Nei'ver was me dad, or 'is dad a'fore 'im. A cockney 'e was. A fish porter at Billingsgate 'e was. All 'is life. Born in the sound o'the Bells n'proud of it. You? You is different. From a different mould, sorter 'fing. Not any better mind yer,' he added hastily. 'Just different. Gentler. Know wot' I mean?' Titch didn't, but he didn't say so.

Bert took in his hand the gold ring Titch's grandfather had given him, and held it to the light of the last rays of sunlight pouring through

144

the workshop window. The old bricklayer peered closely at it through his glasses.

'S'got a crest of some sort on it. Coat of arms I would 'fink. N'some writin'. Could be a motto. A family motto, most like.' He handed it to Titch and he examined it. The old bricklayer was right, though Titch could make little of it.

'Tell yer wot, Titch. We'll go the library ter'-morrer night n'get one o'they books on 'eraldry and us'll see if we can find as 'oo it belongs to.'

They did – the pair poured over a voluminous book depicting coats of arms of companies, corporations and families from all over the British Empire. It took them over an hour to find the one they sought. A Griffin and a Lion on a shield with crossed swords and a motto *'I DDYRU SYDD YN ENILL.'* in a scroll beneath. Bert James and Titch were nonplussed.

'It ain't Latin, Titch. Don't know much about it but I knows it ain't Latin.' He scratched his head in puzzlement. 'I knows wot. Let's ask the Librarian bloke.' They did – the librarian declared it to be Welsh. They spent an hour looking through a Welsh/English Dictionary translating the motto into English. The result showed the crest to be the family of App-Lugus, described as the Squire of the Manor of Cuffty Mawr, or Big Cuffty in English, in the district of Beddgelert, in the county of Caernarfon in North Wales. The motto translated was. *'TO STRIVE IS TO ACHIEVE.'*

The Manor Estate of Cuffty Mawr was established in 1660 by King Charles II of England who rewarded for his services to the

145

Crown the then Llewellyn Lleu Lugus who led a force of Prince Rupert's Cavaliers against Oliver Cromwell's Parliamentarian Army in the Civil Wars of 1644 to 1660.

Bert James closed the book and felt for his pipe. He slapped his empty pockets and remembered he had left it in 'The Workshop'. He leaned back in his chair in that library reading room and looked at Titch.

'Well Titch mate. I knowed I was right. You is gentry. But born the wrong side o'the blanket, as they say. And that makes it all a bit difficult.' He stood up. 'Let's go 'ome and talk about this.'

They did and the long and the short of it was Titch was going to ask for a week's holiday to coincide with the Easter holiday weekend and go to Wales and discover what he could of his father's family.

Titch Wilkins travelled until it was dark that Thursday evening. Mr Whittaker allowed him to leave early and he was on the road by two in the afternoon. It was a lovely day and promised to be a warm weekend. He managed to reach Aylesbury before dark. The second night he made Oswestry on the A5 road – the old 'Watlin Street' of Pilgrim days; he was in Wales. The later afternoon of the third day he rode into the tiny Welsh hill town of Beddgelert. Titch was tired – he booked into the Youth Hostel and almost fell into his allotted bed; not even bothering to cook a meal in the communal kitchen.

He woke refreshed and hungry. Bacon and eggs at a small café filled his stomach but did nothing to allay his fears of the coming day. The memory of the meeting with his grandparents was much on his mind – he was prepared for the worst; or thought he was.

The locals called the manor Cuffty Hall – old stone pillars of the entrance were overgrown with ivy; the tall iron gates had not been closed for a long time. The gate-keeper's lodge was empty and dilapidated. Titch rode his bicycle up the long drive; ruts showed where cars had driven. The surface was poor and full of potholes; trees cast a deep shade. There were horse droppings, old and new, along the centre grassed area.

Cuffty Hall appeared suddenly standing in an open space above unkempt terraced gardens with trees in the background – woods stretched down the side of the valley in front of the house. Titch stopped as much to look as to get his breath. It was beautiful, neglected but beautiful. The old mansion stood at the head of what the Welsh call a 'coombe', or the end of a valley. The old dark granite house was squat and solid overlooking the woods that stretched below into the distance. The roof was slate – all the windows were large and stood out white against the dark stone.

Titch sat there for five minutes telling himself he was getting his breath after the climb – he knew he was gathering his courage to make that last half mile and knock on the door he could see above some wide steps.

Bert James had offered to come with him, but Titch reminded him of his comments about troubles being custom-made for one's self.

'Suit yerself, Titch mate. But it won't be easy. You may not be welcome, yer know. But you're

147

right. It's your problem and in the end it's you as got ter sort it out wot'ever 'appens. But we'll be a'finkin' of yer. Ma n'me. Might even pray a bit. Know wot' I mean?' Titch did and he was grateful – sitting there looking at the manor house Titch wished Bert was with him.

There was a movement at the house and Titch pushed down on his pedal and covered the half mile at a slow, cautious pace. He propped his Rudge against the stone palisade of the steps and climbed the shallow treads to the paved terrace. He looked up and saw above the door the crest of the Griffin and the Lion with crossed swords, and the motto in weathered stone, but unmistakably *'I DDYRU SYDDYN ENILL'* 'To Strive is to Achieve'. Titch said the translation aloud – it gave him courage; enough to bang on the heavy oak door.

It took a long minute for anyone to come. Titch's heart was beating fast – he would dearly love to bolt. He looked at his bicycle leaning just feet away; he could be in the saddle and down that drive fast. The opening of the door cancelled all that. Titch turned and faced whatever was there and saw the face of an elderly man servant.

The old man looked closely at Titch and seemed to hesitate. His lips trembled and he held on tight to the door.

'Dear God. Is that you Master Rupert?'

Titch almost answered yes, but he could see the old fellow was distressed and did not mean him.

'May I see Mr App-Lugus please. My name is Wilkins. Rupert Wilkins.'

The old man recovered his composure and

opened the door. Titch took it as an invitation to enter – he did and found himself in a large hall that had several doors leading off it. A wide staircase led to the upper part of the house. The old servant showed Titch a chair without speaking and shuffled off towards a door to one side. He was shaking his old head from side to side – Titch heard him muttering.

'Master Rupert is home. Thank God. Master Rupert is home.' He left the door open and disappeared into a large room. It gave Titch a moment to look about him.

The walls were covered with portraits of life size figures, male and female. All in period dress – most of the men in military uniforms; the women in gowns of various styles. Over the large stone fireplace was the crest again, depicted in red and gilt. Old firearms, swords and spears cluttered the wall around it. Across the hall was a picture that caught Titch's eye because the light from the hall window shone on it. It was a portrait of a young man in the scarlet, blue and gold uniform of an officer in the Royal Marine Artillery. Titch looked at the face. It could have been his own. And there was a ring on the little finger of his right hand resting on the hilt of a dress sword. No wonder the old man servant was shocked – Titch was. He knew instantly that this was a portrait of his father. Titch moved closer and saw the caption on a small panel fastened to the bottom of the ornate gilt frame – written in gold lettering was,

'Captain Rupert Montgomery App-Lugus. 19th. b. 1890 – d. 1916.'

Titch had come home, or to his father's house; would he be welcome?

As if to answer his question, voices and footsteps were heard. Clicking heels and shuffling of feet and a 'tap, tap' on the slate floor was loud – the voice was louder.

'What on earth do you mean, Williams. Master Rupert has comer home? Don't be ridiculous.'

The short figure of a man strode into the light of the hall. The servant Williams faded into the background. Titch stood as the Lord of the Manor of Cuffty Mawr approached; man and youth faced each other. They were almost the same height – Titch was perhaps an inch taller; the other was broad of shoulder and a bulging waist line. He had a short crop of greying hair that stood stark on an egg-shaped head. A drooping moustache hung limp and gave him the look of a dejected spaniel. His face was wrinkled and had an unhealthy pallor. He was dressed in a suit of ill-fitting country tweeds with a woollen shirt of a green check – a necktie was tied with a large untidy knot. His age was perhaps 50 years old, though his posture and the poor light made it difficult to assess. He wore thick lens spectacles; he came into the light and Titch saw he had a hunch back and his right leg dragged heavily. The cane in his hand was gripped aggressively. The youth understood the 'tap, tap' on the slate floor.

'What is all this about? Who are you boy? And what do you mean by invading my house?' The word 'Boy' was said in an offensive tone.

'My name is Rupert Montgomery Wilkins, sir. The son of Miss Dorothy Wilkins and, I believe, the gentleman in that portrait there.'

The man hesitated for only a moment before he flew into a rage.

'How dare you. This is a respected family. My brother has been dead nineteen years and you claim to be his son? That is an infamous libel. My God, I'll horse whip you.'

Titch faced him – somehow he found the courage to say.

'I wouldn't uncle. I shall hit back.'

'Uncle!... Uncle! My God!' The words exploded from beneath the man's hairy upper lip. Titch could see that he was at a loss. The lad was about to take off his ring and show him but changed his mind. It was the only thing he had, that and his father's photograph. He produced that. The squire of Cuffty Mawr took it and looked at it for a moment.

'Ridiculous,' he lied. 'It is not even him.'

Before Titch could stop him he tore the photograph into small pieces and threw them into the log fire at his side.

'You bastard!' The word burst from Titch's lips. 'You rotten ugly old bastard. I want nothing from you. I only came to find out where my father lived. Perhaps to find a family. I have and I wish I hadn't. You are my uncle, I can see that but you are the bastard in this house, not me.'

Titch turned to go – he had not expected a welcome, but not this... He just wanted to get away. Titch turned at the door and looked at his uncle's twisted body. The voice came at Titch in a rage. 'You young whipper snapper. If I were 10 years younger I would thrash you.'

Titch looked at his father's brother – saw his hunch back and withered leg, and his face ugly and twisted with rage. He saw what he believed in his youth was a tormented spirit – a man sick to his soul; consumed by Titch knew not what. Titch's eye rose to the picture of his father and a peace fell over the boy. Suddenly he was sorry for the twisted figure standing trembling with rage before him – he remembered his days at Swaffield and how he had fought bullies like him. He had fought hard and won, most times. Albeit with boots, knees, elbows, teeth and claws – all was fair then. Anyway – what was another beating; it was surviving that mattered. Of latter years it was surviving with dignity. When he went down, Titch Wilkins went down fighting; he would do it again if he had to. Quietly Titch said.

'Uncle. If you were 10 years younger, you wouldn't dare.'

The man stood and gaped at Titch – suddenly the lad didn't care. His anger had evaporated but the hurt was there. He closed the door behind him and took the steps in two leaps and was on his bicycle and heading down the drive feeling the great loneliness come over him again. He was the bastard. The leper. A person nobody wanted to know. Except Ma and Bert, and Judy of course.

Titch covered the first half mile at a sprint – his legs pumping the pedals – his breath hard and dry in his throat. He swung into the shaded stretch of the drive that ran down hill; he didn't slow. Tears of frustration and disappointment welled up in his eyes and blurred his vision – he didn't see the pony and rider come out of the path in the woods at a gallop. Titch struck the pony square in the centre striking the rider's leg. The horse reared – the rider was thrown backwards from the saddle – Titch skidded in the mud and fell under the pony's hooves. For moments the flurry of iron shod hooves and a scrambling youth threatened peril to both until Titch rolled clear into the soft leaf mould at the side of the drive.

Titch was the first on his feet, surprised he wasn't hurt. He looked at the rider sitting in the mud of the drive. He was a youth and appeared unhurt but dazed. Titch went to him. He stopped and retrieved the other's hard black hat and riding crop that were in the hazel bushes at the drive's edge. He helped the lad to his feet and looked at his face. He was a youth of about 14 – taller than Titch but thinner. The brown eyes looked at Titch in anger – long fair hair was in disarray; Titch found himself apologising.

'I'm sorry, chum. I don't know who's fault it was but it could have been much worse. You alright?' The other youth recovered from the shock of his fall.

'You clumsy lout. Why don't you look where you are going. You could have killed me.'

'I could say the same of you. You shot out of that ride at a gallop. How was I supposed to know you were there? Let's just thank our lucky stars it wasn't worse.'

'Don't dare speak to me like that you swine. Get off my land!' He raised the riding crop and struck Titch. The blow caught the young bricklayer across the face and brought tears to his eyes. Titch's reaction was instinctive. He landed a clenched fist blow to the stomach and his right knee into his groin.

His adversary doubled over – Titch's knee came up again and struck him in the mouth. The boy collapsed into the mud of the drive edge. He held one hand to his mouth – when he saw the blood from a split lip he sobbed softly.

Titch was ashamed of himself. He had reacted as he had done so often at Swaffield School. There had been no negotiation there. If he did not act, a bigger boy crushed him. It was survival there. Titch subconsciously believed it was survival here; he had acted accordingly.

Titch went over to the lad sitting in the dirt and offered him his hand again. The stranger looked up at Titch through his tears. The victor apologised again. 'I'm sorry chum. I didn't mean to hit you so hard. But you shouldn't have whacked me with that whip of yours. It hurt!'

'Good,' the stranger smiled through his tears and showed even white teeth smeared with blood from his cut lip. 'It makes up for the thrashing you just gave me. Sorry I spoke to you the way I did. A dashed poor show on my part.'

His accent was English Public School, but not excessively so. Titch knew about accents – he knew that try as he may his accent was cockney. He remembered Miss Cuthberson being appalled at his use of words; how hard she worked to eradicate it. The boy took his hand and Titch pulled him to his feet.

'There's more to you than meets the eye. I thought I would have the better of you. Longer reach and all that. We learn to box at Wellington, but not to fight. There seems to be a difference.' He touched his bleeding lip. 'Must remember to be more careful in my judgements.'

Titch was surprised to see they still had their hands clasped in a sort of 'Roman' grip. The kind of grip comrades make when swearing an oath. The stranger noticed, too – they broke apart, both a little embarrassed. Titch walked to his Rudge and picked it out of the bushes. Apart from twisted handlebars it was no worse for the spill. The pony was grazing quietly on the grass growing among the trees. The four of them, horse, bicycle and the two youths were bruised but not broken. Titch straightened the handle-bars and took a bar of chocolate from his saddle bag. With it in his hand he gathered the pony's reins and led it to its owner quietly brushing himself down at the edge of the drive. The boy took the reins with a 'Thanks awfully' and walked to a patch of sunlight close to a rail fence. The top rail made a seat and the youths sat side by side and introduced themselves.

'The name is Rupert Wilkins. What's yours?'

'Mine is Rupert, too. Rupert Montgomery, actually.'

Their eyes met with a look of incredulity.

'This is stupid. Those are my names. Rupert Montgomery Wilkins. What's your last name?'

'App-Lugus. App-Lugus the 21st My people have been here for hundreds of years.'

'Then your father is the Lord of the Manor?'

'Yes why?'

Ten minutes and half the bar of chocolate later Titch had told the purpose of his visit – the story done the other lad exclaimed his surprise.

'How perfectly wizard. So we are actually cousins.'

The other's public school English brought a smile to Titch's lips that went un-noticed by the heir to Cuffty Mawr who continued with his exclamation.

'My name is Rupert Montgomery, though people call me Monty.' He seemed delighted with the news of his new-found cousin. Monty smiled and continued in a subdued voice.

'And my father wanted to thrash you?' He fingered his split lip again. 'I believe he would have bitten off rather more than he could chew. Poor daddy. He's not very well you know.' He laughed a short but memory laugh. 'Besides. You don't fight fair.'

Titch laughed at the last remark.

'I have never seen a whip mentioned in The Marquis of Queensbury Rules, either.' The cousins laughed together.

'Touché. But where did you learn to fight like that?' Monty was looking close at the young bricklayer.

Titch spent some minutes telling his new cousin about his early life – the horrors of the workhouse and the orphanage were spoken of and how it was necessary to learn to be able to cope with bullies. Titch spared him nothing. They were silent when the tale was finished – time spent chewing the last of the chocolate.

Monty swallowed and looked at his cousin.

'My God. I never knew such places existed outside novels. It sounds like Oliver Twist. The workhouse, I mean.' He looked into Titch's eyes. 'And you are my cousin. My dead Uncle Rupert's son. How terrible it must have been for you. And your mother, my aunt. How awful for her to die that way.' He paused again and studied his hands – after a moment he looked again at Titch. 'And to think that this was all here for you.' He turned and looked squarely at the young bricklayer. 'Rupert. If your father had not been killed you would have been heir to all this.' He raised an arm and encompassed the woods and fields of Cuffty Mawr. 'You see our fathers, yours and mine, were twins. Your father was the eldest, by an hour I believe. My poor old pater was born crippled so was always lagging behind your father. He was not in the war. He has always resented that, and has always been unhappy. Believes people look down on him because of it. His brother being killed and all that. Total rubbish of course, but there.' He paused again, perhaps wondering if he was being disloyal to his father. He continued thoughtfully.

'Daddy is hard to live with I expect. Mother left him years ago. She got a divorce. Couldn't stand it I suppose. He is very moody, and has a vile temper. Mother married again. Lives in Shrewsbury with her new husband and his daughter. Terribly happy, I believe. Elizabeth the new daughter is a lovely girl. As girls go you understand.' He sounded embarrassed, as if girls were hardly the subject to be discussed between boys. It made Titch think of Judy and how he felt for her. He wanted to tell him about Judy. About their plans to marry before they left for Australia.

The opportunity never came – Titch regretted that.

Monty looked across at his pony grazing quietly in the spring sunshine. Titch followed his gaze and was surprised how the horse's coat glistened. The 14-year-old continued his story.

'I sometimes think my father must suffer a lot of pain with his back or his leg. But he never complains. It seems he hated your father. Jealous I suppose. Poor Daddy. Your pater had everything my father hadn't. Good at sport and hunting. He could ride well and was an incredible shot. And very popular in the county. Or so my grand-mother told me. She died last year.' He paused again as thoughts came to him – his eyes followed a butterfly as it flew among the flowers in the grass at their feet.

'It has been terribly lonely here since mother left and grandma died. We used to have parties and things then, and the Hunt used to meet here every Boxing Day. Has done since anyone could remember. But not now. Father puts them off somehow. People just don't want to know him.'

He looked towards the house as if he wanted to see his father. He rolled the silver paper from the chocolate between his fingers and continued.

'To make matters worse, your father was in the Corps. The Marines. The App-Lugus' have always been Marines. Right from 1664 when they were formed by King Charles the Second. There was always a Lugus in the Marines somewhere in the world. The first Lugus left the cavalry to go to sea when "Rupert of the Palatinate", that was another of Prince Rupert's titles, formed the Marines for King Charles to fight the Dutch. It was years later that they were called the Royal Marines. It seems our forbear and Prince Rupert were close friends.' He paused again and shifted his weight on the rail.

'It's all written down up there.' He pointed with his chin towards the house.

'The whole family history is there from 1660 when the house was built. Father keeps it up-to-date meticulously, though I doubt he will mention your name. Why it even explains why we have the names we have.' He saw Titch was curious.

'Right from the beginning the eldest son and heir has been named Rupert Montgomery, and the second son Montgomery Rupert. That is why I said you would have been Rupert Montgomery the 20th. The name Rupert after the Prince, and Montgomery after the 1660 Lugus' wife's father. He was another commander of "The Prince Rupert Horse" during the Civil War. I don't know about the girls of the family. I believe the Lugus' just produced children until there were two sons.'

Titch looked at him – he heard every word he had said and was fascinated.

The words just fell from the older boy's mouth.

'What about the App-Lugus? Where did they come from? The names, I mean?'

The sun was shining into their eyes so they shifted positions on the rail.

The 14-year-old heir to the estate cleared his throat and continued his tale.

'App simply means "The son of". It is very Welsh. There are lots of them. The country is full

159

of App-Jones', App-Rees', dozens of them in Wales. Lugus was an ancient Celtic character. Reputedly a God. More likely he was a medicine man or wizard. Originally the name was "Lleu Llaw Gyffes". Or "Lleu of the Dexterous Hand." The legend is that he had a virgin birth by means of the very old Celt Wizard "Math" passing his wand over his mother's body. It was believed in the old days that his mother was the virgin goddess "Aranhod." Celtic for Silver Wheel. She gave birth to a son, Lleu, who was abducted shortly after his birth by his uncle Gwydion, an evil wizard, and reared by him as an apprentice. Aranhod wanted to destroy her son because she believed he would grow up evil, but was prevented by the uncle's superior magic. It is believed that Gwydion was evil. The Devil in Welsh mythology. However, Aranhod was able to cast a spell on Gwydion that prevented him from having a wife so he created a woman out of flowers for himself, but the woman was barren, so he taught Lleu Llaw Gyffes all he knew of wizardry. The boy grew up to be the greatest wizard in the land. Over the centuries the name has changed to Lugus.' He hesitated and seemed reluctant to continue. Titch looked askance at his cousin – the boy sensed the other's gaze; their eyes met.

'You are family so to speak Rupert, so I suppose I can tell you. It is only a story and I have never believed it, but some of the local people here believe that my father is the reincarnation of the old Wizard, Gwydion. Lots of the locals will not venture through the gates of the estate. They believe he has magical powers. Evil powers. Quite

160

ridiculous of course. He is just a rather sick, crippled old man. It's his looks, I suppose, and everyone knows of his temper. Very superstitious are some of the Welsh. Very Christian in many ways but the old beliefs are dear to their hearts.'

The sun was warm and the scene was beautiful. It was hard to believe that any evil could exist amidst such tranquility. All Titch's resentment at his treatment by his uncle had dissipated. The serenity of the woods and fields, the sky, and the atmosphere of the Welsh hills enveloped him. He was at peace with the only relative he had, who had not rejected him; Titch wanted this time to last for ever.

The Welsh lad had shifted his weight again – Titch looked at him and as if by cue his cousin continued talking of the family Lugus.

'There is even a story that one of us was the owner of Gelert. Though I doubt it. Legends are rife in the mountains of Wales.'

'Gelert? Who is Gelert?' Titch's voice sounded incredulous, even to him.

'Was Gelert.' Monty laughed at the bricklayer's ignorance. 'Gelert was a dog. A wolf hound. He belonged, it is said, to Prince Llewellyn, one of the last Welsh princes. He lived in a fortified house close to the river near where the town of Beddgelert is now. The story is that Llewellyn left his house on some errand and told his hound, Gelert, to guard his young son, a tiny baby. While he was away a wolf entered the house which was only a primitive dwelling really and attacked the child. Gelert defended the baby and killed the wolf. When Llewellyn returned the dog greeted him

161

and the Prince saw blood on the animal's coat and mouth. The child's cradle was overturned and there was no sign of the baby. Llewellyn thought the dog had mauled the child and eaten it. In a rage he drew his sword and killed the dog. As the dog died the Prince heard the cry of his child. He went to the overturned cradle and found the baby safe underneath, and a dead wolf concealed by the bed clothes. He ran to Gelert but it was too late. The hound was dead. Prince Llewellyn carried him outside and buried him. He surrounded his grave with a wall of stones and made a shrine to Gelert. It is said the Prince never smiled again. That is how the town Beddgelert got its name. The Grave of Gelert. The grave is still there, outside the town. There's a fence around it now. The Prince's house has long gone. You must see the grave before you go.'

Doubtless the two would have been sitting there talking yet if a bell had not rung at that moment. It struck eight times. The heir to Cuffty Mawr counted every stroke out loud.

'That is the bell for luncheon. I must go. Father is a stickler for punctuality. He was never a marine but he runs the house like he imagines your dead father would manage a Royal Marine detachment. The house is run like a warship in many ways. That was eight bells. Mid-Day.' He dropped to the ground. Titch followed; they stood facing each other.

'Good bye cousin Rupert. I really am most awfully glad we have met. Perhaps when we are older we can be real friends.' He looked at his cousin and Titch knew he meant it.

'I hope so. Good bye cousin Rupert.'

They both laughed. Suddenly, their hands were clasped. Each of them held the right wrist of the other – their left hands clutched the fore arm of the other. Simultaneously they tightened their grip – their eyes met in an understanding they could not express. They broke apart – one ran to his pony – the other retrieved his bicycle. Neither looked back – when the muffled hoof beats had died, Titch mounted his bicycle and rode down the hill.

After a lunch of a cheese sandwich and a half-pint beer shandy sitting in the bow window of the 'Gelert' public house, Titch walked across the river to the Grave of Gelert. He leaned on an old fence post and allowed his imagination free rein. He 'saw' the stone fortified house with a roof of rushes. He 'saw' the hound and the wolf – the child and the Prince and the fight between the two animals. In his mind Titch heard the snarling and the growling, and felt the bone crushing blow as the sword struck the dog. The grief he had felt in his young life was what he imagined were feelings of the hound's master when he discovered his mistake. It saw a sad story and one Titch remembers clearly.

An early night at the Youth Hostel and Titch was on the road at first light the following morning cycling the two hundred long miles to London, but feeling his journey had been worth while. He had found a family of his own, albeit a family of one. A boy. A boy who would one day be a man and the 'Lord of the Manor of Cuffty Mawr.' Titch Wilkins' father's house.

Chapter Seven

Years slipped away – German Jews suffered under Hitler; Ukrainian and other ethnic peoples in the USSR suffered even more under Joseph Stalin. For differing reasons 1938 was a momentous year for the countries of Europe. Germany was extending its territorial claims – Austria was occupied by the German Army by a combination of bluff, bullying, propaganda and military might. Czechoslovakia followed – Adolf Hitler claiming he was 'liberating' the Sudeten German minority in the country.

When the League of Nations did nothing more than passively protest the Nazis occupied the small nations of Bohemia and Morovia. The province of Memel in Lithuania was annexed while Mr Neville Chamberlain, the Prime Minister of Britain, waved a white paper of reconciliation signed by Hitler; the phrase, 'Peace in our time' was born, and the world believed him.

The forces of Mussolini occupied Ethiopia – the country's Emperor, Haile Selassie escaped to exile in England leaving the Coptic and Eastern Orthodox Christians to be massacred by Italian Somalia Colonial troops in Addis Ababa.

Spanish Nationalist Rebel Leader General Francisco Franco's army was crushing the Republican Government Forces. His Fascist friends, Germany and Italy, allowed their planes to bomb Spain's cities. German Panzers fought alongside Franco's Moroccan mercenaries. Only Russia helped the Spanish Socialist Government's battalions – the world watched and waited. The Fascist threat to Europe was real – Britain and France armed themselves while the US President F. D Roosevelt continued his 'New Deal' policies with the American people.

The novel 'Gone With the Wind' sold over two million copies world-wide – authorities in British cities were building air raid shelters for their people. Titch Wilkins joined The Royal Air Force Volunteer Reserve, and he and Judy Wilson kissed for the first time; altogether an eventful year.

Cycling was still a major pastime for the young bricklayer – his forays took him to places far and near often with Judy Wilson as his companion.

One summer week-end in 1937 the pair rode as far as Broadstairs to find Miss Cuthberson; a round trip of over 100 miles. They found the house where she had her bed-sitter – she was not there and the occupier had no news of her; a visit to her old school had the same result. However, the rector at St Peter's Church gave Titch the news that she had gone to Central Africa as a missionary teacher. Titch was not altogether surprised, as he said to Judy on the way home. 'She was a lady like that. Always thinking of others.'

RAF Flying Displays attracted the pair. The RAF airfields at Northolt and Hornchurch were favourite Saturday afternoon rides. They divided their outings between airfields and yachting harbours on the Thames Estuary – it was a secret ambition of theirs that when they went to Australia they would sail there in their own yacht. Judy's apprehensions of such a venture lessened as she became familiar with small boats – she shared the books on sailing Titch avidly read with Bert James' guidance. The old bricklayer was thrilled that his dream of blue water sailing was coming alive through his prodigy.

Their journeys to the airfields on London's perimeter were always exciting. The two would sit and eat their sandwich lunch close to the boundary fence and watch Gloster Gladiator and Hawker Hurricane fighter planes take off and land. Fairey Battle and Hampden Bombers came and went; on one occasion they saw the new giant twin engine Wellington Bomber. But it was the new Supermarine Spitfire that took their imaginations. The fast, streamlined monoplane soared and dived over the field in a performance of speed and grace. It was that as much the urgency of the Government's appeals for volunteers, and Titch's own inclination, that made him join the Royal Air Force Volunteer Reserve. Judy shared his enthusiasm and volunteered for the Women's Auxiliary Air Force; a force given the collective name of WAAFs.

She and Titch attended lectures and drills at their respective centres, she as a medical orderly while Titch allowed himself to be persuaded to take a wireless operator/air gunners' training course with the rank of Aircraftsman First Class, in RAF parlance AC1.

Titch discovered the swatting on radio frequencies, modulators, electric circuits and conductors was a disagreeable chore, but he persevered – he was no electrical genius; the morse code was less of a bore. Gunnery he found fascinating and he absorbed sighting theory, trajectories and angles of deflection with ease. Practical flying and crew drills came easy. Firing at ground or air targets with the Vickers or Lewis machine guns a never tiring pleasure. Aircraft recognition was all too easy; all it needed was dedication – Titch Wilkins possessed it. With work, night school, reserve lectures and camps both young people were fully occupied. To their sorrow, Titch and Judy met less and less, and only on the week-ends when both of them were free from Air Force duties.

Titch was in his second year as a fully-qualified tradesman – Bert James and Mr Whittaker had done their work well. The youth passed third out of one hundred candidates for the 'City & Guilds' Examinations. A feat that earned him a benefit dinner and the presentation of a gold watch from Mr Waller of his employers Messrs Waller & Franklin. It was an occasion for which Titch hired a tuxedo and bow tie – he invited Judy as his partner. Mrs Wilson made her daughter a dress of deep green velvet that set off the girl's auburn hair and beautiful complexion. When Titch called for her in the chauffeur driven car hired by Mr Waller, he could hardly believe his eyes; she was utterly beautiful. Neighbours gathered around the front of the pork butcher's shop to see them leave. Most of the ladies dabbed their eyes – Mrs Wilson could hardly speak through her happy tears. Tom Wilson just sniffed

167

– old Sergeant Morgan was in the background. Titch met his gaze and the old soldier lowered an eyelid in a wink that spoke volumes. Little crippled Molly hugged her big sister so tight Judy was afraid the orchid corsage Titch had bought would be crushed. The three Wilson boys stood awkwardly to one side – Titch saw the eldest, Billy, now a lad of 16 eyeing the butcher's daughter in a way he would never look at Judy; or would he? As the Daimler pulled away and headed towards the exclusive Cumberland Hotel at Marble Arch, Titch wondered about that look.

At the dinner there was a speech from Mr Waller – Bert James said a few nice words – Mr Whittaker presented Titch with the watch, and perhaps the young recipient drank a little too much champagne. He danced clumsily with Ma James and Mrs Whittaker – Mrs Waller 'claimed the right' for a waltz. She was a tall, well-built lady and Titch felt foolish waltzing with her, and embarrassed when in a swing to the music he occasionally found his face buried in her ample bosom, and he danced with Judy again and again. As the evening progressed Titch found he was holding Judy tighter and closer – they had never held each other before; holding hands was as close as they ever got to intimacy. Judy was perhaps an inch shorter than he and the young orphan found his face buried in her auburn hair. The scent of her perfume filled him with an excitement he could not comprehend. He found his mouth close to her ear – a desire to kiss her ear lobe was strong within him. He wanted to tell her he loved her; he wanted to... The thought died as blood rushed to his face and his heart pounded. His arm around her pressed tight – pressing her young body against his. When he felt his arousal he drew apart a little, but she pressed closer – he felt the softness of her against his hardness, and he loved it. She was so light, so lovely, so desirable – Titch felt he had the strength of ten men.

It was all a heady experience for an orphaned slum boy – a far cry from his beginnings at the Wandsworth Parish Workhouse. Whatever it was, whatever his thoughts, on the way home in the luxurious Daimler he took Judy's hand.

'Thank you Judy.' That was all he said, then. It was all he wanted to say. That's not true – there was so much he wanted to say; they were the only words he was capable of at that moment. Words composed in his mind refused to emerge beyond his brain. Titch found himself looking into Judy's eyes seeing them as emeralds in the passing street lights that made them glitter. Her perfume struck his senses again, almost a physical blow. The closeness of her, then and earlier, set his blood racing; his breath came in short gasps. The intimacy and soft luxury of the car's interior – their closeness, was exotic, erotic; an experience for them both.

Titch felt Judy's breath on his face, he remembered it smelt of the single glass of champagne she had drunk. With a trembling hand he touched her lips – just the tips of his fingers; gently. When she did not draw away his lips touched hers – gently in a quick, exploratory kiss and a hasty retreat.

He didn't know what he expected – what he

169

expected to feel. He did not know what to do. You see it was his first romantic kiss, ever – he was 21 – Judy was the only girl he had ever known romantically; the only girl he had ever really spoken to. The sensation of the kiss was electric.

Most of the young bricklayer's contemporaries seemed thoroughly experienced with girls, kissing and sex, 'snogging or shagging' was how they expressed it. They had experienced the lot, or so they said, and with several girls. What Titch felt was a wonderful uplift of mind and body – his spirit even; he soared. Their lips touched again; neither of them drew apart. They touched and joined in a long, breath-taking kiss that melted their souls. With their third kiss Judy's lips parted and Titch felt the soft moistness of her – he breathed the perfume of her breath; inhaling deeply; wanting to absorb the essence of her. Judy's arms reached out and gathered him to her – Titch felt the softness of her breasts through the material of his dinner jacket; his arousal was instant, real and thrilling. His hand clumsily reached round to her back – he felt the warmth of her bare shoulders underneath the borrowed shawl. It was electrifying. The stopping of the vehicle outside Judy's home brought them to earth, Titch had time to say doubtfully.

'We said we wouldn't kiss until we were properly engaged.'

For a moment there was silence except for their breathing. Judy recovered first.

'I remember,' she said shyly, then added. 'Shall we tell mum and dad. Tell them we are engaged I mean.'

'Do you think they will mind. They might not like it. You being only 17, I mean.'

'Eighteen. Or I will be in a month. Anyway. Let's risk it.' Judy's brown furrowed a little in puzzlement. 'You still want us to get married one day Rupert?'

'Of course Judy. Oh yes. But I don't want to upset your mum and dad. And…' Titch struggled to pull his father's signet ring from his finger. It took a moment and he grasped Judy's hand. 'And I want to give you this.' He placed the heavy gold ring on the third finger of her left hand.

'No, Rupert. This was your father's. You mustn't.' The ring was too big, but it fitted the second finger so Titch left it there. The young swain smiled. 'It looks better on you… Keep it until I can buy you a wedding ring.' He was a little stunned at his nerve at making the remark so added, 'But will your parents mind?'

'I don't think they will if we tell them that we are only engaged and won't get married until we leave for Australia. And that may be a long time yet.' She paused, the chauffeur was about to open the car door. 'And Rupert. It will mean we can kiss again.' She paused, looked into his eyes and smiled. 'I'd like that.'

Titch detected a laugh in her voice. It was the last remark that settled it.

Like I said, 'It was his first romantic kiss' – he found the experience delightful; with Judy anyway.

With a 'Good night and thank you' to the Daimler and its driver Judy led the way to the rear of the pork butchers and the stairs that went up to her home.

Sergeant 'Scrapper' Morgan was sitting in the Wilsons when the pair entered the flat. The three elders looked questioningly at the two as they closed the door. Perhaps their happiness showed on their faces. Titch looked at Judy – his heart felt it would burst; she looked so lovely. His gaze took in the trio sitting relaxed with several empty brown ale bottles on the table littered with glasses and the debris of sandwiches, peanuts and a pack of playing cards and a cribbage board. They had obviously enjoyed a pleasant evening together. Tom Wilson looked directly at his daughter and her escort.

''Ad a good time 'ave yer both?' Then addressing Titch. 'You looks like the cat wot's just pinched the cream young Titch. Wot' you bin' up to wiv' our Judy, then?'

His tone was friendly but it had Titch worried – defensively he blurted out. 'We want to get married Mr Tom.' Tom Wilson's face changed to a big grin. His eyes glowed with instant happiness, but Titch was worried.

'Not yet, though.' The words tumbled from his lips. 'We just want to be engaged,' he added hastily. He bit his tongue – he almost said 'So we can kiss again.'

Mrs Wilson rose from her chair – walked around to Judy and enveloped her in her arms. The sergeant and Tom Wilson competed to shake Titch's hand.

'This 'ere calls fer a celebration. Open a'nuvver bottle Scrapper. We'll drink to the young'uns.'

Judy and Titch slipped away to the family's

front parlour – there they held hands and kissed again, several times. It was cold in the over-furnished room, used only for christenings, weddings and funerals as they say, but they didn't mind. The settee was big, yet they were close – for the first time they whispered their love without hindrance or self-consciousness.

It was raining. The sexton worked solidly in the rain digging a grave close to Titch. His old back was stooped from years of toil – his face lined and tired from exposure to wind and weather; his hands crooked and gnarled. Spadeful after spadeful of chalky soil was thrown up from the small trench. The rough jute sack over his thin shoulders did little to keep him dry, but did not impede his movement. It surprised Titch how neat the old chap could dig a grave. The sides were steep and straight – the ends perfectly square though the old labourer never used a set square. The old man left after levelling the surrounding soil and Titch speculated with his neighbours as to who would be the occupant.

'Another o'they bomb victims if ye be a'askin' I.' Was the guess of the old Lifeboat Coxwain; Constable Higgins agreed. Miss Burnet thought it might be a sailor drowned in the storm that had raged a few days ago. Titch's guess was that it would be another RAF aircrew as the bomber stream passed over them the night before on its way home. They were all wrong; though when the RAF funeral party assembled Titch thought he had guessed right. When the coffin arrived it was draped in the German flag – Titch saw by the look of the chap hovering over it he was no RAF flyer. He was a German. A Luftwaffe pilot.

Titch was speechless – the lifeboatmen were curious, the policeman's looks were non-committal; Miss Burnet was plainly mortified.

'A German! Really! They caused us no end of bother in the Cape. Very friendly with the Boers they were. Always stirring up trouble for us British. I remember...'

Her words were cut off by the sound of the funeral party going through its paces. It was the same padre who buried Titch – the old Rector was there too still in a grubby surplice and a dewdrop on the end of his nose. Probably worrying again about what to put in the Parish register. The firing party fired the five volleys – sods were thrown onto the coffin and the usual words chanted over it. The dozen airmen marched off with their officer – the padre and the Rector had their heads together. It was all too familiar. Not until the old sexton had returned to fill the grave were they able to introduce themselves to the newcomer.

The policeman opened the conversation by introducing himself. 'Constable Bill 'iggins o'the Kent Constabulary. H'at your service.'

The German looked at the policeman not sure of what he saw. Titch called to Bill Higgins. 'He's a German Bill. Probably doesn't understand a word you say.'

'On the contrary.' The enemy pilot looked for Titch's name on the wooden cross at the head of his grave. He gave Titch a closer look. 'I am sorry Flight Sergeant. No. I understand perfectly.' He

174

looked across at Bill Higgins. 'Thank you, Constable. I do understand you. I learned my English as a boy at Wellington. The English Public School near Crowthorne.' He smiled and gave a short bow in the constable's direction. 'In the county of Berkshire, I believe.' He added as a way of explanation.

Titch remembered his cousin, Rupert App-Lugus, had attended Wellington – he wondered if they knew each other, they were about the same age. 'I must remember to ask him.' Titch stowed the thought away for another time.

The German's smile encompassed them all – if he was put out by being in enemy territory he didn't show it. Miss Burnet would have liked to say something to him but she was 'out of bounds' as far as he was concerned. The pilot had Titch, Bill Higgins and the portly medico for near neighbours. Straight away the doctor monopolised the newcomer and talked his leg off for the next hour. It took that long before they could learn anything about him. But time means nothing to them.

The country GP turned to the old colonel to confirm a remark he had made. The old cavalry officer took the opportunity to delve into an argument on the difference between Foxhounds and Beagles and the pleasures of the chase. Only then were the others able to get a word in themselves.

The German was Luftleutnant Otto Myer, pilot of a Focke Wolfe 190 single engine fighter/bomber that had been shot down strafing a British convoy running the gauntlet of the Straits of Dover. He baled out over the Channel but his parachute had been struck by one of the Spitfire's cannon shells and it 'candled' into the sea with him. He had died upon impact. He continued his story.

'I come from a small town in the Black Forest. Frieburge. You have heard of it, yes?' Titch shook his head. 'No? It is of no consequence.' His English was excellent with only a trace of an accent which gave it charm. 'It is a beautiful place. Very old. Lovely buildings, and the forest so close. A...h. It was a beautiful place to grow up. My father was sent to London in 1934. To the German Embassy. Nothing very romantic I'm afraid... Just the officer in charge of Embassy records. We lived in Chelsea and I was sent to Wellington for my education.' He laughed. 'I learned to play cricket among other things, and that hooligan game of yours that gentlemen seem to enjoy. Rugby Football. Both games I enjoyed but for the life of me I never understood what they were about.'

He looked at Titch – he knew at once that he was an aviator by his dress.

'You are RAF, yes? Fighters?... No. Perhaps not.' He looked again at the cross at the head of Titch's grave. 'No I can see you were not. Your pilots do not wear such clothing and I can see you were an airgunner. So... You must be one of the "Terror Flyers". The Lancaster bomber crews. Yes?'

Titch said that he was and expected an argument – he resented the expression Terror Flyers though he had to confess he was not sure what it meant – as to who experienced the terror;

the people in the target zone or the bomber crews. The German laughed when Titch told him he was a reargunner.

'What you chaps call "Tail End Charley". Yes. The deadly sting in the tail I call it. I have flown against you over our cities. We like to get you silhouetted against the fires and the searchlights. It is the only way us day fighters can find you. "Wild Boars" the Luftwaffe call us, we have only ground to air radio and you fellows jam it effectively.' He thought for a moment and looked closely at Titch. His voice had a serious note to it.

'I shot down one of your Stirling Bombers one night. The rear gunner fired at me and gave me a fright. He damaged my 'plane but I was OK. The poor chap caught the full blast of my cannon. The plane crashed outside the target zone.' He swallowed and looked a little crestfallen. 'There were no survivors,' he added to no-one in particular. The small group were silent – the policeman and coxwain were not sure what the two men were talking about and the doctor was engrossed with the colonel.

Otto, as Titch got to call him, continued.

'Ach... It is a stupid war. My brother was shot down over Coventry. A senseless raid. As senseless as what you are doing to my cities. I have been to Coventry. That beautiful old Cathedral burned to the ground. And you fellows doing your best to destroy Cologne Cathedral. Madness. All of it madness. Madness the Fuhrer starting it all and madness you English believing you can win. Gotte verdamnt. Won't you Englanders understand. No one will win this war. We will all be losers.'

It began the first of many discussions they had of the war – all wars, and the madness of men.

Judy and Titch were together when Neville Chamberlain said to the people of Britain, 'A state of war exists between His Majesty's Government and the German Nation'.

It was a beautiful day, Sunday September 3rd, 1939. All Service Reservists has been mobilised – Titch and Judy had been serving with their respective units for weeks and were stationed in London. Titch doing a radio course at the London Polytechnic – Judy doing nursing training at St George's Hospital at Hyde Park corner. Both were in uniform and sitting in the hospital canteen to hear the broadcast. They left quietly as the nurses and orderlies broke into noisy discussion about the war – not a word was spoken as they walked into Hyde Park intending to buy a sandwich at the Serpentine tea rooms. They had just entered the gates when the air raid sirens sounded the alarm – they began to run to the nearest bomb shelter; as if by a signal they stopped.

'I don't want to go to a shelter, Rupert. I'd rather be above ground. Let's stay in the park?'

'Right'o.' Titch looked into the bright blue of the sky as he agreed. 'It's too nice a day for anything to happen anyway,' he laughed and took Judy's hand and together they ran through the trees. How young and naive they were.

They lay on the grass in the sun by the Serpentine – a breeze rippled the water of the lake; hire boats gently rocked at their moorings. Within minutes it was as if they were the only people in London. The Park was deserted – the roar of traffic had stopped. The distant sound of a fire engine or a police car came across the Park – the bell sounded foreign to them in the silence.

They lay back and allowed the sun to warm their faces. Titch's arm was about Judy's shoulders – it was inevitable they should kiss. Titch looked deep into Judy's eyes and she into his. The newly fledged airman poured his longing into his gaze, and Judy understood.

'Let's get married Rupert. Now. Don't let us wait. It will be years before we can get to Australia.' Her breath caught in her throat. 'I want you, Rupert... You know... All of you. I want your babies. I want us to be together always. I don't want to wait until the end of the war.'

Titch said nothing – he had fought against telling her of his desire so many times. Telling her of his frustration at the wait until they could go to Australia. Their kissing and petting the last few months was getting almost more than he could bear.

'I don't want us to HAVE to get married. I want us to be happy – beautifully happy; free from worry or guilt.' Had been his rational when he lay in his narrow bed in the little terraced house in East Acton – now there was a war and he was going to be flying. The tragedy of his own parents was a frequent nightmare. His father's death and his mother's loss haunted him.

'No, Judy... People say it will be over in weeks. But they said that in 1914. I remember reading

179

about it. Tom Wilson, Bert James and Scrapper Morgan say that the Germans were hard to beat last time. Will they be hard to beat this time?' He spoke aloud but his thoughts were of his dead parents. They must have had the same feelings before his father went to Jutland. They had surrendered to their love – the result was a bastard. Titch could not do that to Judy and their child.

'My God, Judy. How I want you. I have wanted you since that night going home from the Cumberland, but we mustn't do it. I don't want you to be a widow. I don't want you with a child that has no father. I know if we married he wouldn't be a bastard. But you would be alone with it if anything happened to me. Let us wait. We must wait. It won't be for long. It can't be. The whole thing is madness. The world will wake up to itself and stop the war.'

Judy's eyes flooded with tears. She said nothing immediately – she just looked at Titch.

'I wish I had your strength Rupert.' She sniffed away a tear. 'I'm sorry darling. You are right. We will wait.' She paused and Titch saw her struggle within herself. 'We'll wait... We'll wait for everything. I know I have your love and I have this.' She held her hand into the sunlight and allowed the sun to play on the face of his father's signet ring. She refused his offer of a diamond ring.

'I'm happy with this my love.' Were her words then – as if she remembered them she repeated them again.

'I have your love. I am happy with that. And I am happy with this.' She reached up and kissed Titch as the 'All Clear' siren sounded. It was so

180

loud Titch nearly missed her words when she laughed and added. 'For the time being, Titch Wilkins.'

Service training went on a pace. Weeks fused into months of what was called 'The Phoney War' – Judy and Titch were serving on Operational Stations. She was at Biggin Hill with Fighter Command, while Titch was in the Training and Reserve Flight of Number 12 Bomber Squadron RAF. The Squadron was stationed in France with the British Expeditionary Force (BEF) at Amifontaine. Titch was at Bicester, near Oxford. The task of the Reserve Flight was to train replacement crews to be sent to the Squadron as and when needed.

It was a bewildering time for them all. They were trained to operational pitch and yet the war was at a standstill. The BEF reported 'Patrol Activity' by both British and German Forces. RAF communiques from France said the same thing. England-based RAF bombers dropped bombs on German shipping at Kiel and Cuxhaven, and leaflets were dropped all over Western Germany telling civilians the evils and consequences of waging war against Britain and France.

Titch had a crew at Bicester. Sergeants Keith Gale and Andrew Wragge – Pilot and Observer, respectively. Titch was a lowly Leading Aircraftsman, an LAC in service parlance. True he had the 'Clenched Fists with Sparks' of the wireless operator and the winged bullet of the airgunner, but he was only an LAC with the grand income of 4/6d per day, plus trade pay and flying allowance.

Six shillings a day, less income tax.

Keith and 'Hanky' as they called Andrew Wragge were old friends. ('Andy Rag, 'Hanky'.) The name suited him to a tee. Though they were sergeants they were on Christian name terms. Titch was confined to the airmen's mess and they in the palatial quarters of the sergeants' mess.

Keith was a mystery at first. He maintained a silence about himself that was puzzling. His accent labelled him English Public School or similar. His standard of dress was well above the ordinary. He wore expensive Vanheusen woollen shirts and an exotic silk scarf when flying. His number one blues were tailored; his shoes hand-made in Regent Street. All very puzzling for a boy from the Wandsworth slums. Titch had quite a savings account but considered this pilot's tastes beyond his own financial range.

Hanky was un-ashamedly a Communist; he recited Karl Marx to all who would listen. In 1936 he had been wounded serving in the International Brigade in Spain and called all officers, 'A disease. Part of the Bourgeois system that has to be eradicated for the betterment of the workers'. He was a man of 30-or-so – tall and unkempt; a shock of red hair dominated his rugged good looks. He was volatile, conscientious, dedicated to the downfall of Hitler, and a damned good navigator. As a former Trades Union organiser he had a pathological hate of Nazis and was a devotee of Joseph Stalin. He was constantly harassing Keith and Titch in their efforts to volunteer to join the force planned to help the beleaguered Finns fighting invading Russians. Their volunteering efforts and his objections came to naught when Finland surrendered to the Russians in January 1940. To his loss, the RAF hierarchy hated Hanky to a man – a pity, for apart from his belligerent dislike of authority he was a good and loyal Squadron member.

As a crew the trio flew cross country navigation exercises, bombing details and air firing practices. They flew when commissioned pilots were able to stand down for a trip 'To town' and its diversions. Training schedules had to be maintained. It meant flying hours had to be recorded, practice bombs had to be dropped, specified practice ammunition had to be fired. It was often the NCO crews that made up the number of hours at the end of each week. Logically it was the NCO crews who became the most proficient.

Such was the state of affairs as the hard winter of 1939-40 passed into memory and spring emerged in a burst of splendour. England was never lovelier. Judy and Titch were able to spend leave together. Titch lived with Bert and Ma – Judy at her home over the butcher's shop, but they saw each other every day. They walked the London Parks and the city's labyrinth of alleys and lanes. They ate at market porter's cafes, and drank beer in little off-street pubs that had seen the great fire of London in 1666 – on a memorable night they went to see the 'Crazy Gang' at the London Palladium; and they talked of the things lovers the world over talk about. Their love making was confined to kissing and gentle caresses – their words spoke only of love and hope and a future together. Titch drew a hundred pounds from his savings and bought Judy a diamond engagement ring. She protested, but wore it with pride. Too soon they had to return to their units to resume the dreary rounds of training – the way the war was going hostilities would peter out like a damp squid on a wet Guy Fawkes night, or so the nation thought.

In mid-April orders came for Sergeant Keith Gale and crew to proceed on embarkation leave prior to a posting to France as a replacement crew. Judy was stationed at Biggin Hill – Keith invited Titch to stay with him at the house of a wealthy aunt in the Kent village of Westerham Hill, a short cycle ride from the fighter airfield. His aunt Katharine had left England to stay with her sister in America for the duration of the hostilities; an elderly housekeeper was now the only resident. Judy and Titch were together most of the ten days.

More importantly for Titch, he and Keith were able to get to know each other. Neither of them were heavy drinkers, but both enjoyed a glass of bitter and the atmosphere of old country pubs. The 16th century pub, 'The Kentish Man' was to their tastes and saw them on most days for a round of drinks and a yarn.

The spring weather was glorious and the garden of the old inn was ablaze with new blooms – the two would talk over their modest half pints of ale sitting under a cherry tree as old as the pub – blossom fell on them as they sat. They talked of themselves and the war – their comrades, their loved ones and what the future held. It was after their first drink that Keith spoke of his dislike at the name Titch for his gunner.

'It's very descriptive but rather impersonal. What do your friends call you. Your close friends, I mean?'

'Titch. Everyone calls me Titch. Always have. Everyone except Judy... And a teacher I had once. They call me Rupert but it was sort of private. Know what I mean?'

Keith wasn't sure but he continued his line of talk.

'May I call you Rupert ... Titch?' he laughed. 'Would you mind? If only in private.'

'I'd like that,' said Titch thoughtfully. 'But only in private. Other times it had better be Titch, like everyone else.'

And that is how it was.

Keith spoke of himself – he was the son of an Anglican missionary couple working in Tanganyika. They were of 'independent means', as Keith put it – Titch believing he meant they had money of their own. The pilot lived in Tanganhika as a boy speaking Ki-Swahili before his mother tongue. He talked at length of his parents and their life in Africa – talk of lions and leopards wandering through the garden shrubberies and wild boar and elephants wrecking the family vegetable garden gripped Titch's imagination. Tales of charging rhino and hunting safaris with Wa-chagga and Masai tribesmen had the gunner enthralled.

Education made it necessary for Keith to return to England – he was a boarder at Shrewsbury Grammar School; he hated it. Cold, unfriendly England was a far cry from the African sun. As a

'Colonial' with no close family support he had his share of bullies and the indignities they inflict. This led to Titch speaking of his own childhood. The former bricklayer unburdened himself as he had done to no other than Bert James and Judy. The workhouse, orphanage and the incident with du Canne were experiences he touched on – the happier side of life he told in more detail. Keith laughed as Titch quoted some of Bert James' philosophical homilies. He muttered his incredulity at the behaviour of Titch's uncle in Wales. It took two rounds of drinks to complete the tale – Keith leaned against the gnarled trunk of the old cherry tree; his brow furrowed as he spoke.

'It's understandable Rupert... Your uncle's rage I mean. If he accepted you as his older brother's son he was as good as saying you are the heir to the estate. What is its name?'

'Cuffty Mawr.' Titch was incapable of saying more as Keith added.

'That's right. It explains everything... It creates a whole set of problems for him. Of course you will have to prove it all in court. The old devil is sure to fight you. But it shouldn't be too difficult.' He laughed and looked directly at Titch. 'How would you like to be Lord of the Manor?'

Titch joined in the laughter. 'Better than being a bloody LAC Wop/AG.' Keith drained his glass.

'I bet it will... A problem occurs to me though. You will have to learn Welsh.'

Titch raised his own tankard.

'That won't be too hard. All the Welsh kids speak it, so I reckon I'll soon learn.' He drained his glass and the two went laughing into the bar

186

for a ploughman's lunch; it seemed the most natural thing in the world for Keith's arm to be on Titch's shoulder.

Another warm spring day they were seated under the cherry tree again – empty plates littered with the crumbs of a sandwich lunch were pushed aside; the two friends were drinking their third half pint. Titch looked at his pilot.

'Keith. Why haven't you been commissioned? You have the education and the background and cash doesn't seem a problem. Surely things would be better for you if you were an officer.'

'Different for certain. Better? I don't know about that.' He paused and took a drink from his tankard. 'The truth is, Rupert, I am scared.'

'What!' Titch's surprise was genuine. 'You, scared? I'll not swallow that. Scared of what for Christ's sake?'

'You see Rupert, I am supposed to be in the Army. I joined up at the beginning of 1936 and was accepted into the Officer Training Corps. I was in my third month of training when the CO laid on a cadets' dance. Nurses and lots of local girls were invited. It as quite an evening with a punch bowl the size of a bath tub. Jolly good stuff it was too. My Company Commander's wife was there. With him of course. Anyway she was much younger than her husband and very attractive. For some reason she took a shine to me and we had a couple of dances together.' Keith paused again and smiled grimly. 'I think we both had more punch than was good for us. And, like I said, she was very attractive. Anyway, she invited me for a drink in her bungalow. To cut a long story short, old Blubber Guts, my Company Commander, caught us in bed together. He flew into a rage and grabbed a sabre from the wall. The lady screamed and I grabbed my clothes and bolted.' Keith took a drink from his glass. 'I felt it most unwise to hang about waiting for what I believed would be at the very least a rocket of the worst kind. I got a lift to Woking and a train to London intending to report back on the Monday when the old boy had simmered down. But the more I thought about it the worse it became. I never did go back. I enlisted in the Air Force on the Wednesday, and here I am.'

Titch did not speak – he just looked at his comrade and Keith continued.

'So you see Rupert, I am a deserter. I changed my name when I enlisted from Gail. Spelt G.A.I.L. to Gale. Spelt G.A.L.E. I hoped that it would confuse the chase.'

Titch was even more puzzled, 'But how does that stop you applying for a commission?'

'Because, you sub-human little man. They are bound to check on my credentials and then I would be a gonner.' He laughed. 'I can still see old Blubber Guts with his sabre, to say nothing of the Court Martial they would throw at me. Believe me Rupert old son. The Sergeants' Mess is more attractive than The Glasshouse detention centre.' The young sergeant pilot smiled at his gunner, 'So old chum, you are stuck with plain Sergeant Gale and not potentially Air Chief Marshal Gale.'

Judy and Titch saw each other most days. Her duties at the Station Medical Quarters were light so she was able to get way. They walked and cycled over the countryside of Kent admiring the colour of 'The Garden of England'. Ten days flew – they said their farewells at night under a full moon – there were no tears; this was after all, 'The Phoney War'. Titch was going to France where British and German troops peered at each other through the loop-holes of their concrete bunkers watching French farmers plough their fields and tend cattle. A place where off-duty soldiers of both sides drank wine and flirted with local girls in cafes in villages either side of the lines – there seemed no reason why the status quo between the belligerents should not continue indefinitely; the Summer of 1940 had not begun.

Chapter Eight

Twelve Squadron needed five crews and four aircraft – Flying Officer 'Kiwi' Thompson a tall New Zealander and crew were to be the formation leaders. Flying Officers Reading and Smythe-Jones and flight Sergeant Delany were to fly together in a box formation four replacement Fairey Battles to 12 Squadron's base in Northern France. Sergeant Gale and crew were to proceed there BTBMA (By The Best Means Available) to arrive ASP (As Soon as Possible). So read the travel documents signed by the Flight Commander. Sergeant Keith Gale and crew were instructed to contact the Rail Transport Officer at the Port of arrival in France; as things transpired this was Calais.

The journey to Dover via London was crowded and dirty. Troops packed the corridors of the train – kit and weapons overflowed the luggage compartments; khaki figures slept, smoked, grumbled and cursed their way to the capital.

The 12 Squadron crew spent the night in the city and Titch took Keith and Hanky to stay with Bert and Ma James. It was well after midnight before they turned in. The Workshop was overcrowded with the four of them, but no-one noticed as the conversation went back and forth.

Bert was a perfect foil for Hanky. The two of them were evenly matched – Bert James because of his innate wisdom; Hanky because of his well rehearsed dogmatic arguments. Keith and Titch were superfluous to the discussion – they had heard Hanky's point of view often enough to know his rhetoric by heart.

'S'no good a'sayin that Communism'll work yer know young 'Anky. It will fer a time I grant yer that. It'as appeal dun' it. "All fer one and one fer all". And "All you've got ter lose is yer chains". S'lovely. Sounds abs'erlootly wonderful. A real Utopia. Then people get greedy dun' they. It becomes "Every man fer 'is self n'the Lord fer us all". Know wot' I mean? 'Cept all them there communists is atheist ain't they n'greed and corruption a'creeps in. It's bound ter. 'Uman nature a'bein' wot' it is. N'then the 'ole shin bag'll collapse.'

The old bricklayer struck a match and applied it to the bowl of his briar. It burnt his callused finger before he took it out and took a long swallow from the glass of Brown Ale the crew had brought for the evening. He puffed his lips and blew froth from his moustache, looked at Hanky and continued.

'People 'as got ter see sumfin' fer their h'efforts. Promises of good termorrer'll only work fer a little while. Maybe 50 years. Then a bloke asks where 'e's goin'. N'wot am I a' doin' it all fer? Ol' Uncle Joe Stalin?' He laughed a derisive laugh. ''E sees 'im a sittin' up ther wiv' 'is commy mates on the Kremlin wall every May Day. All of 'em a'wrapped up in nice woolly coats. N'ol' Uncle Joe a' smokin' 'is ol' pipe may be, an' 'e 'finks. "'E ain't a'doin' s'bad. But wot' ab'art me and the kids? Eh?" Where are we a'goin' 'e asks 'is'self.'

The old bricklayer's pipe was drawing well and Hanky was allowing someone else a say for a change. He leaned over and topped up the old man's glass from a half-empty bottle on the desk.

'Ta.' Bert took a long swallow from the brimming glass and looked at the red-headed Observer.

'Besides,' he continued. 'I don't believe any good'll come out of a'killin' all them there h'innercent people as Stalin did all them years ago. Good only comes from good. N'bad from bad. That's wot' I say. Stands ter reason dun' it?' He leaned back in his chair and looked at Hanky perched on the corner of his old desk. The younger man was about to say something when Bert continued.

'Mind you. Sum'fin' 'ad to 'appen in Russia after the Great War. That Tzar bloke and 'is crowd of 'angers-on were a'gettin' away wiv' murder. In a manner of speakin' like. I realise that. But the poor'll never feed the poor yer know 'Anky. Yer got'ter give people a chance ter make a bob or two 'uvver wise we'll all sit on our bums and expect the 'uvver bloke ter do it all. And a'course 'e never does, does 'e?'

Ma's knock on the door of the workshop allowed the old Cockney to have the last word The four trooped into the house and the hot cocoa she had prepared. It was to be an early start to get the troop train to Dover.

Hanky bought a newspaper at Waterloo Station – a Stop Press item announced 'German Troops Massing on the Belgian Frontier'. The date at the top of the page was 9th May, 1940.

Calais was crowded – the RTO gave the three short change when they inquired about transport to Perpignan where they had been told to report.

'Perpignan?'

The red-faced Military Police corporal in the RTO's office studied the wall map. Then a road guide. He came to where the three were standing with their kit around their feet.

'They should 'ave routed you through Dunkerque. There's no trains leaving 'ere fer Perpignan. From Dunkerque, yeah. Not Calais. Not now. Best get up there. Ter Dunkerque I mean.'

Keith as pilot and captain was doing the talking – he was very patient.

'Thank you corporal. When can we get a train for Dunkerque?'

The CMP man studied a time table. He walked into a back room and spoke on the telephone.

Minutes ticked by – he returned to the three.

'Can't say at this stage sergeant. Seems all the schedules is changed. Something's goin' on east of 'ere. All the trains are under the orders of the military until further notice.'

The three of them looked at each other – they remembered the 'Stop Press' item the day before. What could have happened? An officer of the CMP came out of the inner office. Keith pushed through the barrier and approached him.

'Excuse me Sir. Could you help me please?'

It was his accent as much as his manner that made the captain stop and look at him. The police officer's eyes took in the pilot's brevet and Keith's three stripes.

'What is it sergeant?'

Keith looked at him.

'We have orders to report to our squadron as soon as possible. I feel it is urgent and the rail service to Perpignan appears non existent. Have you any suggestions?'

The officer looked at the young pilot. He was a tall man approaching middle years. He sported a row of Great War medal ribbons on his tunic. His red face appeared swollen through the tightness of his shirt collar; it gave his face a bloated look. A small 'Gigolo' moustache looked incongruous on his large florid face. The captain hesitated for a moment. He looked at Hanky and Titch standing the other side of the barrier.

'Those chaps with you?'

'They are my crew. Sergeant Wragge, my Observer and Leading Aircraftsman Wilkins, my Wop/AG.'

'Bring them in here.' The CMP man went back into the office he had just vacated; Keith beckoned to Hanky and Titch to follow him.

The room was empty except for them – it was dusty and bare. A trestle table served as a desk – two chairs looked as if they had been bought from the nearest second hand shop stood before it. There was worn, cracked linoleum with a faded fleur-de-lys pattern on the floor. An old fashioned telephone stood on the table stacked with neat piles of typed paper. A large 'Michelin' map of France covered most of one wall. A 'Bulletin Board' was covered with Army notices of one sort or another. Blow flies buzzed against the glass of the dirty window; it was all very depressing.

'Perpignan you said?' The captain ran his eyes over the map and eventually stabbed with a well manicured finger a tiny dot no bigger than a fly speck.

'Perpignan. About 60 miles as the crow flies. One hundred by foot I should think. Because that, my friends, is the way you will have to go. Trains are out of the question, and road transport will become more difficult as time progresses.'

He looked at the three puzzled faces.

'I tell you this in confidence. Something is happening on the Belgian Frontier to the east and north. Every available means of transport is heading into Belgium with British troops. No other news is coming through. I believe the Boche has broken through Belgium as he did in 1914.' The captain sighed in an exasperated manner. 'The bloody Generals never seem to learn from history.' He looked at the three of them.

'Anyway. You had best make your own way to Perpignan. I'll write you out a chit that may help.' He wrote for a minute in an official pad and stamped it with RTO Calais in bold letters. He scrawled his signature over the stamp impression.

'I don't know if this will help.' He passed it to Keith. 'Now if you will excuse me, I have a railway station to care for.' He smiled – Keith saluted, thanked him and the crew followed him out of the room and into the crowded station foyer where troops were being marshalled and marched. It looked an organised chaos of soot blackened arches and bored and weary soldiery; a situation they were glad to be free of.

It took two days to reach Perpignan. The airfield was occupied by a Hawker Hurricane squadron. Fighters were landing and taking off in rapid succession. A harassed Station Adjutant hustled the three out of his headquarters.

'Twelve Squadron? Left here days ago. Went to Amifontaine I believe. God knows where they are now. Look, I must go. There's quite a flap on. Corporal!' He was bellowing orders as the three left the improvised Station HQ.

Keith learned the 'Flap' was as the RTO captain had predicted – the Germans had broken through Belgium and got around the British lines on the French-German border. The elaborate Maginot Line defence system built by the French and reinforced by the BEF was useless. German Panzers had charged through the 'impossible terrain' of the Ardennes. The Allies were taken completely by surprise.

It took four long days to reach Amifontaine –

their kit was heavy and cumbersome; kit bags containing flying clothing began to weigh a ton and their money was running out. Roads were almost impassable with the flow of refugees. Rumours of the German advance were rife – tales of their speed and terror of their atrocities were on every lip. Keith's school French was good enough to get the necessities of life, but they hadn't had a good meal since leaving Perpignan. Amifontaine at least fed them and supplied them with a bath and bed for the night; Twelve Squadron had moved to Echemines.

The three were refreshed and the cookhouse at Amifontaine supplied them with corned beef and cheese sandwiches – enough to last a month; so they thought when they saw the pile. The accounts section supplied some French Francs and they left confident they would catch up with the Squadron and get into the air; foot slogging was not to their tastes.

An army supply lorry gave them a lift north – roads were packed with refugees fleeing to the south. Men, women and children – in cars, vans, horse and carts and on bicycles – even baby carriages and wheelbarrows were pressed into serviced; all laden with household goods. Many were walking doggedly – shoulders bent under personal belongings – eyes and minds oblivious to all else but the pave at their feet heading south. It was a journey of many halts caused by congestion and broken down vehicles – they pressed on until stopped by the Military Police who made them get out of the lorry and ordered the driver to turn round and head the way he had come. Two burly

CMP corporals in full battle order and wearing pistols demanded papers and details of their destination.

'Don't reckon as 'ow you'll make it serg. You c'n see 'ow the roads are. The further north and east you go the worse it'll get.'

'I see there is a railway heading north. Is there a train?'

There was indeed a line – they had passed it just yards back down the road and the metals pointed a little north of east.

'Not a bloody 'ope serg. Not goin' that way. The last one passed 'ere this morning. 'Eadin' south. There's fighting just a few miles along the road. Ask these Froggies 'ere. They're all runnin' from it.'

The three put their heads together and thought it useless continuing along roads increasingly choked with traffic – the railway seemed a good alternative route if they had to walk; it was at least clear of refugees. The decision was made for them when they heard a distant roar of aeroplane engines and the stutter of machine gun fire. Titch looked towards the sound and saw two Messerschmitt 109 fighters breaking away after strafing a road to the north. As he watched, two Hurricane fighters swooped and chased the MEs over the horizon; it was their first sight of the enemy.

Two sets of gleaming tracks stretched ahead of them as far as Titch could see. The sky was a deep red to the west and they were beginning to look about for some shelter for the night. An embankment had been left behind and the railway lines passed through a cutting and disappeared round a bend. Titch had his eyes on the railway sleepers and measured his steps to tread on each one. He had tried stepping over two, but with the load of kit he carried the strides were too long – too long even for Hanky's long legs. Left, right, left, right. Titch concentrated on the sleepers and tried to forget his aching shoulders and sore feet. Hanky's heels in front were the focus of his life.

Titch almost collided with the tall observer when he came to an abrupt halt; he looked up. Four very black ferocious looking French Colonial soldiers were pointing rifles with fierce looking bayonets at them. One had the point of his touching the base of Keith's chin. Titch looked at his intrepid captain and saw he had his hands above his head in surrender. If the gunner hadn't been so scared himself he would have laughed – Keith was standing on his tip toe to get out of reach of the long bayonet point. The pilot managed to stutter in school French.

'Aviator Anglais!'

Nothing happened. The bayonet point trembled at Keith's throat. The pilot stood taller; his arms stretched higher.

'RAF Britannic. Anglais! Anglais!' The young pilot's voice rose an octave – his hands clutched the air above his head. The three Africans peered from under steel helmets – they looked hot in heavy equipment and heavy great coats. Brown eyes with bloodshot jaundiced whites looked deep into their captive's. They eyed Hanky and Titch with looks that said clearly they would love to pierce the white men's frail frightened bodies with their long pointed weapons. The African closest to Titch grinned; his teeth white against the blue black of his skin. Titch was alarmed further when he saw that the man's teeth were filed to sharp points.

'Perhaps we are going to be killed and eaten'. The thought was no sooner in Titch's head than he was convinced it was a distinct possibility.

Bushes parted to the right of the line and a white man in the uniform of a French Infantry Non Commissioned Officer came towards them followed by two native troops. He gave an order in some unintelligible tongue. The soldier who had his bayonet point at Keith's throat withdrew his weapon – very reluctantly. Titch thought. The white sergeant, for that is what he was, spoke to Keith in French. Titch was sure his pilot's teeth were chattering as he answered. There was an exchange in rapid French that was quite beyond Hanky and the Wop/AG. The only words were, 'La Boche'. The Frenchman pointed to a village two miles down the line. A pall of smoke hung over the houses plainly seen in the evening light.

There was a further brief exchange of words – Keith and the sergeant shook hands and the pilot headed back down the line towards the south. He told the others as they walked that the Germans were just a couple of miles behind – the French Colonial troops were from the French Cameroons and were taking up defensive positions as part of a rearguard of a force that they had somehow walked right through on their way north. He also explained that their RAF blue uniforms had confused the African soldiers who were sure we were Germans in field grey.

In minutes they reached the embankment that fell twenty or more feet into drainage ditches either side. Not a word passed between them but as if by a command they tipped their weighty kit bags containing heavy flying clothing down the slopes and watched them roll into the ditches. It was obvious to the three, they were not going to find 12 Squadron this side of the English Channel.

The journey to Dunkerque was long and dangerous. They were strafed by enemy planes. Briefly locked up by an irate Gendarme for stealing an ancient Citröen. Shot at by their own troops and bombed by high flying Dorniers as they waited to board the ship at the quay of Dunkerque harbour. It was a relief when the little collier 'Whitby Lass' packed to the funnel with troops docked at Shoeburyness; they were safe in England.

It appeared Keith had relatives everywhere. He had an uncle and aunt at the small resort of Leigh-on-Sea a few miles from Shoeburyness. The little port was in complete confusion. A former pleasure steamer had docked before them and there was another waiting for 'Whitby Lass' to off-load its human cargo and allow it to discharge another several hundred troops. The reception services were inundated. Red Cross ladies served tea to the thirsty soldiers – local people served sandwiches and cigarettes. Officers and NCOs hastily brought in to organise the reception of returning personnel were swamped. Keith approached the only RAF officer he could see in the ocean of Khaki. The man was near breaking point.

'My God sergeant, are you an imbecile? Use your own initiative man. Find your own way to your unit. God alone knows what we are going to do with this lot.'

From where the three stood they were looking over the heads of hundreds of dishevelled men – some clamouring for attention; others standing or sitting with eyes glazed with fatigue, their kit and weapons spread at their feet. All appeared lost and exhausted, not knowing the whereabouts of their units. It was at that point that Keith suggested they head for his uncle's house at Leigh. A walk of 15 miles, but after three weeks of fruitless marching in France it was child's play.

The trio arrived at the little house on the outskirts of the small town late in the evening, very dirty, very hungry and quite exhausted. The kindly old couple were overjoyed at being able to help. The three bathed and loaned an assortment of clothes that fitted them, more or less. Titch was in the school clothes of their son who was serving with his regiment in the Middle East. They were old – the trousers too long but Titch was able to turn them up and look presentable. Aunt Ann as they were instructed to call their hostess would take their uniforms to the cleaners in the morning; their shirts and underwear she laundered herself.

The enlarged household listened to the BBC news that early summer's evening – it told of the BEF's evacuation from Dunkerque. After a large supper the crew collapsed onto the luxury of feather beds; they slept as never before.

The morning was old when they woke – a June sun shone through the window and the three were ready for a new day. Aunt Ann was shopping in the town – she and her husband 'Uncle Rolf' had taken the uniforms as promised. The three dressed in their borrowed clothes and went down to eat breakfast prepared for them and left to warm in the oven.

The old couple came home as Titch and Hanky were washing the dishes. Aunt Ann was excited at the commotion in the town.

'All the yachts in the club are leaving to go to France. It seems they are needed to take our troops off the beaches at Dunkerque. I was talking to Commander Willis. He is the Club Commodore,' she added hastily. 'He was terribly excited trying to get crews to man the boats.' There was more. The three left the house and walked down to the water front.

They heard the Commander long before they saw him. His voice was strident as he badgered and chivvied men and boats out into deeper water where a Royal Navy launch was assembling about 40 yachts of all shapes and sizes into some semblance of order. The tiny vessels were being positioned line astern prior to towing them out of the estuary. The tall ex-navy officer caught sight of the three dressed in an assortment of civilian clothes.

'I say. You there. Lend a hand!' It took the trio seconds to reach him.

'Give a hand here.' The old salt strode towards a sleek, beautifully varnished motor yacht tied up at the club house pier. The Commodore's flag of 'The Estuary Yacht Club' fluttered above the burgee of the Club and the 'Royal Navy Cruising Club' and several lesser pennants. A considerable amount of the peppery old officer's income must be spent on club membership fees.

'You chaps know how to sail?'

Titch was about to blurt out that they were Air Force men when Keith piped up.

'Yes. But sailing. Not motoring.'

'Really. Splendid. Which club?'

'Dar-es-Salaam Sailing Club.'

'Good God. Dar eh? Haven't been there f'years. Beautiful spot. Chota Peg and Beer moja n'all that, what! Wonderful life.' He looked directly at Titch.

'I say. Don't stand gawping, man. Look to the forward line. You fellar!'

He looked at Hanky peering at the boat's compass.

'Get aft. The pair of you. Cast off at my order. You stay close to me.'

He addressed Keith and scrambled into the deck house followed by the pilot.

Titch looked at Hanky at the stern – he could see his navigator's egalitarian feathers were ruffled. Titch lifted the forward mooring line off the shore bollard and rove it ready for the order 'Cast off'. Hank followed Titch's example.

This was Titch's first time afloat in a small boat. He racked his brain for all the theory he had read during his evenings with Bert James. The yacht's engine roared into life and made Titch look to the task allotted to him.

'Cast off forard!' Titch heaved on the line and it played through the hawse – he began to coil it on the deck as he had seen pictures in the books he had read.

'Cast off aft!'

Hank was alert – his line snaked in; he copied Titch's efforts and began coiling it down. The sleek motor yacht *'Maid of Honour'* edged her glossy hull away from the jetty and crept out to the waiting line of yachts.

There was more activity for Titch and more shouting by the Commodore before they were secured to the last vessel – a bull-like bellow of:

'All secure aft!' from the bridge of the *'Maid'* as the owner called his boat, and the line of yachts began to move. They had gone a mile when Titch remembered; he couldn't swim.

The water around them churned and swirled in the wake of the line of small craft. It worried Titch that they were last – if he fell overboard he knew he was a goner. As if he had read his thoughts the Commodore called him to the bridge.

'Get below into the galley there's a good chap and make a cup of coffee. Or tea if you prefer it. It's all there. Sort out the galley. The little woman said she had victualled us for a month.' He laughed a roar of a laugh.

Titch lit the small gimbaled stove and filled the kettle from the galley tap – he smiled as he remembered his tea making days in the building trade. No black buckets here – everything in sight sparkled in enamel or brass. Shelves were lined with oil cloth and wide based mugs hung from hooks; plates were stacked in roll-proof lockers.

Titch found the tea and sugar – milk was in a small ice box; he straightened his back and admired the layout of the yacht's cabin. It had everything – cushioned berths, a gimbaled table and a chart table with the chart of the Thames Estuary laid on it. Brass gimbal paraffin lamps gently rocked as the yacht rolled in the turbulent water. It smelt, it felt, it looked nautical. Mahogany and teak varnished to a satin finish – brass fittings gleaming. How Bert James would have loved it.

The whistle of the kettle brought Titch back to his task – he made the tea and poured it into four mugs, he saw they were lettered 'Skipper', 'Mate', 'Navigator', 'Cook' and 'Stowaway'. It was quite deliberate; he handed the 'Stowaway' to the Commodore.

'Sorry Sir. There wasn't one with Commodore, or even Commander. Keith's the skipper with us.'

The old man's eyes twinkled. He finished lashing the wheel then took his mug.

'Is he b'Gad. I should have you flogged around the Fleet f'that.' His laugh took any malice from his remark. 'Here Cookie. Hand the jug round.' He took a large stone one gallon flagon from the bridge cupboard and handed it to Titch. It was marked with a garish label. 'PUSSER'S RUM'; beneath in smaller print, 'Guaranteed 99% proof'. It was decorated with Navy signal flags and the figure of an 18th century sailor, and Nelson's *HMS Victory*. Titch poured a liberal dollop into each of the mugs – they drank each other's health and looked about them.

The scene that met Titch as he got 'top-sides' appalled his landlubber's eyes.

He had felt the motion of the yacht getting more lively but had not anticipated the long estuary swell that he saw. The 30 or 40 yachts being towed line astern bucked and rolled. Masts rocked alarmingly. The wakes of so many vessels churned up water passing hulls with a design speed of perhaps six knots at a rate of about ten. The transom of the small 25 footer ahead of them was alarmingly close to the water as the hull 'dug a hole' in the swell with the excessive speed. 'The *Maid of Honour*' coped better than most, though she rolled alarmingly. She was a trim vessel – narrow beamed; built for river cruising rather than ocean voyaging. Darkness came and they lost sight of blacked out England – the French coast was a night's sail away.

An RN launch patrolled the small fleet the whole of the short June night.

'Like a damned Collie rounding up sheep. Totally unnecessary really. Calm as a mill pond.' The old Commodore's remarks seemed an exaggeration; Titch was glad of the Navy's vigilance.

Dawn found the flotilla rolling a mile off the French coast. They had seen the flash of falling bombs or shell fire as they approached. Orange light lit the sky; an occasional explosion sent flames into the air. Dunkerque and the area around it was on fire. As the light improved a pall of smoke enveloped the scene. The Navy launch chugged down the line of yachts bobbing in the short Channel swell. An officer with a megaphone shouted instructions.

'Go into the shore as close as you can and the troops will wade out to you. When you have a full complement, head out to sea to the ships in the deeper water. Then return for another load.' He paused for a moment. 'Any questions?'

A woman's voice from a yacht just ahead called out.

'What about petrol?'

'Cans of petrol and food will be distributed by the Navy. If you need either fly a "P" or "F" signal flag from your mast head. Anything else?' There was silence except for the slapping of halliards against varnished masts and the sound of water against the hulls.

'No! Then God be with you ladies and gentlemen. Good luck.'

The launch picked up speed and headed for the beach. Forty yachts started their tiny engines – tow lines were dropped; in twos and threes they followed the Navy launch.

Titch was ordered to the bow. Hanky was ordered below and instructed to stand by the engine and operate the hand throttle if the bridge control failed. Keith was at the Commodore's side to act as messenger – the old sea dog pulled his cap down firmly – gripped the wheel and steered the *'Maid'* towards the shore.

Titch stood holding onto the pulpit. Small waves and spray broke over his bare feet; he was surprised how warm the water was. The sun was creeping out of the east, red and angry. He was able to look into it – it was like a very red apple, but rounder. The colour changed as he watched – two dots he saw he thought were birds; at first. He heard the noise of the engines – the sound was drowned for the three in the bridge house.

Titch yelled and waved his arm. 'Stukas! Two of them!'

The Commodore's face at the wheel looked puzzled. Keith poked his head out of the sliding door. Titch pointed to the planes that were right above. 'JU87s!' he yelled. Keith and Titch both looked, transfixed. The scream of the plane drowned the screech of the bomb, but they saw it falling. It was coming straight at them. A mountain of water grew before their eyes. Titch remembered it was a dirty brown with a white flat top. It fell all around the yacht. The noise was deafening. Titch was knocked off his feet – the next he knew was when he struck the coarse sand of the sea bottom. Somehow he surfaced – for only a moment; time enough to gulp air and to hear the stutter of a machine gun and the roar of a plane's engine. Water closed over his head again. Titch struggled and kicked. Unbelievably he didn't open his mouth. The water was a dirty grey before his eyes. Salt stung them but he kept them open and his mouth shut. Incredibly he remembered Sergeant 'Scrapper' Morgan's words from his days at Park Mansions. 'I keeps me eyes open and me mo'wf shut, Titch boy.'

His lungs were bursting – he surfaced again and struck his head on something hard; he took another gulp of air and sank again. This time Titch struggled less. A torpor came over him – almost a peace. His feet touched the bottom again; he found the energy and the presence of mind to jump. The effort expelled what little air he had in his lungs. He saw bubbles pass before his open eyes – he choked on the water that rushed into his open mouth. Red lights flashed before his eyes – he closed them but the lights didn't go away. He coughed – with each convulsion he swallowed water. Something pulled his hair – suddenly he saw the sun. It was a bright golden yellow – air was gulped into tortured lungs with each cough. An arm reached around his neck and he found himself on his back and being held up.

'Steady Rupert. You'll be OK. Don't struggle. Relax.'

Relax! Impossible – he was drowning for God's sake!

Titch Wilkins recognised Keith's voice through the mist of his half dead senses – he knew then there was hope. The drowning man fought down the urge to panic and willed himself to be calm. Water splashed over his face – he coughed and choked again, but was able to breathe. With a strength of will he calmed and heard Keith's laboured breathing. Then a voice.

'Bring 'im 'ere matey.'

Titch felt a gentle bump on the head and looked up. It was probably the ugliest face he had ever seen, but it looked beautiful at that moment. A filthy oil-stained hand reached down and grabbed the collar of his shirt and heaved. There was a tearing of cotton but Titch didn't care – a grey, cement encrusted deck was an inch from his eyes. Titch Wilkins retched and vomited sea water – he coughed and felt his lungs were on fire. He closed his eyes and willed himself to composure. He opened them again and saw two hair covered feet with long black toe nails.

''E'll be alright. Swoll'erd 'alf the bloody Channel. But 'e'll be as fit as a coster's randy jack donkey in a couple'a minutes.'

Titch recognised the cockney accent but not the speaker; everything was a blur.

'You okay, Rupert?'

It was Keith's voice. The fug of near unconsciousness cleared. Titch looked at his pilot kneeling over him. Water was dripping off his clothes, his hair and, oddly, from his nose and eye lashes. Titch thought how strange it was.

He sat up and retched again. Hands helped him to his feet and he struggled to the rail. Great gut heaving convulsions seized him as he vomited sea water over the side. Tears flooded his eyes. In the blur he saw a waterlogged yachting cap float by. The white top and the velvet and gilt badge identified it as the Commander's. With an effort Titch straightened his back and looked at his pilot through his tears.

'Where's Hanky, Keith?'

'He was below with the engine Rupert. I don't think he got out. The Commodore was trapped, too.' Keith sniffed and looked at his Wop/AG. 'The "Maid" capsized. They were both trapped. The thing filled and sank like a stone. It seemed to have broken its back. Probably under the weight of water from the bomb blast.'

Titch looked at his captain, then at his surroundings. They were standing on the filth encrusted deck of a cement barge – a spritsail barge, common to the River Thames and its estuary. It was just another of the fleet of small craft that answered the call for volunteers to

210

venture out of safe waters to evacuate the French and British troops from the besieged beaches. The grubby barge's stumpy mast reached up into the pale blue sky; a rust coloured mainsail was furled untidily on the sprit.

'Right'o Ginger! Start the bloody engin' and leg's get on wiv' it then!'

There was a report like a rifle shot – the engine exploded into life with a cloud of smoke – a single powerful cylinder beat a throb that vibrated through the vessel. Smoke rings the size of dinner plates puffed out of the funnel exhaust pipe protruding a rusty finger of doom above the engine house.

'When yer've done that you st'oopid ginger sod get below and put the kettle on.'

A tall red tussled-hair man moved to obey. His great freckled face grinned at his captain, the mouth showing a row of yellow teeth. It was a puckish face – a button red-tipped nose dominated the centre of it; a thatch of long tangled red hair waved in the chill breeze that blew from the sea. Ginger's head was level with the deck, a pair of green eyes peered at his captain. The barge master's voice bellowed again.

''N'get some dry duds fer these gents a'fore their bollocks break off wiv' the cold in this wind. Give 'em any'fin' 'ceptin' my best cords! D'yer 'ear me!' There was no answer from the ship's single crewman – he ducked his head and disappeared. The master of the barge looked at the two flyers.

'h'I 'ad better h'intr'dooce me'self. I'm Oats Smif'sern. Master n'owner o' the barge *'My Nell'* out'er Gravesend though I lives in Stepney me self. When I'm ashore like,' he added as a way of explanation.

Titch looked towards the voice. 'Oats', a cockney name for Charley. (Oats and Barley, Charley) The name was unbelievable to Keith; for Titch with his cockney background it was familiar enough. Oats Smithson, their saviour, peered at the *'Maid's'* survivors – he removed a stub of clay pipe from between cracked lips and his face broke into an embarrassed grin.

Keith made the introductions for Titch and himself – without details he explained their presence on the *'Maid of Honour'*.

Oats Smithson was indeed an ugly man. He was short and squat with a barrel of a chest. Long coarse black hairs protruded like wire from the open front of an oil and food stained blue shirt of heavy wool. A waistcoat of blue serge hung open to reveal garish coloured braces that supported a pair of tight-fitting moleskin trousers that shone from wear at the knees and seat; the fly was a flap pinned together with two rusty nails just below a big brass buckle of a wide leather belt that fitted loosely around a narrow waist. The bottoms of the moleskins were rolled up and showed hair muscular calves and filthy feet. He had a three or four day growth of beard and his black hair was clipped short. His eyes were as black as his hair – eyebrows made a continuous thick black line above his eyes. A very old, black and battered clay pipe was clenched between broken and decayed teeth; the glowing bowl almost touched his thick nose that showed signs of many a fight. The organ was wide and flat and covered with blackheads and blacker hairs – two cavernous hairy nostrils were like black holes of infinite depth; a cyst the size of a cherry on one side added to its charm. Large hairy arms showed beneath the rolled-up sleeves of his filthy shirt, and enormous dirt-engrimed hands gripped the barge's tiller that was little better than a length of four-by-four timber slipped into the groove of the rudder stock protruding three feet above the soiled deck. Oats Smithson exuded a crude animal strength and virility; he was a man of generosity and good will as his treatment of the two airmen proved, but a bath would not go amiss.

His language went with his accent; both a product of his tough environment. The former, the rough company he was compelled to live with all his life – company where every second word was an obscenity from meaningless habit; the latter simply the accent of the cockney longshoreman. Coming as it did from this rough master bargee his crude blasphemous profanities were not offensive for his generosity and courage far outweighed his shortcomings.

His one man crew Ginger was no cleaner, though Titch suspected there was less intellect under the thatch of red hair of the taller man. They were to learn that the red-haired crewman suffered brain damage at birth that left him speechless and simple-minded. He understood every syllable Oats spoke and his looks conveyed his understanding, his answers were the simpleton's grin. Abandoned by his parents when a child, he grew up on the 'Nell' and worshipped

213

every step of the deck his skipper trod.

The four had time to drink their tea and Keith and Titch to change into soiled, though dry, clothes before Ginger was ordered to

'Drop the bloody kedge!'

This was a large anchor dropped at the stern as *'My Nell'* crept forward towards the beach.

Lines of waiting soldiery stretched two hundred yards from the edge of the surf out to where the spritsail barge's keelson was grinding on the sand of the sea bed. Some of the troops were up to their necks in water as the barge gently passed them; the iron studded stem dug into the sand bringing the vessel to a halt. Men began to clamber aboard – some with kit; some with loot.

'Chuck that bloody rubbish in'ter the bleedin' drink. This ain't a fuckin' Carter fuckin' Patterson bloody delivery service. Chuck it over the side Ginger. N'them wiv it if they argues.'

The burly crew acted – those who hesitated were threatened by a fierce grimace from the red haired giant; none risked being thrown overboard with their kit.

'Just bodies. That's all I'm a'takin' to England. Two o'they kit bags takes up the room fer one man. There's only room fer men 'ere. Them wot' doesn't like it c'n fuckin' stay be'ind.'

Titch had no idea how many troops were aboard before a bellow from Oats had Ginger at the stern winch. With the engine going at full revolutions and puffing smoke like a steam train the barge was slowly hauled off the sand into deeper water. It took an hour to chug out to a navy destroyer waiting to take the men. As the soldiers passed Titch to take their places on the boarding nets he saw their wet uniforms were caked with cement from head to foot. A glance up at the deck of the warship and Titch saw the look of distaste on the face of the Petty Officer in charge of the deck; the gunner smiled imagining the navy man's thoughts, 'Oh, my lovely deck'.

It was about all there was to smile about that day, and the next. Afterwards neither Keith nor Titch could remember how many times they went back and forth to the beach, or how many troops old Oats saved, or how many days the four of them laboured. The end came when the beach was bare of the living; though the sound of small arms fire was clearly heard from behind the dunes.

As the *'My Nell'* pulled away with the last load the four took a moment to look at the beach – they saw the strand littered with vehicles, kit and equipment, and the bodies of the dead; a figure staggered from the cover of the sand dunes. It fell a hundred yards from the surf to lie motionless. Dead, or wounded; Titch could not tell; they could not go back.

The *'My Nell'* had been lucky – for some reason the Luftwaffe had left them alone. German shells fell in the water from time to time but none were close to the old barge. As the vessel gathered way Titch looked for the last time along that unfriendly coast – he was surprised to see a small yacht sailing parallel to the beach, quite close inshore as if looking for the last straggler. Its sails were filled and tight hauled and it heeled to the stiff land breeze that had picked up. It reminded

Titch of a petulant duck seeking a lost duckling. From miles out to sea the exhausted troops lying in heaps on the engrimed deck saw the smoke of the fires of Dunkerque as the city and army stores burned; if they felt any emotions, fatigue dulled them.

A RN Destroyer chivvied them along. *'My Nell'* had her mainsail up and drawing. If they had looked they would have seen the old girl had a 'bone' in her teeth, a small bow wave showed white against the grey water of the English Channel. The spritsail barge's engine was belching black smoke – Ginger stayed at the throttle while Keith and Titch tended the blocks and tackles that worked the sheets and halyards; Oats stood unwashed and unafraid at the tiller. At one time the navy vessel came close and Oats was addressed by the loud hailer.

'Can't you get a little more speed out of that rust bucket captain!'

Oats didn't need a loud hailer – he just opened his mouth and bellowed.

'This 'ere ain't the fuckin' Blue Bird yer snotty nosed dick'ead. N'I ain't Malcolm fuckin' Campbell. If yer don't like our company piss off 'ome by yer self.'

The destroyer tooted and shot ahead, but it didn't leave them. It immediately opened fire with its multiple pom poms when a Messerschmitt 110 came in range.

It was dark when they were escorted into the harbour at Margate. As tired troops filed off, Titch looked at Keith, Ginger and Oats standing on the coach roof of the little cabin. How tired

216

they looked. How dirty. Titch felt more exhausted than ever before in his life. The last soldier, a sergeant of the Grenadier Guards, stopped at the boat's side. He saw the tired, dirty, dishevelled group – the guardsman walked the deck to confront the four.

'I didn't see one o'them bastards thank you skipper.'

The foursome were all so dirty and unkempt he had difficulty seeing who was the skipper. He chose Oats because he was the oldest, and held out his hand.

'On behalf of the British Army, and the Grenadiers in particular, I thank you Sir. And you too gentlemen.'

He shook hands with each of them. Oats stood with his mouth open. Ginger grinned – Keith and Titch smiled an embarrassed smile. The guardsman took a step back, smartly shouldered his Lee-Enfield rifle and brought his right hand up in slap across the butt in a salute. He about-turned and leapt over the side onto the quay and joined his men. The four watched speechless as twenty-odd guardsmen 'dressed off', sloped arms and marched off at attention with not one man out of step.

'Well fuck me.'

It was almost a sigh from Oats.

'Sir, 'e said. Charley Smif'sern bein' called bleedin' Sir. Fuckin' marvellous.'

Oats' oath came out in an explosion of breath.

'The 'ole bloody Kate Carney a'fankin' Charley Smif'sern. Well fuck me dead.' He paused as the significance of the sergeant's words sank in.

'Cor. I wish my old Mum could've 'eard that. And me old man. Would 'ave made 'em feel real good it would.'

Ginger was laughing; Keith and Titch joined in.

''Ere. This calls fer a drink.' Oats was almost jumping with joy.

'Yes, sir! Captain, Sir!' Titch called out, and they all laughed again.

The four of them retired to the grubby little cabin and Oats dug out a bottle of rum from beneath the cabin sole.

'I 'id it from them f'eivin' bastards. They nicked me best cords they did. An' me only clean shirt. The bastards. Some of 'em would take the milk from a baby's fuckin' bottle. 'Ere, Ginger, pour a slug apiece n'remember the best drop is at the fuckin' bottom.'

He passed the bottle to his tall deck hand who grinned and silently poured a generous tot into each chipped enamel mug.

It was morning when Keith and Titch crept ashore – a June sun was creeping over the horizon as they clambered lethargically over the *'My Nell's'* rail onto dry land. Oats and Ginger were still in the arms of Morpheus.

The two airmen were awake – their heads were throbbing agonies – their tongues thick from the rum and their throats sore from singing the ribald songs they had sung until a drunken torpor overcame them and they slept where they sat. Oats had quite a store of rum hidden in the bilge.

The walk did them good. The exercise settled their stomachs and the sea air cleared their heads. With each pace their shoulders lifted –

they straightened their soiled, ill-fitting, cement-covered civilian clothes and ran dirt-stained hands through their unruly hair; the stubble on their chins they ignored. The railway station was ahead of them; the sight of a pair of patrolling red-capped military policemen made them think of their immediate future.

Chapter Nine

The gravel foot-path between Police Constable Bill Higgins and Titch was generally only used by visitors to the church yard. Funeral parties seldom passed, preferring the macadam drive from the church. It was a surprise when a party slowly passed them going to a grave out of sight to the south of the cemetery. It was headed by a middle aged undertaker in a suit of sombre black and wearing a black silk top hat with a veil of black lace at the back.

He was tall and thin – though it was a pleasant enough day, he looked cold and miserable. The poor man had a head cold: as he passed Titch he sniffed a dewdrop from the end of his inflamed nose. His eyes watered and his lips were chapped and raw looking: a cold sore on his mouth did not improve his looks. He was a sick man in need of a day in bed rather than performing the rites at a funeral. Two assistants followed, both similarly dressed and looking equally solemn. Next came the coffin mounted on a wheeled bier and pushed by another two sad looking professional mourners. The 'spirit' hovering at its head was that of a nice looking lady of about fifty in a long white nightgown.

There was a hold up. The bier stopped between the graves of Bill Higgins and Titch. Otto Meyer was within range of any conversation but was disinclined to talk; the old life-boat coxswain just stood and watched. As usual it was Titch that opened the dialogue, but he waited until the lady looked his way.

'Hello,' Titch's greeting was pleasant enough. The old darling jerked her head in the gunner's direction; she looked alarmed at Titch's voice.

'What sort of place be this then young man? Where be I? What do be 'appening? N'who be all they there people then?'

She looked at the other 'spirits'. She spoke in an awed voice, her accent a warm Kentish country drawl.

She was naturally worried – none of life's experience had prepared any of them for the 'life' they were leading. Between them Bill Higgins and Titch did their best to reassure her that at least it was all painless.

'But what'll 'appen to us all then? Be this the end like?'

The pair couldn't help her – it was something they wondered about themselves.

'If this y'ere be not the end, then what is?'

Miss Alice Shearsmith, she had told them her name, had lived in the village of Reading Street, a few miles north of the town, but had been born in the country, inland from Broadstairs and lived there most of her life; she had chosen to be buried in the church-yard of the church she had attended as a girl. Bill Higgins answered her question.

'That be 'ard t'say Miss. None on us do seem to know. Sometimes a person do leave like. We don't know where they do go. It's like they be sent fer like. One minute they be there. The next...' he raised his arms in bewilderment. 'Nothin'. We never do see 'em again. Some o'them 'ave been y'ere fer years they 'ave. Then bang!... They be gone.' He paused to allow his information to sink in.

'There were an ol' sea captain next to Miss Burnet over yonder. Saw him every day fer years I did. One day he weren't there. Miss Burnet quite missed 'im for a while I should think. Spent all their time a talkin' they did. Quite a yarn spinner was the old captain by all accounts. Sailed all over th'world in sailing ships. You know. Round Cape Horn and all that sort o'stuff. Then 'ad ter die o'fish poisoning a year after 'e left th'sea. Real bad luck that.'

Miss Shearsmith looked a little sad.

'I 'ad 'oped ter meet Jack Fraser again. I always 'oped we'd meet again in 'eaven.'

'Jack Fraser? Were 'e a Broadstairs man Miss? If 'e were I can't say I ever did 'ear o'a Fraser family in th'town.' The police constable was shaking his head.

'Oh no. 'E were an Australian. We did meet during th'war. The Great War that is. He did come to England to fight the Germans in 1916. A lot o'they did. Most on 'em were tall bronzed

221

young men. Anzacs they did call they selves. Wore big slouch 'ats a turned up on one side they did. Very dashing they looked. Us met when 'e were on leave afore he went to France. His granddad 'ad come from Kent and 'e were a looking round at where 'e imagined his granddaddy 'ad been as a lad.' She looked sadly at Titch as if he was sure he did not understand her.

'We did meet at a dance in th'church hall y'ere. 'E were older than most o'they Australians 'ere he said. Then so were I older than most o' th'girls at th'dance. Older by years I were. Going on thirty as I do remember. Too old to be a dancin' at a church dance, or so my ol' dad said. Spent my time on th' farm wi' mum an' dad, I did. 'Ad little time ter meet young men in them days.' She looked down at her hands – she turned them over and studied the palms before she looked up and continued.

'Come to see I when 'e got leave from France 'e did. Several times. Stayed wi' us on th'farm. Loved it 'e did. Reminded 'im of 'ome 'e always said. Then when 'e was a goin' 'ome to Australia in 1918 us went ter London together. Lovely it were.' She looked down at her hands again a little shamefacedly. Titch wondered what had happened during that leave – they were not old, and they were in love. He thought of his own feelings with Judy and later Mary and how he had yearned for them both.

'They 'ad all come from Egypt after fighting at a place called Gallipoli. The Australians I do mean. Terrible Jack said it were. A fighting th'Turks I think they were. All a waste o'time

222

'n'lives Jack said. I do remember 'e told I nearly eight thousand o'they Anzacs 'ad died there. 'N'lots o'British and French lads too. Lord knows 'ow many o'they poor Turkish lads besides. Must 'ave been awful, 'specially as they all 'ad ter leave wi' no-one a winnin.' 'Cept they Turks I suppose.'

The sick looking undertaker walked between them completely unaware of their existence, or non existence. He chatted to the two assistants quietly. Alice Shearsmith looked surprised at the three men. She looked at Titch and he smiled a reassurance; with his encouragement she continued her story.

''E 'ad a farm in Western Australia. A place called Serpentine. A nice name, I do always remember it. 'Ad lots o'cows he told I. He used to tell I about 'untin' kangaroos in th'forest in th'hills when he were a lad. It all sounded so exciting 'n'romantic.' She looked at them both. Otto was listening but was content to just listen.

'When he went back home he said as 'ow he would send for I and us would get wed. I waited. I did love 'im so but a letter never did come. No … that not be true. Just that I never got 'is letter. Not until a tractor knocked down me letter box a few years back. I still lived on th'farm then yer see. Stayed there after mum n' dad died. When I did pick up the broken letter box I did find his letter between th'wood and the piece o'lead my ol' dad put in t'keep it dry in th'winter. Slipped between the two it 'ad. Been there twenty years 'n' I never knowed. 'Ad th'steam ship tickets in it and some Australian money.' The old spinster looked into the distance as her mind travelled

223

back through the years. 'I wrote to 'im but he had died th'year before. 'Is sister wrote I a lovely letter. She said as 'ow 'e were upset that 'e 'ad never 'eard from me. Swore 'e would marry no one else. An' 'e never did, bless 'im. Neither did I. We was very much in love. Still am I suppose.'

Whatever had held up the burial was clear. The funeral people began to move off. The bier began to move – the lady gave a sad little wave and went with her body bumping over the gravel path.

It's just as well they can feel nothing – such a sad story would surely have made Titch weep. He thought of his own love for Judy and Mary. Love has a funny way of cheating some people. It seemed that lady and Titch were born to miss out.

Titch watched the cortege pass. The old rector was there and one or two friends Titch supposed they were. Rector and mourners returned in a short while – another plot had been filled; the old sexton would be busy filling in the grave. A pity she was not closer; she looked a nice motherly old thing.

Twelve Squadron was in Yorkshire re-forming after the fighting in France. The squadron had lost several planes and crews – some killed, others 'missing'; hopefully either 'walking home' or were Prisoners of War. One Fairey Battle had crashed itself into the bridges over the Albert Canal at Maastricht. The crew of three killed. The Pilot, Flying Officer Garland and his Observer, Sergeant Gray were each awarded a posthumous Victoria Cross. The Wireless Operator Air

Gunner LAC Reynolds, an old chum of Titch from training days, was never mentioned; the letters on his grave after his name are simply, 'Killed on Active Service'. Such is life for a lowly gunner.

There was a shortage of aircraft so much of their time was spent ground training, and swapping yarns about France and the A.A.S.F., pronounced 'ARSE EFF', as the Advanced Air Striking Force was irreverently called by airmen of all ranks. Keith Gale and Titch just listened – their own adventures seemed dull compared with the actions of their more fortunate comrades.

Weeks went by – the squadron made several moves as Britain recovered from its losses. Fairey Battles joined other bombers in raids on the German landing barges assembling at the Channel ports – Keith and Titch were not called on to fly on these operations – they had no observer after losing Hanky and a replacement could not be found. It was while they were at Eastchurch on the Isle-of-Sheppey that Titch saw Judy again. She was able to get a forty eight hour leave pass and travelled to Sheerness to be with him. She booked a room in a boarding house along the sea front and arrived about noon. Titch was stationed close by so they saw each other during the short time allowed. His promotion to sergeant helped his finances – eight shillings a day now; he felt quite wealthy. All aircrew were now at a minimum rank of sergeant. Keith was a Flight Sergeant – as Titch's room-mate he was able to cover for Titch when he sneaked off early to be with Judy.

Austere Sheerness was not an attractive place

the weekend of July 31st and August 1st 1940. The weather that year was glorious – blue skies and warm summer sun. Corporal Judy Wilson and Titch walked the deserted streets and fore-shore watching soldiers build defences against the German invasion they were sure was imminent. All ranks were made to carry arms against the possibility of German parachutists dropping from the skies. Soldiers carried rifles as they walked with their girls; Titch sported a .38 Scott-Webley revolver in a webbing holster. Twelve squadron was at a state of continued readiness as was R.A.F. Fighter Command. The nation knew the real test was yet to come, and soon.

There was little for Judy and Titch to do in Sheerness other than walk and talk. The closeness they felt was real and amounted to almost a pain – a delicious pain; an exquisite agony of frustrated desires. Titch was so afraid that they would fall into the trap that had consumed his parents, though God knows they wanted each other. Because of this they decided to risk all and marry. The wedding was to be as soon as possible; they talked excitedly about it walking the deserted promenade. Together they wrote to Judy's parents, and Bert and Ma James for them to make provisional arrangements. They telephoned Scrapper Morgan at Park Mansions to invite him for when the date was set. He was delighted.

'Yer cheeky little bugger. I f'ought as 'ow you n'Judy was never a goin' ter tie the bloody knot. Well done you lucky little sod.' The friends talked of where and when the wedding was to be and about the wedding reception – Titch thought

226

they had said all when the sergeant's voice almost burst the gunner's ear drum.

'Hey Titch! I 'ave a flat vacant. The Toffs 'ave gone to America fer the duration. Gave me the key ter look after it for 'em. Furnished real good it is. Carpets, chairs, beds, the lot. Reckon wot they don't know they can't grieve about. Stay 'ere mate. It'll be OK. That fat little bastard du Canne discovered 'e 'ad urgent business in Ireland. Pissed off there a month ago 'e did. The little yellow bastard got the first train 'e could. Couldn't get away fast enough. 'E's left me in charge a'fings.' He paused a moment as if thinking. 'So wot abart you n'Judy 'oneymoonin' 'ere? I c'n see as you ain't disturbed. Know wot I mean ol'mate?' He gave a chuckle.

'Fix it sergeant. And that's an order.'

'Yes sir! Group Captain bloody Wilkins sir!'

They both laughed – and so did Judy when told of their old friend's words and invitation.

It was all arranged – all they needed was a date; that would depend on how soon they could arrange leave together. That evening they were very close – their whisperings and caresses on a bench overlooking the sea were very intimate; they were sure that soon they would be together, for ever.

Titch and Judy parted at the railway station convinced they would be married in a few days, weeks at the most. The train pulled out of the station and Titch waved to Judy leaning out of the carriage window. She had removed her service cap; her auburn hair flowed across her face as the train gathered speed. Too soon it was

227

lost from view. Sadly Titch caught his bus back to the squadron.

Luftwaffe Marshal Herman Goring began his air offensive on Britain the following day. Masses of German planes attacked R.A.F. airfields in the south and east of the country. Biggin Hill was the first to feel the weight of German bombs. Day after day the enemy came, bombing and strafing. Day after day Hurricanes and Spitfire fighters 'scrambled' to battle with them.

Titch was called to the Sergeants' mess telephone on the evening of the 6th August. East-church had been bombed again, but the damage was minimal; all were tired and dirty from the dust and exertions of the raids. Titch hurried to the telephone, he thought it might be Judy. It was her father. He told Titch the news of Judy's death.

'She was wiv an ambulance Titch. A lookin' after the wounded she was. A bloody fighter strafed the airfield n'cut our poor Judy ter pieces. Looked like a little broken doll was 'ow 'er friend described it when I phoned to find out 'ow she died. Shot ter pieces my little girl was. The German bastards.' There was a sob on the other end of the line – Titch waited dumbfounded. Judy dead!

'It was only last week I saw her.' The thought flashed through his mind.

'I'm sorry Titch. Abart it all I mean. You a gettin' married n' that. Know wot I mean ol' son?'

Titch heard his sob again – Tom didn't wait for a reply; the sergeant gunner was incapable of speech. Titch suddenly felt his world had crumbled about him. The voice at the other end of the wire continued.

'Look son, I've got ter go to Mum and Molly. Fair cut up they are. Look after yerself now Titch. Oh, by the way. Young Billy's joined up. Lied abart 'is age the little bugger.' There was the sound of something like a sniff. 'Got ter go Titch... Mum sends 'er love... S'long son... Don't let this get cher down now... S'long.' There was a click and the phone went dead.

Apart from saying 'Hello', Titch had not said a word; he was too stunned. He felt as if a hole had opened up in his stomach and a lead weight dropped on his chest. He was holding the telephone hand set when Keith Gale appeared at his side and saw something was wrong – he led him quietly to the room they shared and the young sergeant wept on his pilot's shoulder.

Titch had not cried for years – there was no shame in his tears; no rage or guilt. Not then. It was grief – pure and simple grief with a fair mixture of self pity. That great loneliness came over him again. He felt it was Titch Wilkins against the world as it used to be. Until he saw Keith Gale and knew he had a friend. Memories of Bert and Ma James, Freddy Silk and Broadstairs flooded Titch's mind and he was comforted.

'VOLUNTEERS ARE WANTED TO TRANSFER TO FIGHTER COMMAND.' There were further details on the squadron's 'Daily Routine Orders'. Many of the squadron's air crew read them and responded. Keith and Titch were of the same mind – they wanted to fight in this war, to hit back at the enemy after the blows they had received, and they wanted to be together when they did it. A bond had built up between them, born partly out of shared experiences and partly for liking and trusting each other. As people they were opposites, scholastically and socially. Titch an orphaned cockney slum boy with a poor education – Keith with a family, connections, education and wealth.

They knew there were two seater fighters operating. Boulton Paul 'Defiants'. Heavy single engine fighters that boasted a four gun turret behind the pilot. As fighters they had had an initial success against the Luftwaffe but had been withdrawn from day fighting after drastic losses and now relegated to the task of second line night fighters; they were no match for Goring's ME109 and 110 fighters, but lumbering Dorniers and Heinkels? The Defiant's four Brownings and fighter capabilities made them a match. The two applications were in the orderly room in minutes, they were on their way in a week.

After a crash conversion course on the new planes they were posted to Speke, an airfield on the edge of Liverpool. There they flew every hour they could – mostly at night. When they weren't flying they were standing by, but the war stayed in the south of England.

August passed into September – R.A.F. Fighter Command was flying and fighting for its life, and the life of Britain. Casualties were heavy on both sides; fighter bases were bombed relentlessly. On September 7th the Luftwaffe changed tactics and made its first big raid on London. It started in daylight and went on into the night. Over one thousand German planes flew against the capital – Londoners fought the fires, tended their wounded and died in their hundreds. The city burned. The word 'Blitz' entered the English language; Britain held its breath. Keith and Titch along with millions of others fumed with impotent rage. The news of Bert James and Ma's death came as another blow. They had died that Saturday. 'Bleak Saturday' the newspapers called it.

'C' Flight was on 'Second Reserve' when Titch got the telegram from the friendly newsagent. Being on second reserve meant they could sleep in their beds for three nights without disturbance. With the telegram in his hand Titch asked his squadron commander for compassionate leave and was allowed forty eight hours.

The little terraced house and its near neighbours had disappeared – there was just a shallow hole in the ground; hardly one brick stood on the top of another. Titch staggered among the debris looking for he knew not what. Life? Impossible. A memory? He had a million of those. Some bric-a-brac that would tell of the lovely old couple that had made this hole their home for over thirty years? Titch just didn't know – the exploding bomb had blown their lives away, and Titch's world apart; what explosives had spared, incendiaries had consumed.

The wind ruffled the pages of a book on the fringe of the devastation – Titch picked it up. The edges were charred and the cover totally burnt but he saw the title, 'Sailing alone around the world' by Joshua Slocum. Tears had been very close all day; now they overflowed. Titch sat on a piece of masonry among the shattered treasures of a lifetime and wept silently. He was sitting there when he felt a touch on his shoulder; it was Tom Wilson.

''Eard as 'ow you was 'ome Titch. F'ought I'd come round.'

Toms grip was hard on the younger man's shoulder – Titch's hand crossed his chest and lay on the top of his. The former bricklayer felt Tom's love and understanding passing through to him. He stood and looked up at the old guardsman.

Tom Wilson had aged – lines of fatigue and grief had cut grooves in his normally cheerful face; the war was touching them all.

'Scrapper was killed the same night. 'E was on dooty as an Air Raid Warden and 'is post caught a direct 'it. Like Bert and Ma. Nuffin' left of any of 'em ter bury. Bad as Ypres in the last lot I reckon. N'this is England. Not bloody France.' The two began to walk away from the site. Tom reached into his pocket and handed Titch Judy's rings. The Lugus signet ring and the engagement ring Titch had bought.

'They sent us these. Bein' next of kin like. F'ought as 'ow you might like 'em. Them bein' yours an' all.'

Titch looked at them and placed the signet ring on his finger.

'Give the other to Molly Mister Tom. She would like something of Judy's.' The old soldier looked down at Titch and sniffed away a tear.

'Fanks Titch mate. I knows she will. She'll treasure this 'ere.' He put the ring into a waistcoat pocket; took out a handkerchief from a trouser pocket and blew his nose loudly.

A policeman approached.

'Sergeant Wilkins is it lad?'

Titch didn't answer – just looked at him through his tears.

'They told me at the station you were here. Thought I'd come along. Don't mind I hope.'

The middle aged constable stood tall in front of Titch – the solid arm of the law. Tall and resolute with his steel helmet on his head and his gas mask slung over his shoulder.

'Terrible business all round. I was on duty along the road when it happened. Saw the bomb floating down on its parachute. They call them land mines. Though why beats me. It landed on the roof of Mr James' house. I saw the parachute caught up on the chimney. Couldn't do a thing. I was running to warn them to get out of the house when it went off. The explosion knocked me flat. Knocked me out it did. When I recovered the street was alight from incendiaries.' He paused and touched Titch's arm. 'Sorry lad. I heard you and the old couple were close.'

Close. Dear God – old Bert James was a father, brother, uncle and friend all rolled into one; and Ma? Words were useless to describe her generosity and kindness. The kindly copper stayed a while but he could see there was nothing he could do and excused himself. Tom was in the Auxiliary Fire Service and had to report for duty. Titch said he would get the first train back to Liverpool and his squadron. He put the charred copy of Slocum's book in his pocket and trudged off to the underground station.

St Pancras railway station was a shambles when he arrived. An unexploded bomb had been found on number three platform – all trains had been cancelled and the platforms were cordoned off. Titch looked for a pub where he hoped to get a meal. 'The Gun' was a seedy little public house. Titch was unfortunate that it was the first one he saw. He was not in a discerning mood and simply walked into the first bar he came to.

The R.A.F. sergeant airgunner noticed the four soldiers sitting at the bar as he ordered a half point of bitter and sandwich – got the drink but was told there were no eats available. The blowsy barmaid looked at Titch through the smoke from her cigarette.

'There's a war on Ducky. Or aren't you Brylcreem boys aware of it?'

Titch looked at the female and hid the contempt he felt by taking a long drink – with each gulp he heard the sniggers from the four khaki figures at the bar. They all looked at Titch, he looked at the woman behind the bar and spoke quietly. 'Yeah. I read something about it in the papers.' Titch took his drink and walked to a table near the door.

He wasn't thinking straight – grief and confusion were heavy on his shoulders. First Judy, now Ma and Mister Bert and old Sergeant Morgan.

'Damn the bloody war.'

One half pint followed another – Titch didn't even taste the stuff and he was not a heavy drinker. It must have been the third or maybe the fourth drink he bought – he began to feel the effects of the beer. One of the soldiers approached his table.

'Hey! Nancy boy! Me mates were wonderin' where were you bunch a pansies at Dunkerque, 'cos we didn't see any fin of yer bloody fighters over the beaches.'

Titch peered at him through the haze of tobacco smoke. The man had a cigarette in his mouth – before Titch could reply he removed it and blew a stream of smoke into Titch's eyes. He then leaned over and slowly and deliberately put his cigarette butt into the fresh glass of bitter.

Titch knew he was in no condition for a fight. He was no match for them. Even the smallest of the foursome was taller than him; he could see it was not going to be a one to one match. These four were out for some sport and Titch Wilkins was going to be it.

Titch stood, hoping a discreet exit on his part with no altercation would satisfy their vanity. He had his respirator and steel helmet in his hand and walked to the door. The barmaid smiled superciliously – her lip curled and showed a gapped row of yellow teeth. Her peroxide hair and heavy mascara eyes gave her an evil look; her finger nails were long and showed dirt under the layer of bright red nail varnish.

'Goin' 'ome ter mummy are we Nancy boy? There, there. Ever so there.' She giggled and drew on her cigarette.

Titch should have ignored her but there was something about the way she spoke that made him angry that this slut was alive and Judy, his lovely Judy, was dead.

'Shut up you bitch.' Titch's words were not

loud but they burst from his lips like bullets. A fury erupted in his breast – all the anger at his loss exploded; he wanted to strike, to kill.

Titch Wilkins swept the bar clear of glasses and ash trays with a wild sweep of his arm. The barmaid screamed. The four soldiers stood as one man. A fist was aimed at Titch's head – he weaved and brought his steel helmet attached to his gas mask round in a swing. It caught the first soldier across the face and he collapsed crashing against the bar; his face a bloody mess.

Adrenalin pumped through Titch's veins. He saw this fight as a way of avenging Judy, Bert and poor old Ma and he fought. The second khaki figure he managed to disable with a kick to the groin. The third caught a side swipe with the heavy respirator that made him falter, but only for a moment.

It was the chair aimed at Titch's head that was his undoing. The enraged sergeant parried the blow but the remaining army man piled on top of him as he staggered away from the falling chair feeling his arm was broken. Titch saw a boot aimed at his crutch and twisted his leg to take the blow on his thigh. The pain was excruciating – it made him forget the pain in his arm; then his leg collapsed under him. Great nailed boots pounded his head and torso as he sought to cover more fragile parts. Titch was almost senseless – he felt himself picked up and dragged across the floor and through the door into the dark street. The light from the open door went out as the door closed. He was alone in the London black out, or so he thought.

Titch felt himself being rolled over. In his semi conscious state he thought he was being robbed, but he didn't care. A hand touched his face – Titch could have cried from the pain of it; all he did was moan.

'Are you all right?'

In spite of himself, Titch laughed. It sounded terrible to him but he laughed. He had just had the beating of his life and he was asked, was he all right? What he wanted to say was, 'Don't be ridiculous. Of course I'm not all right.' All that passed his lips was another moan. A soft hand touched him again. Titch opened his eyes, more exactly he opened his undamaged eye and saw in the darkness the pale face of a woman.

'Are you all right?'

She asked the same question. As a reply Titch tried to get to his feet. An arm went around his shoulder and helped him. He would have fallen again as he put weight onto his injured leg, but that arm saved him.

'Can you walk?'

Titch groaned again but managed to put one foot in front of the other – they walked a few steps together – it hurt but Titch felt stronger with each pace; his whole body was floating in an ocean of pain but he was walking and feeling stronger.

Titch managed to say a thank you between his swollen lips. His escort did not reply at once – when she did she spoke in a soft, rather uncertain voice.

'I live close by. Let me look at your injuries. I know a little about these things so don't worry.'

Titch Wilkins did not resist. He had nowhere to go so he allowed himself to be led along a dark street. He saw some iron railings in the darkness and an iron gate. The pair walked down some steps and Titch leaned against a wall while the woman opened a door. After they had entered and a black-out curtain drawn, the woman turned on the light.

'Oh you poor boy. What happened?' The words reached him as Titch felt the pain of the bright light in his single open eye. He could not have answered even if he could have found the words. Standing before him was a pretty woman. She was a little taller than he but slim and well made. Even in his distress Titch noticed how tight her dress was across her breasts. She was about his own age, possibly a little older – and pretty, but Titch saw lines on her face that could not be accounted for by age; there was a sadness about her.

Her face was small and heart shaped – her hair a mousey shade of brown. Hazel eyes flecked with green smiled from beneath long dark eye lashes. And her lips? They were pink, a pale pink. Titch thought of Judy's lips and wanted to cry. He noticed a small dimple in her chin – he remembered thinking of a saying Ma James used. 'Dimple in the chin? Devil within.' Titch looked closely at her with his good eye; there was little of the Devil in her he concluded.

The young gunner's leg hurt and he made to move. Pain exploded in his brain and desperately he clutched the door jamb to save himself. Her arm came to help him again and she guided him to a chair.

'Here, sit down. I'll put the kettle on. There's nothing like a cuppa tea.' She left the room – Titch heard the clatter of crockery through an open door. He cast his eye around the room. It was small. He realised he was in a small basement flat – one of thousands in London; probably a former kitchen or servants quarters of an old Victorian house. It was neat and spotlessly clean.

The tiny sitting room in which he was sitting was furnished with the conventional three piece suite of two arm chairs and a settee. Bric-a-brac cluttered shelves scattered around the wall. Photographs littered the mantelpiece. It was all neatly untidy. The room had a lived-in-look without being cluttered; a happy look; warm and friendly. Titch was surprised at his summary.

He turned to face the open door and saw a photograph of a group of young people dressed in odd looking uniforms and carrying ancient rifles. It was a mixed group and they there laughing. Close to it was a picture of a young man wearing a foreign looking forage cap. He was wearing a cartridge bandoleer across his shoulder and held a rifle in his hands. He was a pleasant looking fellow with a pleasing smile. Titch suddenly felt a pang that he could not analyze – a heaviness deep inside himself. Guilt? Envy? He was puzzled.

Titch was saved further speculation with the return of his Good Samaritan – she entered the room carrying a tray loaded with tea things. She placed it on a small table and looked at Titch.

'I should have told you. The bathroom is through there.' She pointed with her dimpled chin at a door the other side of the room. 'Through the bedroom. You'll find everything you need there. But mind. The black-out curtain has not been drawn.'

Titch suddenly felt the need to urinate – he rose; the pain in his leg made him wince.

'Are you all right?'

He nodded his thanks and limped over to the only other door in the room.

It opened to his touch and he entered the darkened room; he paused to allow his night vision to adjust. It took a minute – the bathroom door showed as a pale shadow against the lighter wall. Titch made for it and closed the door behind him. Only when he was sure it was tightly closed did he fumble for the light switch and flooded the room with light. His saviour had been right – there was what he needed standing a yard away.

His need satisfied, he glanced around the room; it was large for a bathroom. A large bath tub in the room's centre dominated – there was a shower cubicle in one corner and a wash hand basin set below a mirror. He looked into the mirror and gasped.

'My God Wilkins. What a bloody fool you are.'

The words were whispered as he examined the image. The left side of his face was one large bruise from eyebrow to mouth. His left eye was puffed and closed. His bottom lip was split, and there was blood still wet on his chin, and his neck hurt. He touched the spot and his finger came away wet; wet with blood. It confirmed what he already knew; he had had the beating of his life. He washed his hands and made for the door –

carefully he switched off the light before he opened it; he limped and groped his way back to the small sitting room.

The young woman was sitting in one of the armchairs waiting for him. With a gracious gesture she indicated to Titch that he was to sit in its companion; he did by lowering himself carefully into its deep comfort.

She didn't speak for which Titch was grateful. Lip movement hurt his mouth and he was afraid he would have to make a reply. She seemed to understand for she poured the tea without a word. With another silent movement she offered a plate of sandwiches.

Titch managed to eat two; they were cucumber and cheese between thin slices of buttered bread. He remembered how they hurt his mouth as he chewed but his hunger was real and he persevered. The tea was good too; sweet and soothing. It was as if this saintly patron knew his tastes.

The injured gunner looked across at the young woman with curiosity. She sat with her shapely legs crossed modestly. The coffee table was close to her and she reached and took a sandwich for herself. She bit into it and chewed for a moment before her eyes looked into his. She swallowed and spoke in a low voice.

'My name is Patricia. Or Pat if you like. Pat Tilson.' She paused and swallowed daintily. 'Mrs Pat Tilson if you prefer it. But I like to be called Pat.'

Titch swallowed the morsel in his mouth at a gulp and found his gaze fixed on the ring on the third finger of her left hand. She followed his look and smiled.

'If you are worried about my husband bursting in and catching us, don't be. He was killed in 1937, in Spain.' Pat pointed with her dimpled chin to the photograph of the wall. 'That's his photograph. His name was Harry. Harry Tilson. Harry Tilson from London was how he introduced himself the day we met.'

Titch looked at the framed picture of the young man in the foreign forage cap again. He muttered an unintelligible apology. As if she had not heard, Pat rose to her feet and poured him another cup of tea.

'Drink it. I'll do you good.' As an afterthought she added, 'Help yourself to another sandwich.'

Titch drained his cup and fidgeted uncomfortably. Pat finished her own tea and gathered the tea things and made for the kitchen; she stopped and faced Titch. 'I'll look at your injuries presently.'

He had eaten another sandwich and drained his cup before she returned. She looked at him and smiled. 'This way. We'd best do it in here.'

She walked past him into the bedroom. Titch scrambled painfully to his feet and followed. He was in time to see the shadowy outline of Pat drawing the black-out curtains. He waited in the darkened room not knowing what to expect. It was pitch dark – there was a movement from where Pat Tilson stood and the room was flooded in a soft pink light from two wall lights above a large double bed, and another above a gleaming dressing table.

The room was a wonder to Titch Wilkins. He

had never been in a woman's bedroom before. Judy's had been out of bounds. Mrs Wilson had seen to that. Besides, Judy shared a room with her sister Molly. Ma and Bert James' room was never entered and the Wilson's marital chamber was sacrosanct. Titch remembered Tom Wilson's gentle reprimand one day when Titch hovered close to the couple's bedroom door.

'No Titch mate. That there ain't for you. Sorry.' Then as Titch hesitated he continued. 'Yer see Titch a couple's bedroom is a sacred chamber like. Secret only t'them. Lots o'secret whisperin' an'loving a goes on in there. Sacred only to them as wot shares the room. Know wot I mean?'

Of course Titch did not know what he meant when he said it but as the young man observed the affection the couple shared he knew that it was something very special.

Titch's embarrassment increased as the memories flooded back; he looked about him. Everything in Pat Tilson's bedroom was either pink or a deep burgundy colour; carpet, rugs and bed coverings. The furniture was painted white and gilt. The walls were covered with a silver and burgundy striped wallpaper. Between the wall lights over the bed was a large gilt framed painting of a peaceful mountain scene; in the shaded light walls and furniture reflected the colours of the room. It was all rich without being overpowering – warm without being stuffy and very intimate. Titch searched his mind for a word to describe it. It took a moment for his limited vocabulary. Erotic? When the word came to him he was not sure it was right.

Erotic? The word was unfamiliar but he remembered reading it once to describe the boudoir of Marie Antionette; just one of the books in Bert James' small library. Erotic! The word and its meaning impinged on Titch's mind; looking about him he was sure it fitted. It was a room of infinite intimacy that made him feel an intruder.

Pat Tilson stood before a large mirror framed in white and gilt. She turned and smiled at Titch. He winced as he tried to avoid the sight of the tightness of her dress over her breasts. He winced because he felt a wave of guilt; was he betraying Judy? Pat misinterpreted his grimace.

'Take off your uniform and shirt. I'll look at your injuries right away. I can see you are in pain.'

To cover his confusion at the proximity of a pretty woman and the intimacy of the room, Titch slowly removed his tunic. There were splatterings of blood on the serge. His own? Or the blood of the soldier he had swiped with his tin hat? The blood on his shirt was undoubtedly his own – it came from a wound on his neck where a nailed boot had found a target; his vest was no better.

'Better take off your vest.' Pat went into the bathroom and returned with a small basket containing an assortment of medical equipment. She looked at Titch disrobing. 'And let me see that leg of yours.'

Titch placed his shirt on a bedside chair. Embarrassment had superseded his pain. To cover his feeling he began to wonder about those four soldiers, especially the one he clobbered with his steel helmet. They must have a hate of some sort against the R.A.F. Titch could not imagine one service having such a strong dislike for a brother service; were they not fighting the same war?

With a jerk Titch brought his mind back to the present. He looked down at himself standing dressed only in his unattractive service underwear; the image in the mirror caught his eyes. He was indeed a sorry sight. His face was one large bruise; one eye was completely closed. The cut on his neck was bleeding again and blood trickled down his chest soaking into the material of the vest.

Removing his undervest was the most painful thing. Pat heard his groan, she saw his difficulty as he tried to reach it over his head and came and helped. Titch gritted his teeth for the pain was almost unbearable. The vest was free at last and was dropped on the chair with his tunic and shirt. He stood naked from the waist up.

'Move over here to the light.'

Pat helped him over to the direct rays of a wall light over the dressing table and began to run her hands expertly over his back and chest. Titch was just marvelling how soft and warm her hands were when she touched a tender spot.

'Ouch!' He winced and pulled sharply away from her touch.

'Hurt there does it?'

Her fingers probed gently the sore area. Titch closed his eyes and gritted his teeth and was able to suppress the groans that threatened to pass his lips. Pat's hands moved away and found another tender spot, and another; warm fingers pressed into the area of his kidneys. He felt no pain as she dug deep into his flesh. Titch felt her move – her voice came to him from very close.

'Badly bruised ribs but nothing serious. Your kidneys seem OK. Now let me look at your face.'

Pat moved round and faced him. She lifted his chin gently to the light. Her fingers pressed the bones of his face and travelled around to his jaw. Titch was able to look directly at her with his undamaged eye. He found the picture of her face quite pleasing.

'Move your jaw.' Titch did as he was told. 'Now your neck.' He obeyed. Pat's hands were manipulating his neck; they moved gently but firmly round his shoulders then back to his neck where they lingered for a moment, probing the wound.

'Nothing wrong there. Just a flesh wound.' She expertly cleaned it and dressed it with a plaster. 'Your eye is a mess and will look worse tomorrow. Now let me see your leg, but you will have to remove your trousers and underpants.' She saw Titch hesitate and laughed. She turned away.

'I promise not to look.' She turned her back. 'By the way, I don't know your name.' Pat laughed a bell like laugh. 'If I have to have a man in my bedroom we really should be introduced.' Titch growled a response through his swollen lips.

'Rupert. Rupert Wilkins. But everybody calls me Titch.'

'Titch?' She turned and faced him as his underpants slipped to the ground – he stooped hurriedly to pick them up and cried out with the pain. Pat's friendly hand was there to help him again.

'I think I will call you Rupert. It's much nicer.'

Pat Tilson examined the large bruise on Titch's thigh – she probed and she prodded and was at last satisfied there was no fracture.

'It will be sore for a day or two but there is no serious damage. Just an injured muscle.' She gathered her equipment and left the room.

Titch had a hot bath and in a pair of borrowed pyjamas he was made to get into the only bed in the flat – his protests were of no avail.

'You need that bed more than I do tonight. Don't worry about me. I have a way of managing. Besides I am on duty in an hour, and will be until six tomorrow morning. So sleep tight.' With that she turned out the light and left the room. Titch heard the outer door slam shut a little later and fell asleep wondering about Pat Tilson.

The drawing of the black-out curtain woke him. It was daylight; bright September sunlight poured into the basement flat window. 'Good morning. How do you feel?' Pat Tilson stood over the bed looking down at Titch. For a moment he wondered where he was. Memories of the evening before flooded back. He went to rise and felt his body scream a protest.

'Don't move. I have the kettle on. We'll talk if you want to after a cup of tea.' She left the room and Titch flexed his limbs. He found after the initial pain they were surprisingly supple. His ribs hurt and his eye was tender. His leg hurt when he touched the bruise but otherwise he was well.

Titch heard the rattle of cups as Pat returned. She placed the tray on the bedside table and began to undress.

'Now it's your turn to look away.'

Titch did by lying back and covering his head with the bed-clothes. He lay in the darkness and his mind played havoc. Minutes passed. Titch heard water running in the bathroom; he could not imagine what was going to happen next. About the last thing he expected was to feel her form slipping into the bed beside him. Titch's mind and body froze. He felt her nearness, the warmth of her, damp warmth and her perfume, faint and sweet. She smelt of soap and lavender water.

Pat reached across and took the sheet from his face. 'You can come out now. And thank you Rupert.'

Titch managed to croak, 'What for?'

Patricia laughed. 'For being a gentleman and not taking advantage of a lady. How do you like your tea? I put one sugar in last night. Was that all right?'

Titch muttered that it was and made to get out of bed.

'I'm sorry Pat. I have never done this before.'

'Done what?'

'Been in the same bed with a woman.'

'Never?' Pat Tilson looked at Titch in disbelief.

What could he say? That he was in love with Judy and didn't want to get her pregnant? That he was twenty three but had never slept with a girl? Titch was beginning to feel a fool. He remembered all the jokes his work mates had made at his expense. Jokes about him being a virgin. Titch had not cared then because he had Judy and their love was precious and not to be tarnished by the sordid romps his fellows described so often. Titch always thought of what his mother had suffered through a lapse of will power, as he believed it was. He recalled Bert James' words when he queried the whole sex problem.

'When it 'appens Titch you'll know ol' son. And when it does 'appen, be gentle and make it beautiful fer both of yer. Know wot I mean.'

Titch didn't understand then but after Bert had explained further he understood a little of what he meant.

Pat's hand came onto Titch's shoulder.

'You think I want us to make love Rupert? That might happen for I am sure you are a decent man but not today. Not any day unless we both want to. You see I loved my husband. I still do I believe. I should have explained that before.'

She turned and tried to face Titch. He was too embarrassed to meet her gaze. 'Harry and I met in Spain. During the Civil War. I was a Medic in the International Brigade, he was an infantry sergeant. He was an Englishman, a Londoner like me. This was his place before he went to Spain. It is all I have of him. This and the memory of us together before we were married. We fought hard and long in the same unit. But we had some good times. As comrades, but never as lovers.' Pat's voice was little more than a whisper and her hand was still on Titch's shoulder. She dropped her hand onto the bed and lay back. Titch looked into her face and saw the faraway look that had come into her eyes.

'We were holding the Fascists back from Madrid. Italian mercenaries were facing us and we were waiting for dawn and our bombardment before we attacked. We were married on a rainy afternoon just before the battle of Jarama in February 1937. Our wedding night was a night in a bombed ruin, on a bed of straw. It was the only time we ever made love. He was so afraid that I would get pregnant and he would be killed before we could marry. He was afraid I would have his bastard. He didn't want that.' Her hand went to her mouth to suppress a cry. She recovered and drew a deep breath. 'But I wish I had. I would have had something of him to love other than memories.'

Titch's heart leapt for her, and for the man who had died. He realised he was not alone in thinking as he did about Judy and their lovemaking, or lack of it. If Pat's husband had thought that way, and he had, there must be others. A feeling of relief came over him. The feeling of guilt and foolishness at his thoughts dissipated until he wondered if Judy would have wanted his child, no matter if he had been killed and it was their bastard. And his mother? Was she proud to bear her lover's bastard?

Patricia moved beside him and Titch turned to face her. Her words were hardly heard as she went on.

'I never saw him again. He survived that battle but was on the move with his company for weeks afterwards. He was killed a month later at Guadalajara. He was captured and shot by the Fascists.'

She paused and looked at the tea getting cold in the cups on the bedside table.

'I was with the Brigade until the end. It was a

pointless thing. A gesture to mankind I suppose. There were a lot of grand words spoken but little action by world powers. Only the Russians helped us by sending small arms. But it was tanks and aircraft we needed, and the men to drive and fly them. Harry and others like him did their best against overpowering odds. They fought hard and well but Germany and Italy were too much for us. I believe we could have beaten Franco by himself. But we had not the arms or the men to beat all the Fascist nations against us.' Pat paused, lifted her cup from the saucer and took a sip of tea. She replaced the cup and continued.

'I escaped with a dozen others over the Pyrenees into France. They were terrible days. It was so cold. I was the only woman left from the five in our unit. All the others were dead. We all slept together for warmth crossing the mountains. All huddled in a heap in whatever shelter we could find.' She laughed a rippling little laugh. 'So you see Rupert, you are not the first. Though I never made love with any of them.' Her laughter stopped. Titch had taken her hand in his. 'And they never tried. They all remembered Harry and respected his memory, and his widow.'

As if to close the conversation, she turned to the tea things again.

'Now let's have another cuppa before it gets cold.'

The tension had eased. They drank their tea and both lay back on the pillows. Titch was silent. His cup was empty and he was holding it on his lap. His bruised lips hurt. He touched them gently, then looked at his fingers. There was blood on them. He closed his eyes and relaxed.

'Another cup?'

'No thanks Pat.' Titch did not open his eyes.

Pat Tilson poured herself a third cup of tea and drank it. Titch heard the saucer being put down on the tray. She reached across and took his. Titch felt the pressure of her hand over the blankets and wanted to touch it. He didn't. She took the cup away and turned towards him.

'What happened to you last night Rupert? You don't strike me as being a drunkard or a mauler. How was it you got such a beating?'

There was nothing for it but for Titch to tell her. He had nothing to hide; he had done nothing to be ashamed of and she surely deserved an explanation. One word led to another and Titch found himself telling her everything; about Judy dying, and Bert and Ma James' death. It was almost his life story. Patricia listened to every word without an interruption. Titch Wilkins didn't know what stage their hands touched but when he had finished he found they were holding hands.

They didn't make love; they lay together and talked. She told Titch more about Spain and about herself. She was 'working for the War Office' as a translator she said. Titch believed her; why shouldn't he?

It was noon when she fell asleep in his arms like a child. She had been on duty all night but was off for two days from then. Titch lay feeling and enjoying the soft warmth of her. He thought of Judy and all the things they had enjoyed, and missed together. Pat Tilson was real and living and Titch had to admit, pretty, even desirable, though in his innocence he was not sure quite what that meant. His mind considered this last thought until he too dozed off.

Evening light was shining through the window when Titch woke. He had not intended to sleep but somehow he had. Immediately he remembered the morning and looked at the other pillow. Patricia Tilson was not there. Titch lay back and wondered about this strange situation. Was this normal between people? He found it puzzling.

The bedroom door opened and Pat entered carrying his uniform, shirt and underclothes. They were all cleaned and pressed.

'I took them to an all night cleaners last night on the way to work.' She smiled. 'You were in no condition to argue.' She paused, looked at the gunner and smiled again. Titch had a fleeting thought that she was a beautiful beginning of the day, albeit that it was evening. Pat walked to the door and stopped. She looked at Titch sitting up in the bed.

'When you are ready I have a meal waiting. It's not much. There's a war on you know.' Her smiled belied the seriousness of the remark.

'Will it wait until I have a shower?' Titch remembered she hesitated, then spoke softly. 'Of course.' It was all she said. Titch was afraid he had offended her.

The noise of the gas water heater and the running water was loud. Titch didn't hear the bathroom door open. The first he knew of her presence was when the shower curtain parted and she entered the shower. Her hair was loose; she was naked and close to him. The water was pleasantly hot and Titch's arousal was instant. He held his head back and allowed water to wash over his injured eye and tried to collect his thoughts. When her hands found him it was as if his mind exploded. Titch held his breath as she washed him where he had never been washed by another before. The soap slithered obediently and deliciously in her hands.

Titch Wilkins looked at Pat for a long moment. As if a magnet pulled their lips together, they kissed. His lips hurt; blood was salt in his mouth but the pain was exquisite. Water rained on them and formed a pool on her breasts as they clasped each other. Their hands had developed minds of their own as they stroked and caressed. Titch's lips travelled down; down to her throat and further. At her breasts they lingered. A pink nipple was hard in his mouth; his tongue toyed with it and all the time their hands were doing wonderful things.

It was as if Titch's legs could not hold his weight for he sank to his knees and kissed and fondled, first her navel and then as she pressed his head downwards his lips found the soft fold of her thighs and the silk of her mound. Titch Wilkins was drowning in the ecstasy of her and had to gasp for breath as the water cascaded over his head and still she demanded him. Pat Tilson demanded more and Titch gave and the giving was a joy beyond his imagination.

Suddenly the deluge of water ceased. Titch stood and looked breathlessly into her eyes. Water was streaming from both of them. Titch threw back the shower curtain and ignoring the pain in his body, he picked her up in his arms and carried her into the bedroom and laid her gently on the soft pink bed. Her arms were about him and she took him to herself.

Pat Tilson was no more skilled than he was but their mutual longing demanded satisfaction and each gave savagely to the other. Soft wet bodies slithered and slid as hands fondled and explored. After the first explosion of passion a tenderness came over them. Each subsequent coupling was as tender as it was sweet. The London night sang to their sighs and soft cries. Their pillows were damp and receptive to their whisperings. They made love. They laughed. They drank Spanish sherry from each others' navels and explored each other until exhaustion overtook them and they slept. They slept to wake and eat, bathe together in the large bath where they romped and made love in the foam-warmed confines of the tub. They made love in the shower and in the kitchen while an omelette burned unnoticed. Time was nothing to them. Day and night were the same. An air raid alert went unheeded and they made love as 'Ack-Ack' fire rattled the window and falling bombs shook the house above them. It was all wonderful and exciting. The world was theirs and they were the only two in it.

It was early evening, Patricia turned on the radio. The BBC announcer read the news. It was another story of more bombing of London. A victory for the Royal Navy. More British shipping sunk by German U Boats and further successes by Fighter Command. An item that made Titch sit up and listen was that R.A.F. Bomber Command was taking strong offensive action against German cities. The fact that ten bombers failed to return from the night's raid did not impinge on his intelligence. What did was the closing announcement. 'That concludes the nine o'clock news for Friday the eleventh of September. There will be another bulletin at eleven o'clock.'

Titch should have reported for duty in Liverpool at eight o'clock that morning. Their farewell was brief and sad. They arranged to write to each other. Titch gave Pat his address. She did not give him hers, said she would write to him first. Her address would be in the letter. Titch took her into his arms and kissed her.

'I will be back Pat. I believe I am falling in love with you.'

'Don't do that Rupert. It may be true and then you could be hurt again. But I could easily fall in love with you. But I won't. I have known too much killing and the grief it causes. It will hurt too much if anything happened to you.'

Titch kissed her again and left. Pat had given him instructions how to find the public house 'The Gun'. He would know his way from there.

The night was black, the sky overcast when Titch emerged from the flat. The heavily shaded street lights were of little help, but he found 'The Gun' and from there he managed to find St Pancras.

Lighting was a little better in the station and Titch hurried to the departure board. The next train for Liverpool via Crewe was waiting at number three platform; he hurried to the barrier.

'Your pass sergeant! And where are your

respirator and helmet?' Titch was confronted by a corporal of the R.A.F. Service Police.

'Sure. But a please would be nice corporal. As for my helmet. I lost it. Respirator too.'

It was a mistake. Titch should have kept his mouth shut. The tall service policeman examined his leave pass.

'You are twenty four hours overdue sergeant. This is a serious matter.'

'I'll be more than that if I miss this train.'

It did not impress the S.P. The sergeant air-gunner was absent without leave and something had to be done. Titch read the message on the corporal's face.

'Do I catch this train or do I go through all your bullshit? Miss it and catch a later one that will make me even later.' Titch could almost hear the other's brain ticking over. 'Here. I haven't time to argue. Take me to your officer in charge.'

An R.A.F. Flying Officer with the blue arm band marked S.P. walked out of a door behind the officious corporal.

'Sir!' Titch's voice was loud – almost an order. The officer came to a halt and faced him. Titch remembered to salute. The officer was a tall man and heavily built. If Titch had to guess he would have said he was a former civilian policeman dragooned into his present job.

'What is it sergeant?'

'I am late returning to my squadron and if I am delayed by this' (he almost said idiot) 'corporal I will be even later. My train leaves in five minutes.'

'Where are you heading?'

'Speke, near Liverpool.'

'What squadron?'

Titch told him.

'Operational isn't it?'

'Yes sir. Nightfighters.'

'You look as if you have been in the wars enough sergeant. One of theirs or one of ours?' He looked up from examining Titch's leave pass and smiled.

'Ours sir. Four of them. Army they were. I thought four of them against me made it evens. I was wrong.'

'I can see that.' He folded the pass. 'Cheeky little bugger aren't you? And tough I would say.' But he was smiling, albeit grimly.

'You've got to be where I come from sir.'

Titch was glad he remembered the sir. The officer struck Titch as being a reasonable man and he didn't want to offend him. The tall Flying Officer returned Titch his pass.

'You had better hurry sergeant or you will miss your train and the war will be won without you. Good luck.'

Titch thanked him and hurried away. He was in such a hurry he forgot to salute. Titch was sorry about that, the man deserved one. Titch turned to look back as the railway inspector examined his ticket. The corporal and the officer were talking. The corporal was standing stiffly to attention and appeared to be getting a ticking off, probably for excessive zeal. Titch watched and his confidence in the officer class soared.

'C' Flight was on Stand By when Titch arrived and reported to the squadron commander to explain his absence. Of course he lied about the whole thing. Well almost. The bit about the bomb damage was true. To explain about his injuries and late return, Titch claimed he was involved in a near miss by a bomb during the raid when Pat and he were making love. The humour of it did not escape Titch but he was able to keep a straight face, though Keith and he had a good laugh when Titch related his story to him, but omitting the intimate details. The experience was too precious, the telling of it a betrayal. It was a sweetness and intimacy to be shared only with Pat Tilson.

Titch was ordered to report sick and was given forty-eight hours light duty. Keith and he were 'Stood Down' for that time and slept each of the nights between clean sheets, undisturbed by the war. For Titch it was to dream, but the girl he was making love to was Judy Wilson. Titch Wilkins awoke puzzled, confused and a little sad.

Chapter Ten

For Europe the war dragged on through the autumn into winter of 1940-41. 'The Battle of Britain' as it became known had been won. A victory for the R.A.F. but at a cost in men and machines and the deaths of hundreds of civilians, men, women and children in British towns and cities; increasingly in Nazi Germany as Britain began its bomber offensive.

The battle over British skies was claimed as

won in that the Luftwaffe was compelled to change its tactics almost exclusively to night bombing British cities. Manchester, Liverpool and later Coventry to name a few, blazed when high explosive and incendiary bombs shattered whole areas of the cities. There were occasional daylight raids; these were confined to the south and east of England.

As a nightfighter crew Keith and Titch flew long and often, seeking enemy bombers with nothing other than the eyes God gave them. With others of the squadron they would scramble and orbit their allotted radio beacon for hours only to be recalled, or forcibly made to return for lack of fuel. Sometimes they would be given a bearing and would shoot off to intercept bombers that they always failed to find, though ground control would say they were right among them.

Over Manchester on the night of December 23rd the pair were shot at by their own 'Ack-Ack', blinded by their own searchlights and compelled to watch the city burn. Helpless and impotent they gazed from 14,000 feet at pillars of smoke that spiralled in the air to 10,000 feet and not an enemy plane did they sight. It was the same when Liverpool was bombed; all tiring and dangerous; dangerous from the amount of 'friendly' fire that came their way. It was frustrating work. It was no wonder the squadron was disbanded in the new year and crews given a choice of converting onto the new twin engine Bristol Beaufighter, or transferring to Bomber Command.

To go onto Beaufighters would have meant an extensive, and for Titch, a difficult, course as a

R/O (Radio Observer); he had no head for electronics. After talking it over with Keith they decided to go to Bomber Command. As long as they could stay together it was okay with them.

Their arrival at Binbrook in Lincolnshire was a surprise when they discovered they were with their old squadron, Number 12. Called by rival squadrons the 'Dirty Dozen', by squadron members 'The Shiny Twelve'. The squadron was now equipped with twin engine Wellington Bombers. Two huge radial Hercules Engines powered them and they had a bomb load of over 4,000 pounds. They could carry a 'Cookie', the 4,000 pound bomb that was coming into service. The planes were armed with two hydraulic powered gun turrets housing quick firing Browning machine guns; four in the rear, two in the nose. Titch was impressed. He chose to fly as a reargunner. He preferred to see what was shooting at him rather than be hidden in a 'cupboard' as a wireless operator and being shot at by an unseen enemy. Such was his reasoning. But like he said, 'I have no head for electronics.' Radio was still largely a mystery to him.

The two were allocated to a crew captained by a Polish Flying Officer, 'Count' Leopold Bronnovski, a tall lean beanpole of a man. Keith as second pilot and Titch as rear gunner. The Count, as he insisted on being called, was an ex Polish Air Force Officer and very correct in all things on the ground and reputedly an ace in the sky over Poland. He claimed he 'had connections', presumably with someone at Group Head Quarters. Connections or not, he was not a popular member of the squadron, either as an officer or a captain but the two friends were stuck with him for the duration of their tour and Count, or Skipper, he was. He demanded that title from them all, loud and often.

In addition to a lank gaunt frame he had a wispy moustache and a face that wore a continuous look of gloom. Thick lips barely concealed large white teeth that when he relaxed, protruded above his lower lip. He was called 'Bunny' by his brother officers, his few friends conceded he did look like one of our little furry rodents.

Titch developed a bit of a fixation about him. He was what Tom Wilson would have called 'A Toffee-Nosed Bastard'. Anyone not out of the aristocratic mould was not of this earth. It was at this time that Keith dubbed Titch a 'Sub Human rear gunner'; an endearment that stuck and was a constant source of fun for both of them.

As a crew they flew, they trained. On a night in March they flew on their first operation. It was Cologne in the Ruhr valley, called by some 'Happy Valley', called 'Flakky Valley' by the N.C.O. aircrew. They sat through the briefing and listened to the 'Gen' as the slang called the information given out. Titch asked a question of the Wing Commander.

'What about the night fighters sir?' No one had mentioned these and it seemed to Titch to be important. The young reargunner thought it odd when there was an ominous silence. The Gunnery Leader answered his question and told him what he wanted to know and he was happy. Puzzled, but happy. It was not until they were out at the aircraft that his captain approached him.

'Oh Wilkins.' Not Titch, not even sergeant, or rear gunner, but Wilkins. Titch's egalitarian feathers stood erect.

'Oh Wilkins.'

The tall Pole towered above his short rear gunner.

'It is customary for crew members to address questions to their skipper. I could have answered you quite well. You do nothing without my orders. Do remember that in future.' He affected an English public school accent that was perfect, with only a trace of a Polish enunciation.

'Right o.' Titch deliberately paused. 'Oh Count,' he said, 'if an ME gets up our arse do I ask permission to shoot the bastard down before I fire?'

'Don't be impertinent,' was his retort. He muttered something in Polish that was quite incomprehensible. It was the best he could do so Titch let it lie. The pilot threw his head in the air hard enough to toss his long dark hair back over his head and with a flourish, twisted the silk scarf he sported around his neck and went to the front of the plane.

A shadow leaning against Titch's turret unwound itself and spoke. It was Lofty Melbrace a lanky L.A.C. armourer from Wapping, in London's east end. He sniffed loudly.

'Calls 'is self a bloody Count 'e does. 'E can't even pronounce a simple four letter word, can 'e? Bloody Polish pansy.' The cockney airman spat his disgust onto the oil stained concrete.

The first operation was uneventful as Ruhr

'Ops' went. Both Keith and Titch thought it pretty horrific at the time; subsequent experience convinced them that it was a fairly easy trip. It was a mission to Bochum two weeks later that was nearly their undoing. The squadron intelligence officer at the briefing convinced them that the flak defences would be slight. He could not have been more wrong. The Germans threw everything at them. 'Everything but the kitchen sink' was a saying at the time. Light, medium and heavy flak and well aimed. The Count had an aversion to 'evasive action', abbreviated to weaving, so they caught more than their share.

'Weaving is for cowards and women' was how he excused his defiance of standard orders. The flight in was easy enough. A little flak as they crossed the coast and when they wandered over a town of some sort.

'Bombaimer to Skipper. Flak and searchlights ahead.'

The target was coming up. Tom Williams their sergeant Observer/Bombaimer was a genial Lancastrian. He would call the Devil Christ, if it gave him an easy life.

'No bloody good a botherin' wi' a bloke like yon. It'll sort itsen out in th' long run. You mark my words,' was Tom's laconic reaction to the Count's passion for titles. Roy Ellis, their Navigator had the same sentiment. Keith, Titch and Sergeant Billy Longbottom their Wireless Operator, predictably called 'Short Arse', were the odd balls. The three hated pomposity, and Flying Officer 'Count' Bronnovski was pompous.

'Thank you Bombaimer.' It would not have surprised Titch if he had said 'Oh I say, good show. Thanks awfully.' He was hardly English enough for that.

They were flying straight and level; they should not have been but they were. A searchlight caught them, then another. Flak opened up around them. They were not able to see it in the glare but Titch felt it strike them. The crump and jarring of exploding shells, the jolting as light flak hit them and passed through the fabric of the fuselage. The tearing of the plane's fabric was loud, even with the noise of two engines roaring. It must have been close to Titch.

Both pilots put the old Wimpy into a dive and miraculously the searchlights went out. God knows why. Titch immediately thought of fighters. He had covered one eye to preserve some semblance of night vision and searched the sky expecting a deadly stream of tracer. It came, but from the ground. Titch saw the pin points of light reaching up to him slowly. Suddenly it rushed past, a stream of yellow lights that he knew were only the tracer. Every fourth shell, unseen between were armour-piercing or incendiary missiles as big as cricket balls. Just one was enough to kill him. If it was an incendiary it would burn inside him; frying his guts and heart. That thought and others bombarded Titch's brain – the stream of fire missed his turret by inches.

'Bombaimer to skipper. Bomb doors open!'

Tom's voice was pitched low. Titch admired his apparent lack of concern. He was terrified back there in the rear turret.

'Bomb doors open.' Keith repeated Tom's

instruction as a matter of routine. Titch wondered in a moment of mad speculation if he had asked the Count's permission. The things that go through a man's head at times like this! Tom's voice came again loud, clear and drawn out.

'Right... Right... Steady.'

The whole plane shook with an explosion; a cloud of black oily smoke swept past Titch's turret. The Wimpy's port wing dipped and began a diving turn. There was silence, except for the roar of the engines and the screaming of the wind past the turret.

'Drop the bloody bombs, Tom!'

It was Keith. The Wellington's wing was going in a steeper angle. There was no reply from the Lancastrian bombaimer.

'Roy get down and press that bloody tit! I believe Tom has bought it. The Count is out of commission. I can't hold this bastard with the bombs on, so hurry!'

Roy Ellis did not answer. Titch didn't know what was happening up at the front of the plane. Suddenly they were on a more even keel and flying normally. Flak poured up at them from a dozen places. Heavy and medium joined the tracer. The flash and crump of explosions made the old Wimpy jerk and bounce. Tracer formed a pattern of fire close above them. It seemed an eternity before they were clear.

'You OK Titch?' The pilot's words came between gasps of breath. It was the only time he called Titch, Titch, when other people were around. All other times it was Rupert.

'Sure Skipper.' In the air that was how Titch

thought of him. He added, 'and to hell with the bloody Count.' Keith supposed it was Titch's sense of mischief – whatever it was it had the effect of breaking the tension.

'Short Arse. You busy?'

'Nothin' that can't wait.'

'Good. Get up here and give Roy a hand with Tom and the Count.'

'Don't bother with Tom, Keith. He's had it. Poor bastard. 'Alf 'is bloody 'ead shot away.' Roy's voice cut through the intercom like a sword of gloom. Tom Williams was dead; who next?

'Get the Count away from the controls and see to him. He looks in a bad way.'

'Roger.'

The Wellington was flying on a regular weaving set of courses. Things looked OK from where Titch sat but then he only looked into space unless he looked down the fuselage. It was pointless doing that, a waste of time; like looking down a dark tunnel. It could be dangerous when there is a risk of fighters.

Minutes passed. The target was well behind them. Titch was disappointed that the fires he could see were not bigger. There were sixty of them on the raid, Wellingtons, Whitleys and Hampdens. They were about the last to bomb so the raid was hardly a success.

'Keith, I've laid the Count down and given him a shot of morphia. He caught the flak in his face, poor sod. His shoulder is all shot up too. His is not bleeding too bad and his breathing is OK.'

'Thanks Roy. Make sure he is warm enough. Then give me a course for home. The shortest.

I'll get the pompous idiot home as quick as we can. Short Arse!'

''Allo?'

'Check the kite.'

'Roger Keith.'

'You OK Titch?'

'Right as rain, Keith.'

'Keep your eyes peeled back there.'

'You bet. I'm not a bit sleepy. I wonder why?' Keith's chuckle was lost as his mike was off – but Titch was far from cheerful.

The Wireless Operator reported that all was intact with the airframe. They had holes and rips in the fabric, and several pieces of the aluminium geodesic frame of the fuselage near Titch's turret were shot away. The tail plane spar had a few holes in it but they were flying so all was well.

It was a long ride home. It was their third operation and the worst so far. The worst in terms of the flak defences and in terms of being shot up. One dead and the captain wounded.

When they saw the old Wimpy in the daylight the next day, they were shocked. The whole tail section was riddled with holes. How the flak missed Titch, he will never know. There was a hole a man could crawl through in the nose that caught the blast of the heavy flak shell; the shell that killed Tom Williams. The perspex canopy over the 'throne', as they called the first pilot's seat, was shattered and starred with holes Titch put his fist through. He looked at Keith who was standing beside him.

'It must have been draughty flying all the way home in the blast from those holes. Weren't you

268

cold Keith?'

'I was near frozen Rupert, but I had to get us home. The central heating wasn't working. We ran out of coal over the target.' He laughed at his own joke and made light of his suffering. Titch knew how cold it could be in a rear turret with the wind pouring in on one's face. He shuddered. It must have been agony and Keith made not one word of complaint.

'Flying any time is bloody dangerous. Flying over the Ruhr is raving bloody madness.' Short Arse's words said it for all of them.

The crew were stood down while the squadron commander sorted out the problem of a new captain and bombaimer and the fitters repaired their aircraft. They licked their wounds, buried Tom Williams in the little church yard in Binbrook village and went to see the Count in Lincoln Hospital. They went as a duty rather than love. The Count was badly wounded. His face would be scarred for life and he was permanently blind in one eye. His shoulder would recover but his flying days were over. Titch believed the Pole was secretly glad of that.

Keith Gale was awarded the immediate award of the Distinguished Flying Medal for his magnificent effort at bringing them and the damaged Wellington home. He was made captain of a new Wellington, 'C' Charlie and they saw the arrival of a second pilot and a new bombaimer. They were now an all N.C.O. crew and happy about it. They shared two rooms between them in the sergeants' mess. They lived together, drank together and nearly died together on several occasions.

Five operations later they were allowed six days leave. Keith asked Titch to join him in Cornwall to stay with another of his aunts and uncles. Titch remembered him saying earlier that he had relations everywhere. The gunner refused his offer; he wanted to find Patricia Tilson.

The weeks had dragged. Every day he had looked for a letter. He had pestered the station post office to check if they had mislaid her letter. All with a negative result. After six weeks it seemed final. Being Titch Wilkins, he was not prepared to give up that easily.

He caught the train to London and found 'The Gun' public house. He tried to find her flat. It had been dark when he had entered it and dark when he left; he had not stepped out of the door between times. He and Pat had been too busy inside. How then was he to recognise it? In daylight every house was a mirror image of the other. Tall Victorian terraced houses, most of them with iron railings, though several had workmen cutting them down. 'For salvage for the war effort' was the reply when he asked why. Titch searched north, south, east and west of 'The Gun'. He knocked on doors and received many shakes of the head.

It was late evening. Titch was about to give up; something made him go down this last flight of steps to the door of this particular basement flat. Had he been there before? There was no reply to his knock. He thought he would try again; it had a familiar look. He knocked again – louder this time. The sound echoed through the building and he knew it was empty but he knocked again.

A waste of time. He climbed the steps wearily to the street level.

'Lookin' fer Mrs Tilson are yer young feller?'

Titch looked in the direction of the voice. It was a woman leaning out of a ground floor window. She had a mob cap on her head and what hair Titch saw was protruding from the elastic and was tied in curlers. She had a round red face and seemed a cheerful soul. The pinafore she wore over her floral print dress was clean.

'Yes. I am an old friend. I'm on leave and thought I would look her up. I knew her husband,' Titch lied.

As if she knew it was a lie the woman gave him a suspicious look and sniffed. 'Friend eh? Knew 'er 'usband yer say? I fought as 'ow she was a widder woman.'

'She is. I knew him. Her husband, I mean. I knew them both before they were married.' Lies poured from Titch's lips. He began to feel desperate for a sight, a touch of Patricia.

'Can't 'elp yer much. Left 'ere monfs ago. War work she said it was. Didn't leave a forwarding address. I cleans fer 'er yer see. Yer know. Airs the place. And set traps fer the mice. Know wot I mean. Sorry I can't 'elp yer.'

Titch wrote a note and asked the woman to be sure she gave it to Pat.

'Dun'know when I'll see 'er. Monfs maybe. But I'll give it to 'er when I does.'

Titch could see he was at the end of the line and made his way to the station. He thought he would go to the Wilsons but changes his mind at the booking office and booked a ticket for

271

Penzance to be with Keith.

They had a wonderful leave. The elderly uncle and aunt were kind hosts. Titch almost forgot Patricia, almost. In quiet moments the memory of her flooded back. This brought thoughts of Judy and his betrayal of her. Titch realised that for whatever reasons, the relationship with Pat, short and beautiful as it had been, was at an end. Keith convinced him it was more lust than love, whereas with Judy … to quote Keith.

'You must turn the page and open a clean sheet and start our life again Rupert.' And he did. He was going to live a life of a monk. Well, until the right girl came long. His first adventure into a loving relationship had been too wonderful to cut himself off from the prospect of such joys.

For five days Keith and Titch wandered the deserted beaches of the Cornish coast. In the fishing harbours of Newlyn and Mousehole they ate freshly caught lobsters. They drank beer in old pubs that had been the haunt of smugglers and wreckers. They drank rough cider from a leather 'jack' in the cellar of an old stone farm house and as they so often did, they talked.

Keith continually impressed on Titch the need to improve himself.

'You have a quick mind Rupert. Learn how to use it. Educate yourself. Read. More importantly, debate. Search for truth. Seek it with argument as much as by reading and experience.' The sun was warm and the sea blue. The pair were sitting on the beach. Keith lay back on the sand and looked at Titch. 'No matter where you have to look. No matter what you do. Don't clutter your mind with trivia. Cultivate intelligent friends and read. Never take "I don't know" for an answer. There is a wealth of knowledge out there. Don't try and learn it all. Learn where to find it. Learn how to speak and be understood. Learn how to listen and understand. To do this you must be articulate. Improve your vocabulary and modify your mode of speech so that you will not be stereotyped and lampooned, be it Londoner, or Scot. Be international. Conan Doyle had the right idea but he retreated into Switzerland rather than out in to the world to preach Internationalism.'

Many an hour they spent talking in this vein. Long conversations that Titch listened to and learned. Together they planned a new world; a world of peace and prosperity where poverty was outlawed and freedom was a right for all men, but with responsibilities and obligations.

Keith had a grand scheme, what he called 'A Union of English Speaking States' where all the English speaking nations of the world would form a cultural, economic, scientific and defence union as a prelude to a world union.

'If it works an Asian Union would be formed. A Latin, European and so on. A sort of United Nations where people debated issues of contention instead of fighting over them. Then together set about righting wrongs. And make it work better than the League of Nations.'

They discussed the existence of God and the effect of Jesus on the world. Islam, Jewry and Buddhism were discussed in some depth. They talked of world population control and whether the world could feed itself in the future; the future of world trade and the possibility of another great depression. The possibility of another world war if peace broke down and its catastrophic effects on humanity.

It was all heady stuff for an orphaned slum boy but Titch listened. In the months that followed Keith guided him through a library of books. As a game Titch added a word a day to his vocabulary. Whenever he could Keith would correct Titch's speech and between them they improved his grammar. Titch remembered thinking how hard Miss Cuthberson had tried during his few short moths at Broadstairs. She would have been proud of their efforts.

The summer of 1941 was a turning point in the war. Germany attacked Russia and had to fight on two fronts. The Luftwaffe stepped up its night bombing of British cities and blasted Liverpool for ten nights in a row. Coventry was almost destroyed and of course London had almost nightly visits.

The U.S. was doing all it could for Britain, short of going to war. Ships, tanks and planes were shipped to British ports and found their way to the fighting men. Food was strictly rationed but there was enough for all – just.

Twelve squadron, as part of Bomber Command, were doing their best to pound German industry and population centres, hoping to cripple the Nazi war machine. The losses were heavy. It was said that the average life of a bomber crew was ten operations. Keith and his crew didn't count, except that every operation was one closer to the finish of the tour; six minds concentrated on that. It was survival, something Titch had been practising since birth. Their tour came close to an end in June. A near fatal end.

It was their twenty-first 'Op'. The target Essen, their third visit to the home of Messrs Krupps and his armaments empire. They hated Essen. All bomber crews hated Essen.

'We get the key to the city tonight, blokes.' Short Arse tried to make light of the crew's apprehension about a revisit to the Ruhr city.

'Not if we go for a shit in the mean time,' Bill Davenport their new second pilot was the eternal pessimist. English tabloids claimed there were twenty thousand flak guns defending the Ruhr; Essen was about the centre of the huge industrial zone. Perhaps Bill had good reason for his pessimism.

It was to be a big raid; two hundred Wellingtons, Halifaxes and Stirlings. Two types of four engine bombers that were coming into service. The Wellington was becoming the old lady of the bomber force. Its altitude and speed were superseded by the four engine super bombers that were to accompany them.

There was nothing new in the briefing. Flak, nightfighters, German decoys, weather, flying procedures and aiming points were all gone over. There was nothing left but to take off.

It was a beautiful June evening. They took off in daylight and Titch enjoyed the sight of England stretching behind him as they gained height and headed east. The North Sea looked benign. The few clouds looked friendly; the sun as it set was a ball of glorious colour behind them. Only the thought of the target spoiled Titch's reverie.

It was dark before they reached the Dutch coast – there was no moon. Titch had seen one or two other Wellingtons of the bomber stream, the four engine kites were well above them and behind. Their superior speed allowed them to catch up before the target was reached. Titch began to feel they were alone.

Flak shells burst like instant stars way over to their beam, probably a Wimpy off course and flying over a defensive zone. A search light probed the sky searching for an errant bomber. Keith weaved the Wellington gently to throw off the prediction apparatus of the flak gunners, or the nightfighter radar controllers that may be plotting their courses. Every fifteen seconds he changed course and height. It was gut heaving, nauseating work.

Bombing times were co-ordinated so that the bombing would be spread over a long period and so strain the defences to the utmost. They were briefed to bomb early in the raid.

Tiny Willis their bombaimer piped up that he could see the target ahead. A brilliant display of flak and searchlights at Titch's back and out of his sight showed that they were not the first. As they approached their aiming point the Ruhr's guns really opened up.

A Wellington Titch had been keeping an eye on astern of them blew up from what could have been a direct hit from a shell. It must have struck the plane's bomb load for it disintegrated in a holocaust of flame that dripped fire for a minute until the wreck hit the ground in another explosion. Their altitude was such that they were exposed to every calibre of gun. Tracer snaked up to them, medium and heavy shells burst around 'C' Charlie and made the aircraft jink and bank. A shell burst very close on Titch's port. Shrapnel starred the Perspex of his turret, yet he saw no flash, just an elongated column of black oily smoke. It was his first experience of German 88mm flashless shells. Titch knew then the barrage was even worse than what he saw.

They were knocked around over the target but their bombs were gone and they were on the way home intact and all systems working. The target fires were a distant glow. Titch marvelled that men could live in that inferno let alone fire their guns. Such were his thoughts when he saw a shadow pass over the lighter sky between him and the target. In the instant he saw it silhouetted against the fires of the target he recognized it as a Messerschmitt 110; a German nightfighter. There was no mistaking the twin engines and the twin fins and rudders. Titch warned the crew to prepare for evasive action. He saw the fighter again, closer, but still out of range of his guns and still a silhouette against the ground fires.

'Watch it, Titch.' Keith's words came like a breath over the intercom. The reargunner didn't reply. All his concentration was on that shadow some four hundred yards astern of them. He was tempted to fire a burst to frighten it away, but he knew it would be up there another night and he may not see him then. He waited. His mouth was dry and he felt a moisture around his anus. Keith gently weaved the plane in the usual way.

The fighter was at two hundred yards and had not committed itself to an attack. Perhaps it had not seen them? The reargunner felt the knife thrust of fear – palpable as a sharp double-edged sword of ice that pierced his heart and chilled his veins.

'Dive starboard Go!' Titch screamed the command into his microphone and opened fire all in the same breath. In the split second before the Wellington fell out of the sky in a diving turn, Titch saw his tracer biting into the soft skin of the fighter. He continued to fire and saw fire in the engine of the ME. It did not return his fire and it did not break away. It was flying straight at them – following their evasive manoeuvres? Titch kept up his fire. When it was closer than perhaps fifty yards it exploded in a ball of flame.

Titch was about to breathe again when a stream of tracer fire passed over his head. He saw the flash of another fighter's guns in the dark. A quick shift of aim and a scream of 'Keep weaving for Christ sake!' and he opened fire on the new target. It was too close and fired another burst. Titch felt the impact of the shells from its cannon and the tracer was all around him. Miraculously he was not hit. Only three of his four guns were firing. Titch kept his fingers on the triggers and 'hose-piped' his tracer into the Messerschmitt. A second gun stopped and the fighter disappeared below the Wellington. As it passed, Titch saw a flame spreading from its port engine. The nightfigher spiralled away into the darkness of the night.

'I've lost it but keep weaving Keith. The bastard's not dead. Just damaged.'

The temperature was freezing but Titch was sweating and his heels tapped a nervous tattoo as he shook from the reaction of the combat. His gut heaved. With a wrench he tore off his oxygen mask and vomited his fear and shock onto his lap. The realisation that he had personally killed possibly six men in a matter of seconds sickened him further.

'But they were shooting at me.' Even as he tried to control his nerves and forebodings his mind rationalised his action, but the sick feeling remained.

Miles slipped away beneath them and Titch Wilkins knew that he had to learn to live with that remorse and the thoughts that people died from the bombs he was dropping on them. Black darkness stretched away from him. He searched it for a hidden enemy and wondered if the German who dropped the bomb that killed Ma and Bert James had any remorse and the fighter pilot who strafed and killed Judy. What about him? Titch mentally grabbed the straw of thought that he was avenging their deaths but in the loneliness and darkness of his turret he became aware that it was an empty feeling. It did nothing to lessen the pain of his loss. Minutes ticked away unseen and unheard. Keith Gale weaved 'C' Charlie to and beyond the Dutch coast, then straight and level for home.

It was customary after each operation that crews were greeted with a cup of hot coffee before they were interrogated by the squadron intelligence office. The same two W.A.A.F. NCOs were on duty at the door with the coffee urn. Every operation it was the same pair. They were both sergeants and each had a smile and a cheery word as they doled out coffee, cigarettes and biscuits.

Titch had noticed the small brunette – he had seen her in the sergeants' mess and was pleased one day when she smiled at him but W.A.A.F.'s seldom lingered in the ante room after a meal. They retired to their own room for their after dinner coffee or drinks.

Keith and the rest of the crew were in a huddle with the flight commander and Titch was alone after arriving late; his flying clothing was a mess of vomit that had to be cleaned. The brunette sergeant W.A.A.F. was alone behind the coffee urn as her companion had left for a moment. The W.A.A.F and Titch were quite alone.

'Had a good trip sergeant?'

Titch took his nose out of his cup.

'Don't know about good. One more anyway. A bit special this time though.'

'A good prang was it?'

'Pretty good. The bombing was on the ball. No… What I meant was we got a bit shot up. But no blood spilt. Not like last time.'

'Badly?'

Titch drained his cup and looked at her.

'Pretty bad. But none of our blokes got hit. Not like last time. We lost our bombaimer then.'

'Yes I know. It was sad about Tom Williams.'

The reargunner looked closely at the girl standing a yard from him. Tom Williams had been dead and buried for weeks. Just one of twenty or more casualties ago. There were fifty odd crews on the squadron yet this girl remembered the laconic Lancastrian.

'You knew Tom?'

'Yes, we came from the same town. I went out with him a few times.'

'Must have been tough for you. Sweet on him were you?'

The W.A.A.F. sergeant blushed and Titch smiled his delight. The colour made her cheeks rose red.

'No... Not really.' She smiled at the grinning tail gunner. 'He was just a friend.' She paused and blushed even further. 'He wasn't really my type of bloke,' she added shyly.

Titch noted the twinkle in her eye. He meant it as a flippant reply and grinned even wider. 'If old Tom wasn't your type of bloke, who is?'

The W.A.A.F. sergeant seemed to smile with the whole of her face. She looked at the begrimed figure the other side of the counter.

'You really want to know?'

'You bet. It might be me.'

'You're right. It is. I mean you are. Cheeky monkey that you are.'

Titch choked on the dregs of his coffee. He dribbled coffee down his battle-dress blouse, was about to stammer a reply when he saw Keith breaking off from talking to the flight commander. Their eyes met and the pilot beckoned his reargunner.

Titch Wilkins cleared his throat.

'Sorry. Gotta go. Duty calls.' He grinned, placed his empty cup on the counter, grabbed a biscuit

281

from a plate and hurried to the table where his crew were sitting.

The interrogation proceeded and word that one of their number had had a successful brush with a nightfighter ran through the room. Two nightfighters! The crew of PH 'C' Charlie had had a double combat and survived; a rarity indeed.

The table for interrogation was crowded with standing aircrew keen to hear the details. Titch was explaining the whole thing, the sighting, ranges, length of burst and combat manoeuvres he ordered. There was a silence directly behind him. Titch felt the presence of something, or someone. Before he could decide which, a voice broke through the silence; a voice that had a ring of authority.

'Never mind the details sergeant. Did you shoot the bastard down?'

Titch looked over his shoulder. He saw a well built man of middle age. He saw too the gold braid on the man's cap, the broad bands on the sleeve of his tunic that seemed to reach to his elbow. Titch's eyes travelled to the face and noted the moustache and the deep set, piercing eyes under bushy eyebrows. The gunner's answer was immediate.

'Yes sir.'

'You sure?'

'Positive.' Titch's clipped reply left no room for doubt. The omission of 'sir' went un-noticed.

'Splendid. And the second Hun?'

'Only damaged sir.' Titch suppressed a giggle brought on by his nervousness. 'He'll have a headache though, I reckon.'

Titch Wilkins saw a grim smile break the severe mouth of the man towering above him. A hand squeezed his shoulder. Words came like whiplash. 'Well done laddie.' He turned and walked away. The silence of the group remained for some seconds.

'Who the bloody 'ell was that? He 'ad more scrambled egg on 'is 'at than I could get on a bloody dinner plate.' The words exploded from Roy Ellis.

'Christ! Don't you know Butch Harris?'

Titch could never remember who said that. He was speechless. Bomber crews revered Air Marshal Sir Arthur Harris, second only to God.

The crew of 'C' Charlie left soon afterwards. Titch passed the dark haired W.A.A.F. sergeant and smiled. On an impulse he turned back. The young woman smiled a welcome.

'If I'm really your type of bloke, what about stepping out with me on the next stand down night? We could go to a flick in Grimsby.'

'No thank you.'

Titch was visibly disappointed and felt a fool for asking. He was about to apologize when he saw the twinkle in her eye and the broad smile on her lips.

'Not Grimsby. Make it Lincoln and I'm your girl.'

'Lincoln it is then. What about your chum?' Titch pointed with his chin to the second W.A.A.F. sergeant wiping down the counter. 'Would she like to come if Keith comes too? We could make it a foursome.'

The question hung in the air as she looked at

her colleague who had heard every word; a signal unseen by Titch passed between them.

'I'm sure she would.'

'Good. We'll see you both later then.'

Titch caught up with the rest of the crew before they got to the mess and broke the news to Keith. He was far from enthusiastic at first, but warmed to the idea as they ate their bacon and egg post-operational meal.

Wellington PH 'C' Charlie flew the following night and the night after that – three nights in a row and all on the Ruhr. The fourth day was a Saturday and the squadron was stood down for seventy-two hours. Such a thing was generally greeted by Keith and Titch with a trip to either Grimsby or Lincoln with the view to some shopping, a film show, a meal and a few drinks. They invariably returned to the mess an hour before midnight and joined in the 'high jinks' that a stand down demanded. They seldom got to bed before two in the morning. The following two nights were less festive; the third night generally with an early night between the sheets; the fourth night might mean another operation.

On this occasion they had a different programme. They met the two girls at the bus stop outside the guard room and sat together on the way to Lincoln. It was a pleasant trip through the Lincolnshire Wolds. The girls introduced themselves as Mary Golding and Sheila McDonald. Mary hailed from Lancashire, Sheila from a tiny village near Helmsdale in the Highlands of Sutherlandshire on the north east coast of

Scotland. They spent the hour long journey getting to know each other.

Mary and Titch hit it off at once. If he was her type of bloke she was certainly his type of girl. They laughed and talked their way to the city and were surprised when they arrived. They did their shopping together and after a light tea the four of them went to the cinema. The film 'It Happened One Night' starring Claudette Colbert and Clarke Gable was the main feature. It was an old film; one Titch remembered seeing with Ma James before the war. He pushed the memory of that time from his mind and concentrated on the film and the girl sitting close to him.

The rest of the evening passed in a whirl of laughter and talk. On the last bus back to the airfield, Mary and Titch were holding hands and telling each other how much they enjoyed the day.

The following day they met again, just the two of them. It was a Sunday, PH 'C' Charlie was not on the battle order. They walked together across the Wolds to Tealby, a small hamlet where they were served tea and scones with home-made strawberry jam. They sat in the cottage garden soaking up the sun and listening to the birds playing havoc among the raspberry canes behind them. On the walk back they were holding hands. At a stile at the top of a hill overlooking a field of new mown hay they stopped to look for the distant spires of Lincoln Cathedral. There was a heat haze and they were difficult to find; it took them a minute or two. Titch lifted Mary onto the top rail for a better view. He looked up at her. She had removed her tunic and cap and his eyes were level with her chest. Her regulation shirt was stretched tight and Titch saw the swelling of her breasts and the whiteness of her skin through the gaps between the buttons. The young sergeant found it hard to tear his eyes away but he did.

Mary looked down from her elevated position and their eyes met in a glance of frank understanding. Titch was surprised to find Mary's eyes were a deep blue, he had told himself they were brown. Her dark brown hair had escaped the tight roll at the back of her head and was blowing in the soft wind. Her perfume came to him, faint but sweet. He breathed the soft aroma of lilac and fresh perspiration. He felt the pressure of his arousal and wanted to take her in his arms and kiss her but he was afraid.

Titch's eyes travelled over her face and took in every feature from the rounded chin to the dimpled cheeks. He noticed how thick and arched her eyebrows were. When she smiled, as she often did, she parted full red lips and showed small even white teeth; her tongue was a delicious shade of pink. Titch noticed too her nose was small and wrinkled when she laughed.

Everything inside Titch demanded a physical contact. His intuition told him to be careful; this girl was as delicate as a fawn and would frighten easy. It was a surprise to him when she bent her head and kissed him full on the mouth. The shock lasted a full second before he returned the gentle pressure of her lips. He wanted more. He wanted to crush her to him, to possess her and be possessed. Titch lifted her down and they kissed again, each of them breathing the other. Titch tasted a lingering of strawberry jam on her lips. She parted them and he felt a warm moisture; her tongue sent electric currents through him. They walked a few yards down the hill to a stook of hay and sank into its fragrance.

Titch could never recall exactly what happened next but they were naked in the pile of hay thrilling at the sight and feel of each other, ignoring the scattered clothing that littered the hay around them. Frantic fingers fondled and touched. Frantic hands cupped and caressed. Titch and Mary made love with an urgency and passion that had them both breathless. She reached up to Titch as he thrust into her. Her arms were about him pressing him to her. She arched her back to take more of him and he gave, cupping her buttocks with trembling hands and thrusting deeper. They cried out softly in the ecstasy of their climax. A timid rabbit in the hedgerow eyed them with a frank stare – only it and a high flying lark heard them.

Minutes later they lay exhausted and allowed the sun to bathe them with its glowing warmth. Their hands sought and found each other with soft caressing movements. Their lips did not tire of their kisses, their hands from searching, exploring, finding and holding. Soon arousal demanded more satisfaction and they made love again under the blue Lincolnshire sky with only that lark to see them. The silence from worldly things was heavenly. The lark sang to the soft accompaniment of buzzing insects. They lay naked until the chill of the evening made them dress and continue their walk, each holding the other close.

They learned a lot of each other during that walk to Binbrook village. Mary told Titch that she had been a junior librarian before she marred a school teacher in late 1937. In 1939 he was mobilised and sent to France. He was killed with the B.E.F. in 1940; one of the half-trained Territorial Army Volunteers that were rushed across to Calais in the early days of the phoney war. She was married at twenty – her husband was twenty four. For two years they had wanted a child. She had wanted his child before he left for the front but it was not to be. After a miscarriage she discovered that she was barren and could never have children. When her young husband was killed she thought it was the end of life for her. The W.A.A.F. had been her salvation. As a well educated woman she found service life fulfilling and trained as an Intelligence Clerk, she soon reached the rank of sergeant. Her work at Binbrook in compiling and copying Intelligence Reports to send to Bomber Command H.Q. was confidential and rewarding.

By the time they reached the doors of the 'Marquis of Granby' public house in the village, Titch had told her much about himself and his hopes for the future. He told her of his fears when flying and the need he had to fulfil the expectations of what Bert James thought he was capable of. He talked of Bert's dream that was now his, to sail single handed around the world.

Mary Golding listened and all the time they walked close together though, because of it being daylight, and with the presence of so many airforce personnel in the village, they had their arms to their sides.

The old pub was open and they had a drink before they walked through the water meadows below the airfield to the W.A.A.F. living quarters. It was dark when they arrived and they stood close against a tree kissing and whispering. A new moon showed a tiny crescent of light in a cloudless sky.

'Turn your money over and wish Rupert.' Mary looked at Titch and laughed as she said it. They turned their money and wished.

Titch remembered his wish. It was for a long life and happiness with such a woman as Mary. He corrected himself midway and thought, 'Should I wish for a woman like Judy?' Titch felt the presence of his teenage sweetheart; he felt her smile on him and was happy.

Mary and Titch kissed and whispered a little longer. They didn't want to part but it had to be. At last they did. She turned to go.

'Thank you Rupert. Thank you for a lovely day. Thank you for everything. For laughing with me. For listening to me. Nobody has listened to me for a long time. Not like you have.' She paused and looked at him with the pale moonlight shining on his face. 'And thank you for loving me. Perhaps we can fall in love Rupert. I hope so.'

The words were like a caress and held a question. She reached up and kissed Titch again and was lost in the darkness before he could hold her and tell her again that he loved her.

The walk back to the sergeants' mess gave Titch

time to think. Was he in love with this girl? He remembered Patricia Tilson. He compared his feelings for her and with Judy and now Mary. Were they different? Was this as Keith explained, 'lust, not love'? Even when he joined his crew for a last drink before bed he could not make up his mind but sleep came easy and was dreamless.

The following day the battle order showed Flight Sergeant Gale and crew were operating. For them the stand down was brief. The crew of 'C' Charlie were out at their aircraft when a message came to order Titch to report to the Wing Commander immediately. He left the dispersal with the W.A.A.F. driver who had been sent for him. Questions tumbled around his mind. Why had he been seen sent for? What had he done? Titch said nothing as the service utility drove around the perimeter track to the squadron offices.

It was a dark contrast when Titch entered the orderly room from the bright sunlight. Again he was wondering what he had done for such an urgent call into the holy of holies, the C.O.'s office. The squadron adjutant showed Titch into the 'Wingco's' presence without a word.

Sergeant Wilkins saluted smartly and looked at the man sitting behind the desk. He was smoking a pipe, a good sign thought Titch. If I am going to have a strip torn off me I know he would not be smoking.

'Ah Wilkins. The very man. Sit down.' Another surprise this was surely not a strip tearing operation.

'Thank you sir.' Titch removed his cap and sat

on the edge of the regulation chair not knowing what to think. The Wing Commander took a grey message form from his 'IN' tray.

'A message for you.' He handed Titch the form. The grey flimsy trembled in the outstretched hand. Titch hesitated. He saw a brief type-written message under the heading 'Bomber Command Head Quarters.'

'Here, take it lad. It won't bite.' The senior officer took the pipe from his mouth and smiled. Titch's eyes travelled from the flimsy to the officer's face – he saw he was smiling. Titch Wilkins took the message form and read.

TO. SERGEANT RM.M WILKINS. 156282.

    Air Gunner R.A.F.V.R.

FROM. COMMANDER IN CHIEF

    BOMBER COMMAND.

CONGRATULATIONS ON YOUR IMMEDIATE AWARD OF THE DISTINGUISHED FLYING MEDAL. I AM PLEASED AND GRATIFIED THAT YOUR COURAGE HAS RECEIVED DUE RECOGNITION.

Signed. A.R Harris. Air Marshal. C.inC. Bomber Command.

Titch remembered his knees felt weak; he was glad he was sitting. The Wing Commander spoke again.

'Allow me to be the second to congratulate you sergeant. Well done. I am proud to have you under my command. On behalf of Twelve, allow me to thank you and wish you good fortune.'

He stood and held out his hand. Titch found himself standing and grasping the outstretched hand. He accepted the message flimsy and a yard of D.F.M. ribbon with, 'Thank you sir.' He saluted, about turned and went through the door into the outer office. Titch stepped from the gloom of the office into the brilliant sunshine, wondering what it was all about. The adjutant slapped him on the back with a muttered 'Well done sergeant.'

The Orderly Room sergeant whispered, 'Whako Titch.'

Sergeant Rupert Montgomery Wilkins D.F.M. walked in a daze to find Keith and the crew. He felt tears in his eyes thinking how Bert and Ma James and Scrapper Morgan would have been pleased with him. A slum orphan with a D.F.M. Titch was not sure how Judy would have felt.

Titch saw Mary in the mess at lunch time and ignoring protocol she embraced him in front of the others.

'I don't care, Rupert. It's wonderful. You didn't tell me about the second fighter you shot down.'

'I didn't shoot it down. I only claimed it damaged.'

'You shot it down. Seven aircraft confirmed they saw it crash and their times and lat. and long fixes match with your own navigator's log. The news came through this morning.'

A series of thoughts flashed through Titch's mind.

'I have personally killed six men. Six men whose only crime was defending their country. Six men with sweethearts like Mary and Judy. Perhaps wives and families; old widowed mothers like Ma James and Mrs Wilson.'

The thoughts drove the excitement of the last minutes from his mind. The medal ribbon looked

292

tarnished in his hand. That old feeling of sadness and loss came over him. The glass of beer that was thrust into his fist tasted sour.

To hell with the bloody war. When will the killing stop?

The question troubled the reargunner. Only the sight of Keith and Mary standing, smiling their love and friendship made Titch feel that he was not totally alone.

Chapter Eleven

Winter 1942. It was wet but there had been no frost. Everywhere was damp; gales had stripped the trees of leaves. The elderly sexton appeared early and began digging a grave close to Titch Wilkins, as Titch had seen before, he dug quietly and efficiently. The dead gunner watched and marvelled at his skill. The sides of the grave were straight and square. The old man's only tools were a spade, shovel and a pickaxe. Deeper he dug. Chalky soil flew. Suddenly he had finished. A neat six feet by two feet pit was exposed. The depth as far as Titch could judge was six feet. The old man had not used a rule of any sort. His eyes, wise with experience had told him just what to do.

Constable Tom Higgins, the Doctor, Otto and Titch speculated who was going to be the occupant. The old doctor made a guess that it would be another airman as the bomber streams often flew directly over them, day and night. Spitfires and the new American light bombers, Bostons, the R.A.F. called them, swept low daily, heading east in the mornings and returning by noon. The U.S. 8th Army Air Force Flying Fortresses and Liberator Bombers flew high above them most days and R.A.F. bombers most nights. The war in the air was stepping up. Nazi Germany was reaping a harvest from what it had sown in 1940.

Otto and Titch did their best to bring their neighbours up-to-date with the affairs of the world. The former Luftwaffe pilot and Titch did not agree on everything – what they did agree on was the enormity of it all – the wanton wholesale and indiscriminate destruction wrought by high explosive and incendiaries dropped on whole areas of cities in Germany and Britain. No one was safe, soldiers or civilians; men, women and tragically, children, all were casualties. The deep 'bunkers' built for their protection were not safe. People died in their hundreds from suffocation when fires above and around them consumed the oxygen. Even drowning, when water mains burst and flooded underground bomb shelters. A voice interrupted their speculations.

'Of course I knew it was up to England to stop that cad Hitler in the end. All very well these aeroplanes and things bombing and doing whatever they do. But mark my words, it will be the P.B.I. The poor bloody infantry that have to finish the Boche off. The Hun couldn't stand to cold steel last time, and by God he will run again from Tommy Atkins and his bayonet.' There was a pause. Titch looked to the speaker sitting on his tombstone pontificating. It was the doctor. The medico drew breath and continued.

'The pity is that so many have to die in the process. Damned shame really. Blasted politicians. They never learn y'know.' He was addressing all within earshot. 'Every generation of the blighters make the same mistakes, damn it!' He snorted his disgust and turned to his neighbour, the old cavalry colonel, for support in his argument. Otto, Tom and Titch watched the two old friends become involved in yet another of their heated discussions.

The three became aware that Miss Burnet was not in her usual place. To quote Tom Higgins.

'She 'as been a sent fer.' Titch would miss the old lady. She had been good company, an amusing neighbour with her stories of The Cape and the scandals of yesteryear Broadstairs.

It was near noon when the first soldier appeared. The personage of a Company Sergeant Major of the Royal Engineers. He was dressed in khaki; no greatcoat, brasses gleaming, boots polished to a mirror shine, the creases in his battledress so sharp they seemed brittle, as if they would break rather than bend. Two medal ribbons of forgotten Indian or Afghan campaigns decorated his broad chest.

He looked a short bulldog of a man; about forty years of age, pugnacious in the extreme. Small brilliant blue eyes glittered out of his red freckled face, short clipped orange red hair showed on his thick red neck. He wore a peaked service cap set severely straight on his cropped head. A long orange red moustache bristled on his upper lip;

the ends were waxed and protruded beyond the width of his face like the antennae of a hornet. The little man strode around the open grave slapping his thigh with a swagger cane. Titch was not sure whether he was approving of its neatness or wondering if it was up to his military standards. He said not a word but suddenly turned and marched off from the direction he came. The crunch of the gravel under his boots came as a determined sound of 'Right. Let's get on with it.'

Minutes passed. The group of spirits around the open grave looked at each other. Otto Meyer shrugged his shoulders.

'Who the hell was he?' Before any could answer, there was a shout.

'H'atten ... SHUN!' The road crunched under army boots. 'Slo...pe H'ARMS!' There was the slap of hands on rifle butts. 'Rever...se H'ARMS!' Again that slapping. 'By the right, slo...w MARCH!'

Booted feet ground the gravel of the roadway to the beat of a muffled side drum. Domp!... Domp! The beat came with every crunch of gravel. There was just the sound of the drum and of slow pacing feet until they heard the crunch on the gravel of the foot-path between the graves. Along the path came the firing party of eight soldiers in double file. All in immaculate khaki. Battledresses creased, gaiters and belts freshly blancoed a bright green and brasses shining in the morning sun. Each had a rifle at reverse arms; butts shone with new varnish, steel parts brightly polished. Bare headed bearers followed, carrying a coffin draped with the Union Jack. Then came a drummer/bugler. A party of troops followed the cortege and an Army Chaplain accompanied by the same old Rector came at the rear of the procession. The clerical surplices stood out a brilliant white against the drab of the khaki. An officer resplendent with a polished Sam Browne and drawn sword in reverse headed them all. The dog-like C.S.M. brought up the rear.

'Funeral Par...ty! 'ALT!'

The little sergeant major's voice would have woken them all, dead as they were. His face changed from red to purple with each bellow. Twenty odd soldiers came to a smart halt. Titch saw 'people' on their graves looking curiously in their direction. The old colonel had drawn himself up to his full height and was standing to attention. Titch smiled when he saw the former cavalry officer holding his walking stick at the slope sabre fashion. Otto and Tom Higgins were standing stiffly to attention. The Life Boat crew just looked.

The figure hovering over the coffin was invisible to the parading soldiery but not to the audience of spirits standing and sitting close by. The new arrival was in soiled work-worn battle-dress of a Sapper of the Royal Engineers. His steel helmet was on his head at a jaunty angle and he was in need of a wash; a sharp contrast to his neat sergeant major.

The dead Sapper was gazing around in wonderment. He pushed his tin hat back on his head and looked at Titch.

''Allo ol' mate. Where this be to then? Wot be a goin' on y'ere?' He had the accent of an English west countryman though Titch could not place his exact domicile.

'I did never think as 'ow I would see me own funeral. What a fine ol' dish o'peas this be. And I be on time too. My ol' dad always aid as 'ow I be late fer me own funeral. I wish I could tell 'im 'e be wrong.' He grinned at Titch and showed a set of large very white teeth. 'And little ol' electric whiskers there a ballin' and a shoutin' enough ter wake the dead. Blow 'is bloody gasket one day 'e will 'n' no mistake.'

There were more commands from the short C.S.M. Twenty soldiers stamped their feet and turned as they were commanded 'Off...'ATS!'

Even the Sapper on his coffin removed his head gear.

'He doesn't mean you, you know. It's your party. Sit back and enjoy it.'

Titch's words made the man look at him. He was very young. Twenty perhaps. He had fair hair and a ready smile that revealed his white teeth. He was broad of shoulder and about six feet tall, though it was difficult to tell, the way he was perched on his coffin. Quite a handsome young lad, Titch thought. The sort of lad that would break many a maiden's heart before one caught and tamed him.

Six pall bearers placed the coffin on the ground over the open grave. One slipped a little in the mud and nearly fell.

'Steady 'Arry boy. You still be pissed from last night you drunken bugger you.' The newly dead sapper looked at the unfortunate man who received a piercing look from his C.S.M. Only the offender and the watching spirits heard the little man's hissed, 'Steady Wallace.'

The Army Chaplain said the appropriate words over the grave. The coffin was lowered into the ground with a muted rumbling of the single drum. The volley of shots into the Kent sky were hardly louder than Electric Whiskers' loud commands. The drummer switched from his drum to his bugle and the Last Post echoed through the church yard. A minute's pause and it was followed by the stirring Reveille. Sods of earth bounced off the coffin lid, more incantations from the chaplain and the funeral party departed, after more orders were bellowed.

The quickened beat of the drum and the crunch of forty boots at the quick march on the gravel died into the distance. Ragged words of command on the distant road dismissed the bored sappers and silence descended on the church yard again. The old sexton appeared and quietly shovelled the loose soil into the grave. Only then did any of them pay any attention to the new arrival. Surprisingly, it was Otto who opened the conversation.

'A soldier I see komraad. Infantry. Yes?'

The new arrival looked at the German pilot.

'No. A Sapper. The Royal Engineers.' He looked at the German pilot standing close to him.

'Hey. Be you that Gerry pilot us did find last year? Washed up on the beach y'ere you'm were. Right?'

Otto nodded for his answer. The sapper looked about him and continued.

'What 'appens now then? Does us all sit y'ere

like. A doin' nothin'?'

Between them they told him what they knew. They each introduced themselves and as a gesture of friendship they told briefly their own histories. It took some time, especially when the doctor got warmed up, but like Titch always says, 'Time means nothing.' The sapper accepted their comments and introduced himself.

'Sid Mathews be me name. 21st Demolition Company th'R.E.'s.' He began. 'Been y'ere since we did get 'ome from Dunkerque. Laid all they land mines along the beaches fer miles us 'ave. And that pesky barbed wire. Bloody miles on it.' He raised his head and looked into the distance as if seeing the miles of barbed wire entanglements. 'I was a checkin' one o'they land mines fer their condition. Some bloody officer at H.Q. probably thought as 'ow they needed testin'. I stood on one o'the buggers. Blew up in me face, it did. Blew I ter pieces. Not much of I in that there coffin, I can tell 'ee. I doubt they'll test any more. They works all right 'n' I be y'ere ter prove it.'

Sapper Sid Mathews talked of his unit and of the horrors of Dunkerque and the fighting in France.

''Ad to blow bridges 'n' things us did. The demo squad was us. Back with the rear guard. Bloody murder it were. Rifles against tanks. Panzers they do call 'em. And they Gerries 'ad they Tommy Guns like them there American gangsters do 'ave in the pictures I did see at 'ome. Mowed our blokes down when they did try ter get in wi' the bayonet. Like I do say, bloody murder, 'n' no mistake.' There was more in a like vein. It was Tom Higgins that asked him about his life before he joined the army.

'Lived in a little village in Somerset, I did, a workin' in the local smithy. Afore I were called up like. 'Ad an 'ankering ter be a blacksmith like me old uncle Walter. Norton-Fitzwarren th'village be. Nice little place. Just two pubs, a post office, a church, a little ol' school and some 'ouses. Me dad be the game keeper fer th'squire. Ol' General Sir Thomas Armitage. Fat Ol' Sir Tom us lads do call 'im. Liked 'is grub did the general. Spent a lot a time in India, I believe. Fat as an ol' sow in pig, 'e be.' He chuckled as he remembered. 'I be th'eldest o'ten lads. Dad wanted a cricket team, 'e allus said. Cricket, dominoes, cider and a raisin' poultry were dad's passions. Drank a lot o'cider did my ol' dad. 'E liked the ol' scrumpy. Good fer th'kidneys 'n' bladder he allus said.' The sapper grinned at the recollection.

''Ad some fine birds too 'e did. Fowls yer know. Used ter bring 'ome prizes from the Taunton Show 'e did. Every year as long as I c'n remember... No... There were one year 'e didn't. 1938 it were. 'E had a beautiful Rhode Island Red Cockerel. Caesar, dad called 'im. 'E loved that bird did dad. More than 'e did us kids I reckon... Always Rhode Islands dad 'ad. Nothin' to compare wi' them 'e reckoned. We lads used ter laugh when 'e did come 'ome and tell mum, "I 'ad the best cock in th'show, mother." Me Mum caught us a laughin' once and gave us a clip in the ear. "You've got vulgar minds 'n' dirty tongues you 'ave," she said.' Sapper Mathews was chuck-

301

ling at the memory of it all.

'Any road, as I was sayin', Dad 'ad this 'ere cockerel. A beauty it were. Stood nearly a yard 'igh when 'e did crow. Raised it from a chick 'e 'ad. Me ol' dad reckoned it were a matter of breedin' 'n' feedin'. Well, 'e bred 'em, and old Sir Tom did feed 'em, though a course the old General never knowed that. Wheat, corn, and raisins dad's chicks 'ad. Better than 'e fed the General's pheasants.' He paused as the memory returned.

'It were a month afore the Taunton Show, I do remember. We was 'aving a bit a trouble wi' foxes a comin' and taking the fowls at night. Well, me ol' dad 'e slept wi a loaded shot gun under the bed and many a night 'e did get up when 'e thought as 'ow a fox were about.' Laughter was beginning to get a hold of the speaker; he had to stop again for a moment.

'Now my ol' dad allus went ter bed naked. 'E claimed as 'ow night shirts were unhealthy. Stopped air from getting' ter vital parts 'e said. Made mum do it too.' The sapper was shaking with laughter. 'Tryin' fer the eleventh man fer 'is cricket team us older lads said among ourselves. Any road.' He lost control for a moment. He slapped his thigh and wiped a laughter tear from his eye.

'Thus y'ere morning, must 'ave been about five. Just a gettin' light it were. An' cold fer May it were. Any road, we all 'ears a squawkin' and a rumpusin in the chicken house. Dad leaps out a bed and grabs 'is ol' shot gun and rushes out the back and sees a dog fox a chasin' 'is prize

302

cockerel Caesar. Me brother Jim and me follers and we sees dad a bring 'is ol' gun to 'is shoulder. Jim and me's a watchin' 'n' sees ol' Bess, dad's Springer Spaniel crawl out a her ol' kennel. She comes up be'ind ol' dad and puts 'er cold nose right up 'is arse. Gave dad a fright I can tell 'ee. 'E near leapt a yard. Th' gun went off, both barrels.' The west country sapper had to stop as laughter took a hold of him again. He pulled himself together after a minute and continued.

'When the smoke did clear 'n' ol' dad recovers from the shock of ol' Bess' nose up 'is bum, we sees the ol' dog fox a trottin' through the trees and dad's prize cockerel kicking 'is last in the mud o' the chicken run. Poor ol' dad. 'E near cried. Like I said, 'e raised that bird from a chick. Follered 'im around the garden, it did. Just like ol' Bess.' There was pause as the laughter from the listeners subsided. Even the old doctor chuckled at the story. Sid Mathews took up the thread of the yard again.'

'Mum dressed out that ol' bird. Weighed nine pounds it did. Looked well all trussed up ready fer th'oven. We 'ad it fer Sunday dinner. Twelve on us sat down and polished it off. Even ol' dad enjoyed it. "Ain't never seen a cock dressed up so well mother," he said. Jim an' me nearly busted our sides a laughin'. Got another clip in the ear from mum fer that we did. 'Andy wiv 'er ol' 'and, is mum. Quick as lightin' she is.'

Titch could see that there would never be a dull moment with Sapper Sid Mathews as a neighbour.

Weeks passed, the war progressed. The country-side around Binbrook began to take on a winter cloak. Another ten 'Ops' were completed by the crew of PH 'C' Charlie without an incident of any significance. There had been several more to the Ruhr – another to the dreaded Essen, and one each to Cuxhaven and Brest when they tried unsuccessfully to sink the German battle cruisers 'Scharnhorst' and 'Gneisenau' and got several holes in the kite for their pains. They had one 'Op' to go, number thirty, and they were scared.

Mary and Titch were drawn closer to each other during this time. As she had hoped that night after their frantic love making, they had fallen in love. They went on leave together to stay with her widower father in Rochdale. Titch had never been to Lancashire so was interested. He had seen it from the air, but had never been to any of the little cotton towns that dotted the county.

He was disappointed. Titch thought the town of Rochdale a dreary little place. Tall mill chimneys dotted the landscape, terraced houses of the mill workers were a sad collection of buildings set in cobbled streets, the whole, soot-grimed and depressing. Mary's father lived in the mill manager's house of 'Tettly Mill' on the outskirts of the town – one of the better houses – convenient to the moors above the town and it was larger than most. It was on the moors where Mary and Titch spent most of their time. They walked the heather and picked bilberries in the cold sunshine of the high land. They picnicked and one afternoon sheltered in an old abandoned hermit's cave during a thunder storm.

The rain had taken them by surprise and they were soaked before they could get to shelter. Titch made a fire from a litter of dead bracken and gorse and they stripped and dried their clothes. Seeing Mary naked in the firelight, Titch could not resist drawing her to him and stroking the soft flesh of her back as she stood to arrange her clothes near the blaze. He saw her figure silhouetted on the wall of the cave. Her breasts stood proud; the roundness of her buttocks excited him. It was as if his lips and hands were guided. Titch found her breasts with his lips and the soft warm fold of her thighs with his hands. They sank beside the fire and made love.

The firelight threw shadows on the walls of the cave as they strove to possess each other in their frenzy. Limbs waved and twisted throwing images that danced in the flicker of the flames' reflection. Passions spent, they lay on damp clothes, exhausted and allowed hands and lips to do what they would.

If Mary's old father knew they shared the same bed from that day, he did not mention it. Mary and Titch loved as they were sure no other lovers had ever loved. Theirs, they were sure, was the purest, most loving love making that ever had been. They were convinced they were making love making history. For five glorious days and nights they revelled in the glow of each other – until they had to return to the war.

One operation to go. It seemed they were doomed not to make it. Three times PH 'C' Charlie's crew

305

were briefed for a raid on Dortmund. Three times it was scrubbed. Three times, six set of nerves were built up to breaking point at the thought of 'the last one'; three times they had to let down. The third occasion the aircraft had got as far as the runway ready for take off; a white flare fired from the control tower cancelled everything. Everything except the fact that they had all taken their caffeine tablets and were wide awake and ready to go. They were wide awake all night.

The night was spent talking, reading and trying to sleep. Titch read a complete novel from midnight to four in the morning when at last his eyelids drooped and he was able to sleep.

Wellington PH 'C' was called into the hanger the following morning, for modification. The crew all wondered what it could be and wandered into the hanger after lunch. Titch walked around to his turret and saw there was nothing new there. It was when he got into the fuselage he saw things were different. A large hole had been cut in the floor of the plane. The crew were nonplussed and the ground crew could not help. Titch volunteered the idea that it was a new type of toilet. It was no joke. Something was in the wind and the crew had a feeling they were involved.

There was no battle order next day but the message over the tannoy was that Flight Sergeant Gale and crew were to report to the Squadron's O.C. It was then they were told they were going on their 'Last One' that night, on their own.

'Get your kite ready. Air test it. Briefing at 1800 hours. This is a high security job so not a word.' The Wingco's words were short and to the point.

'Like a coster monger's donkey's gallop. Short and bloody sweet,' was how Roy described the interview.

Titch was unable to see Mary to cancel their meeting for that evening. He knew she would understand when she heard he was flying. Titch saw her just before the briefing and was able to touch her hand as he walked past into the Intelligence Officer's map room. Just the one crew, 'C' Charlie, were detailed for flying; the usual briefing room was too large for such a small group.

They really were to be on their own. Their job was to fly low over the sea to Southern France to drop four agents in the region of Bordeaux. It was to be low level flying all the way from base and all the way back. Seven hours flying time. Low flying? Low enough to be below the German radar, that meant very low. A full moon would help them. There were no other operations planned with the night being so bright.

It was Keith and Roy that the briefing was for. The rest of the crew were just passengers, unless something went wrong. Titch's fear was they would have the Luftwaffe to themselves. Not a happy thought. This was going to be their 'last one', one way or another.

The crew were standing around the rear turret, as was customary, draining their bladders. Urine mixed with the muddy puddle on the concrete dispersal. Operational piss' they called them; seven hours before the next opportunity was a long time.

Titch saw the closed vehicle draw up; he hoped it was Mary come for a goodbye. She knew it was to be their last and he was sure she wanted to wish them luck. It wasn't Mary. Four figures got out and walked towards the aircraft. Titch saw by their profiles against the light sky that one was a girl, her hair waved for a moment in the light breeze before she pulled a woollen cap over it. One of the three men was talking in rapid French. He dropped something that sounded metallic and switched on a hand torch to recover it. The stooped to help find it. Titch saw in the torch's light it was Patricia Tilson.

Titch Wilkins was shocked. He could never forget her, but to see her like this, knowing she was a British agent about to be dropped into France set his mind whirling and his heart racing. After a moment he walked casually over to them. The two were searching for whatever had been dropped. As Titch got close the man found the article and made a remark in French. Patricia stood and saw Titch.

It was impossible for her to recognize him. It was a light starlit night, the moon had not risen but Titch was in flying clothing and she would not have expected to see him.

'Hello Pat. How have you been?' Titch's voice sounded flat. His throat was dry and he was shaking.

'Do I know you?... Who are you?' She sounded alarmed.

'Rupert. Rupert Wilkins. Remember?'

Titch heard her catch her breath; it was sucked in with a soft hiss.

'Rupert. Oh dear God. Of all the times to meet with you again.'

'I waited for your letter. And I left a note with your char lady. Did you ever get it?'

'Yes Rupert, but I am involved in all this and I must be free. I am sorry my dear. I thought that perhaps when it was all over I would find you and...?' There was a question in her voice. Titch struggled for words.

'Is this what you meant when you said you worked for the War Office?'

'Yes. I could not tell you more.'

Her voice was little more than a whisper. The man who had done all the talking approached.

'Best get aboard, Cherry,' he said in English.

'Cherry?' The reargunner gasped the name in disbelief.

'It is my code name Rupert. And my call sign. Cherry Ripe. No one must ever know my real name until all this madness is over.' Pat Tilson looked at her erstwhile lover. There was a break in her voice as she said, 'I must go. Goodbye Rupert. Good luck dearest.' On an impulse she reached out and touched Titch's hand then turned abruptly and followed the three men into the fuselage.

'Goodbye Pat. Good luck,' he called to her. For a reason Titch could not explain he added, 'God bless you.'

Pat Tilson, code name Cherry Ripe, turned and looked at Titch Wilkins. Her face was in shadow so he did not see the tears forming.

'God bless you too Rupert.'

Pat ducked her head and got into the plane. Titch went to the tail of the Wellington. With his wireless operator's help he clambered into his turret and slid the turret doors half closed behind him. It was like closing away another life.

All else was blotted from Titch's mind as they took off. 'C' Charlie headed for the dropping zone, keeping low and well out to sea on a course south west, to miss Brest, then south east keeping low all the way about twenty miles from the French coast. It was extreme range for a Wellington, an extra fuel tank was stowed in the bomb bay.

The English Channel appeared as the moon was rising. Titch watched England recede rapidly in the darkness. The moon rose higher as they got into the Atlantic twenty miles off Brest. It rose in a great red ball and rapidly changed colour to a brilliant silver; the ocean was a sheet of burnished pewter as far as Titch could see. The Wellington was low and the sea was close. Titch had never flown so low for so long. Keith handled old 'C' Charlie superbly. The water looked benign as they skimmed the waves. It looked calm too. Titch was glad of that; he could not swim.

'Surely it would be easier for me in a calm sea.' The thought was reassuring to the non-swimmer. As a precaution he blew two long breaths into his Mae West – it made it a little bulky but he felt happier. The water looked benign enough, it looked deep too.

'You OK Titch?'

'Never better.' Titch lied.

'Roy?'

'Fine Keith.'

'Short Arse?'

'Great.'

Keith called up the crew to check all was well. He called up their passengers. Titch's heart leapt when he heard Pat answer that she was fine.

Titch wondered about his feelings and about Mary – until he pushed everything from his mind with Tiny Willis' report over the intercom.

'Ship dead ahead.' There was a pause of perhaps two seconds. 'Shit! They are firing at us. It's a bloody E boat.'

A stream of tracer passed over the top of the Wimpy. It was way out; the seamen gunners were unable to depress their gun. The Wellington skimmed over the vessel at mast height and Titch was ready. The plane rushed over the boat's deck; he fired as soon as his sight came to bear. Four Browning machine guns spewed tracer into the ship and no fire was returned. Titch gave it a second burst before they were out of range.

'You OK Titch?'

'Fine Keith. Just gave a couple a'squirts to keep their heads down. Might cure their constipation.'

'Well done. Keep your eyes peeled and look into the moon. Fighters could come at us from there. And that E boat may radio a warning to the mainland.'

'Your wish is my command, Oh Genie of the sky!'

It was bravado. It said nothing of the looseness of Titch's bowel, the dryness of his mouth or the dread in his mind.

Nothing else happened the whole way in, over the dropping zone or on the way home. The plane climbed to two thousand feet for the drop and Titch reported that all four parachutes had opened. As they disappeared, Titch wondered which one was Patricia Tilson or Cherry Ripe. He wondered what her work involved. Her work, whatever it was, made his war look so simple. He got into his turret and hoped he would step out of it after a raid, then it was peace and quiet until the next 'Op'. Hers? Titch imagined she would be on guard all the time; expecting treachery and arrest and...? Titch refused to think beyond that. Poor Pat and what about the others?

They had the usual 'screening' party the next night and went on leave for ten days before joining their new postings. Keith, Roy and Titch were going to an Operational Training Unit in the midlands of England. The rest of the crew to Lossiemouth in the north of Scotland. What for? They never discovered. They all promised to write, but never did.

Chapter Twelve

Life for Keith and Titch at Number 30 Operational Training Unit, Hixon in the county of Staffordshire, settled to a dreary round of instructing one course of starry eyed pupils after another. Titch's task was to instruct on gun turrets in 'The Flannel Factory' – the class-room complex of the training unit. He saw airgunners for a period of three weeks, teaching them the workings and operation of new four gun hydraulic gun turrets coming through to squadrons. From

312

there students went onto flying training; that was the last he saw of them other than a nod and a word in the sergeants' mess. Gone was the old camaraderie of squadron life. Gone also was the fear that operational flying engendered. Titch should have been happy with his lot; grateful that he wasn't shot at night after night, that he slept each night between clean sheets with a reasonable certainty of being alive the next day. He should have been grateful, but he wasn't. He felt impotent; he felt time and the war passing him by.

Keith felt much the same as his erstwhile reargunner. He was attached to the Flying Training Flight and spent his days teaching new pilots to land and take off in the old Wimpies; the work horses of the unit. He and Titch would meet in the sergeants' mess at the end of the day and spend a lot of off duty time together. They each bought a bicycle and cycled around the county visiting old pubs, castles, ancestral stately homes and churches, in that order when the weather allowed. And of course, they talked.

Keith told Titch his hopes for the future.

'I may go in for law. I spent my screening leave with my Uncle Charles. He is a barrister in the Canterbury circuit. We had a long talk and he has promised to help me if I choose to follow his advice and go to Cambridge after the war.' He paused. 'Then again the church attracts me. Father is keen that I take Orders with the Anglicans after Cambridge. So, whatever, I intend to apply for Cambridge as soon as the war is over. I'll see what develops from there on. Shawri A'Mungoo, so to speak.'

'Shawri A'Mungoo? What the hell is that?'

Keith laughed. 'It's Ki-Swahili. It means, "I will leave it to God."'

Titch looked at his old friend. He was not surprised at his choice of vocation, or his words, though they puzzled him. His old skipper as a lawyer or a priest? It sounded great. He would be good at either but Titch had a question.

'But Keith. The war? Bombing and killing? How does that all tie in with Christianity?' Their eyes met. Titch could see his pilot was puzzled. 'Frankly I don't know Rupert. All the Churches tell me this is a "just war" – whatever they mean by that. I worry about it sometimes. And I always pray.'

'Pray?' Titch laughed. 'I have seen you praying. You only take a minute. That can't be much of a prayer.'

Titch had indeed seen Keith pray many a night, and in the mornings when they got back from a raid. It never took him long. He laughed his short laugh. Keith looked at his comrade.

'At night prayers are easy. I feel God knows what I need. What I want. And what I am thankful for. I simply say "Thank you... Please ... and Forgive Me." He knows I mean thank you for the gift of life and for all the earthly things I enjoy. And for all the gifts and joys I experience in myself and in others. I say "Please". Please for all the things I feel He knows I need and want. Please to take care of my family and friends. Please for... Oh lots of things that would take me all night to say. And I pray for forgiveness for all the wrongs I have done. That's why I take so little time. You see, I feel He KNOWS. I would fall asleep before I finished most nights. He knows that too and I am sure He understands.' Keith looked at Titch. 'You don't see me pray before we leave on an Op do you?' That was true. Titch had never seen him pray then.

'Do you?'

They were resting in a little pub after a long ride in the country and hard ride up a hill. It was a warm early spring day and they were hot and thirsty. Two half pint pots were nearly empty and crusts of bread and the rind of cheese littered their plates on the table in the orchard behind the pub. They had enjoyed the morning visiting an old castle; the cycle ride through leafy lanes where the beeches were a brilliant green and the road sides a russet brown from autumn's fallen leaves had left them in a silent wonder at the beauty of England. Keith took a sip of his ale and continued.

'Oh yes. I prayed then. More than ever as we progressed through the tour.' He laughed again, 'and of course, you are curious to know what I said?'

Titch nodded. The pilot looked at Titch directly for a moment, then his eyes looked into the distance.

'I prayed for wisdom ... for courage ... for strength ... and for forgiveness.' Keith drew the words out; he saw Titch's puzzled look and laughed a nervous laugh yet again.

'I prayed for wisdom to make the right decisions. For the courage and strength to carry them through.' He paused for a moment and

315

looked into the distance again. 'And forgiveness if I was doing wrong or if I made mistakes and people suffered through them.'

'Us, you mean? The crew?'

'Yes of course. And the enemy.' He paused for a moment as if to collect his thoughts. 'You see Rupert I am not entirely convinced it is a just war. I wonder how much is the fault of politicians and the establishment. And what could have been done to avoid it all. There are faults on both sides. Even the Churches. Theirs and ours. The Germans pray to the same God you know.' Keith paused as a thought struck him. 'A Great War soldier wrote a poem in the trenches,' he continued quietly. 'A chap named Squires. He caused a bit of a stir at the time, I believe. The poem went like this.

"God heard the warring nations shout.
'God strafe England. God save the King
God this, God that, God everything.'
'My God,' said God. 'I've got my work cut out.'"

The pilot paused as if expecting Titch to say something, but the reargunner was speechless. Keith took hold of his glass and drained it. The banging of the empty tankard on the rustic table brought Titch back from his thoughts. Keith looked at him.

'There are so many questions unanswered. The only thing I feel consoled about is that Hitler must be stopped. Of that I am sure. And that Fascism is not the answer to mankind's problems.' He

316

laughed again. 'But neither is Communism. And democratic capitalism has a lot to answer for. Meanwhile it is the little people of the world who suffer and die for the whims and ambitions of the greedy and the powerful. Or the would-be powerful.' He added the last with a smile.

It was all very perplexing to a slum boy – brought up as he was to gather hungrily grains of kindness and intelligence that fell within his reach; like a dirty London sparrow pecking at crumbs in the dirt. But Titch believed he understood. From that day he followed Keith's example, and felt better for it.

Days passed into weeks; weeks into months. The war dragged on. Titch's daily letters to and from Mary were the highlight of his day. What they were unable to say to each other with their lips, they did with a pen. Titch even composed a verse or two of poetry for her, but they missed each other.

It was winter – January 1942 – the Atlantic Charter signed the previous August between Winston Churchill and President F.D. Roosevelt began to take effect. The U.S. was at war with Japan and committed to the war in Europe as well as the Pacific. Armadas of ships and planes were crossing the Atlantic to the British Isles. U.S. aircraft were seen over England in greater numbers – some with the roundel of the R.A.F. – more often as the months went by with the star marking of the U.S. 8th Army Air Corps.

Hitler's Eastern Front army in Russia was bogged down by the severe winter weather. Nazi occupation of the whole of Western Europe was complete. The Afrika Corps was in retreat in North Africa; American and Royal Navy ships and aircraft were winning The Battle of the Atlantic and the R.A.F. was stepping up the bomber offensive.

Keith and Titch should had been satisfied that they were training crews to take part in this offensive but they were not. They felt frustrated with their roles as instructors, and Titch missed Mary.

Through Mary's letters Titch heard the squadron news; the good and the bad. It was sad to hear of an old comrade who was reported 'missing, believed killed.' Conversely, Titch was happy to hear when a crew they had known had survived their tour.

Mary and Titch decided to marry as soon as the war was over. They wrote long and often about it and decided that peace bells would be their wedding bells. Neither wanted Mary to be made a widow a second time.

Spring 1942 came in a flood of colour and splendour. Wild flowers, bursting leaf buds and warmer weather made for a wonderful time. Mary and Titch were on leave together in North Wales. Lake Vyrnwy is a delightful place. The lake, reservoir really, is situated in a cleft in the mountains, surrounded by farmland and forests. The lovers walked the twelve miles round the lake. They cycled round it on borrowed bicycles. They rode around it on frisky Welsh mountain ponies. On the only calm day they had, they rowed a hired boat to the end and back.

There were always two stops along the way. The first at the farm of William Evans 'Top' – on the way home at the farm of William Evans 'Bottom'. Each farm at the top and bottom ends of the lake. At each place they would have a meal of home cured ham and farm eggs. Farm baked rough wholemeal bread, thickly spread with home made butter filled the corners of hungry stomachs. The whole washed down with milk straight from the cow's udder.

They made love in the heather above the tree line and lay afterwards in the sun and watched an eagle soaring in a thermal pocket hundreds of feet above them. They watched new born lambs gambol in the brilliant green of the mountain pastures. One memorable evening they walked to the village of Llanwddyn. They drank beer around the log fire and heard forest workers singing in the public bar. Their modest half pints of bitter went flat as they listened. Not a word was said for the hour they sang the plaintive songs of their mountain heritage.

The lovers' thoughts on the way back to their hotel were of the morrow when they had to return to the war. Neither of them spoke for the whole four miles. It was dark, a cold wind was blowing. Mary had her head tucked inside Titch's great coat wrapped around her. They trudged up the mountain road.

'Shout if you want me,' were her only words before she buried her head in his shoulder. He did not disturb her. Their love making that night had an urgency amounting to desperation. Mary's pillow was wet with tears; she wept for all the lovers the war robbed of love.

May 31st 1942. For days there had been unusual activity on the unit. Some of the Wellingtons were withdrawn from the training programme and submitted to severe maintenance checks. Aircrew instructors were crewed in pairs – each pair appointed to more senior pupil crews.

Keith was to be the pilot of a Canadian crew; Titch was the reargunner. It was obvious they were all to fly an 'Op' when a Battle Order was placed on the mess bulletin boards. There were eight crews of seven – five pupils and two experienced instructors of one category or another in each plane. Roy was flying as a navigator with a crew with an experienced pilot as Captain. Briefing was at 1830 hours.

The exercise was out of character for an Operational Training Unit. Titch had a feeling things were going to go wrong even though they all believed it was going to be a 'Nickel', code name for a leaflet dropping raid, usually over France or Belgium. These were generally done by each crew as a 'finalis' to their training before they left for a squadron. As a rule they went on their own – tonight they were taking their instructors with them. When Titch saw they were carrying bombs instead of paper, speculation and apprehension soared.

It was to be the R.A.F's first 'Thousand Bomber Raid' – target Cologne. The crews were all dumbfounded. Titch had never known a briefing so quiet. Crews just sat, most smoked cigarette after cigarette. Some bit their nails or chewed knuckles; others frantically chewed gum. It was all gut wrenching and heavy with foreboding.

One thousand bombers? Unbelievable. Did the R.A.F. have that many? Even to the experienced instructors it seemed impossible. Bomber Command squadrons were reinforced by aircraft from Operational Training Units. Even Training Command Units were asked to contribute. Old Wellingtons, Whitleys even Hampdens were pulled into service.

Keith and Titch looked at each other; the pilot winked.

'Going to be a whopper tonight Rupert. The shape of things to come I believe.' He paused and looked at his reargunner. 'We are lucky. We have another "C" Charley.'

'Yup. The kite's okay. But there isn't an R in the month. I don't like surprises when there isn't an R in the month. Plays hell with my water.'

Titch didn't know what made him say it. Bravado? He didn't feel brave. It raised a nervous laugh from the Canadians; the gunner concentrated on the briefing.

One thousand bombers over the target all to bomb within thirty minutes. COLLISION! The word flashed a neon sign to Titch's brain. It was his first thought when 'Wingco' broke the news. Collision over the target would be as greater danger as flak and fighters. He kept his fears to himself but wished he had some gum to chew like his neighbours; the Canadians' jaws were working like chaffing machines.

Take off was straight forward. Keith had enough experience to do it with his eyes shut, though

Titch was praying he had them open; he hated take offs. A fault with the power and it was a hairy landing; with bombs aboard there was little hope of walking away. He had his turret to beam and the doors open for a quick get away. Better to be thrown clear and break your neck than fry slowly as the plane burned. He remembered a Wellington burning at Binbrook – the rear gunner was the only casualty; trapped in his turret and incinerated.

'C' Charley began to wave 04° east. Up and down, port to starboard, starboard to port. Fifteen seconds this way, fifteen seconds the other. Nauseating. The crew were air sick; Titch's gut turned itself inside out.

'You OK Titch?'

The old question felt good to hear, like old times.

'Only fair Keith. I have lost my sea legs.'

'Stick it out fellar. The first hour is the worst. You OK Wireless Operator?'

'I guess so. Now.' He paused for a moment. 'I felt a little hairy thing in my throat and swallowed just in time. I nearly threw up my anus.'

The man's humour was not lost on the rest of the crew. They were a cheerful bunch; they would make a good team.

'Bombaimer. You OK?'

'Ditto my buddy. My Mom's fruit cake is spread over Holland.'

The navigator and the young Canadian pilot were the only ones immune from air sickness.

'Target five minutes skipper. Course out of the target 355° for four minutes then 088° until the first dog leg. OK?'

'Roger. And thank you.'

The old Wimpy's two Hercules engines purred power. Titch moved his turret from right to left and left to right; searching, searching. Looking for a dangerously close friend as much as for a hostile enemy. His eyes ached, his gut churned and he was cold. Pure oxygen puffed gently into his mask and he breathed deep. One barley sugar sweet followed another – each one popped into his mouth as soon as one was sucked away. The sweets were frozen; he rolled them in his mouth before sucking seriously.

'Searchlights ahead... Shit!'

The Wellington bucked like a frightened filly as several flak shells burst around them. They were flashless 88mm shells. Invisible and deadly.

'What the hell was that?' It was the bombaimer.

'Flak. Look out for the aiming point markers.' Keith's command had a steadying effect on the novice crew. Titch smiled into his oxygen mask, Keith is on the ball was his thought.

'Markers dead ahead.' The bombaimer had control of himself. Titch found he was singing. Crazy? Like whistling in the dark. Between verses he thought of Mary, of Judy and oddly of Patricia Tilson. What was she doing down there in the south of France. Why had Judy to die the way she did? And he thanked God for Mary.

The seconds ticked by and incidents of his life would come into his mind. It always happened. Thoughts ran amuck as he sang songs with the most unlikely lyrics; love songs, hymns, ditties and bawdy ballads. They tumbled from his lips in a flood of escaping fear. Marooned in the tail and his mike on 'off' no one could hear him.

He was once asked by a B.B.C. reporter, 'I say.' He was a rather fat balding man, Titch remembered. 'What do you reargunner chaps do back there by yourselves?'

'Oh,' said the sergeant nonchalantly, 'sometimes I sits and thinks. And sometimes I just sits.' It was a flippant answer that covered the fear, the cold, the loneliness and discomfort; but that was about the strength of it.

'I say. Really? Is that all?'

Titch looked at the butterball of a man; the journalist was not convinced. 'What the hell do you think I do?' was Titch's thought. What he said was, 'Between shooting down nightfighers I masturbate.'

'Good God.' The reporter pursed his lips in distaste and walked away shaking his head.

It was mischief on the reargunner's part but what could he say without sounding dramatic? It was each man to his own and difficult to recall all of one's own thoughts. Suffice to say that they were varied, speaking for himself anyway, but loss of concentration could be fatal.

'C' Charley's intercom crackled with life.

'Kite shot down dead ahead skip. Jeese!... Poor bastards.' The sky was lit up with the explosion of the aircraft's bombs.

'Cut out the natter.' Keith's command was like a whip lash. The bombaimer did not reply. A minute passed – flak was exploding all around them. 'C' Charley reared and banked; seconds were like hours.

'Bomb doors open.' Keith brought the aircraft on a straight and level course. They were on the bombing run. Titch's nerves were at breaking point. He hated those words.

'Roger.' Keith's voice was like a balm.

'Bomb doors open.' The second pilot was doing his stuff.

Titch wasn't smiling. 'Bomb doors open.' Why do those words always threaten to panic him? Thirty one times he had heard them now; will he never get used to it? That same loose feeling in his bowel – the same dryness in the mouth, the sword-like icicles lunge into his head and the cold surge through his veins; the racing heartbeat as adrenalin pumped to muscles. Fight or flight! Titch had read was the purpose of it all. There was nowhere to run. How could he fight against unseen guns, fired by unseen men, firing at unseen targets. Titch felt the target was him, not the plane, just him. And now the spectre of collision raised its ugly head.

Wellington 'C' Charley bucked and reared like a nervous horse; shells burst around them. A Whitley was coned by a dozen searchlights astern. The ungainly plane twisted and turned to extricate itself from the web of lights. Flak shells burst around it; tracer tore into it. Titch watched aghast – its twin fin and rudder fell away from the fuselage and the plane spun out of control into the ground to explode with a blinding flash of fire. Only one parachute blossomed in its wake. Titch watched fascinated. As the chute fell, light flak tore into it. The silk crumbled. Chute and man 'candled' into the fires raging on the ground.

A Wellington exploded on their beam, then another above and astern of them. This was hell. Was it flak? Fighters? Or collision? Titch wrenched his eyes away from the fiery scene and looked for what he could not see. A fighter? Or perhaps a more deadly peril as they approached the aiming point; an all too close friend.

'Left, left!' The bombaimer's Canadian drawl came through the wires of the intercom. 'Right... Steady... Steady.' Titch saw a Wellington closing in on them. 'Left, left.' There was a pause.

'Drop the bloody bombs!' The words screamed silently into Titch's oxygen mask. The Wimpy was very close and above them; Titch saw his bomb doors open.

'Steady... Steady...' The Canadian drawl was infuriating.

'Drop those bloody bombs you bastard! This is no training run.' Titch's voice screamed into a dead mike. He knew better than interrupt the bombing run.

'Bombs gone!' There was a moment's pause. 'OK Skipper. Let's blow this fuckin' joint.' Titch looked aghast at the Wellington above him. The masked face of the bombaimer was very close.

'DIVE STARBOARD GO!'

As they dropped out of the sky in a diving turn Titch saw a shower of incendiaries falling from the errant Wellington. They fell like bundles of kindling wood, hundreds of them; large and small. Three large bombs missed them by a few feet. Dozens of incendiaries peppered 'C' Charley. Hundreds ricocheted off the tight skin; others penetrated linen fabric. Titch felt a jarring of the airframe and a faltering of the engine.

Keith pulled the plane out of the dive; they were flying straight and level; there was a different tone in the engines. Titch had his turret on the beam; he saw flames in the fuselage! Some incendiaries had broken through the linen fabric, they had exploded and were burning.

'Christ! Keith the fuselage is on fire.' Titch's voice was near panic.

'Wireless Operator, Bombaimer, get back there with the extinguishers.' Keith could have been ordering a second cup of tea in the mess. His voice gave not a sign of urgency. The old Wellington was flying but it sounded rough.

'You OK?' Keith looked at the second pilot as he spoke. There was no reply. The young Canadian was slumped forward over the dual controls unconscious.

'Navigator. Look at the second pilot, will you? I believe he has bought a packet. There is a hole in the canopy right above him. Better hurry.' Titch had his turret to the port side. He stretched his neck to see what was happening. The fires in the fuselage were out; the port engine was feathered, his turret was lifeless in his hands and still the flak was coming at them. Arcs of fire swept the sky, searchlights reached like tentacles of a giant marine creature, weaving and feeling for them. 'C' Charley had lost height; a combination of loss of power and that dive to starboard. The turret controls were dead. The hydraulic motor that operated the turret was powered by the feathered engine.

It was over at last. The flak eased as they left the

target area. A searchlight felt for them but gave up. Fighters were now their danger. Most aircraft were shot down on the way home, but Titch's guns were useless.

'You OK Titch?'

'Only just Keith. My turret's stuffed.'

'Keep smiling old friend. The port engine has had it. The second pilot is wounded. I think an incendiary hit him. We have the fire in the fuselage under control. So everything in the garden is blooming.'

'Blooming bloody awful if you ask me. My turret is dead. I am useless back here.'

'Courage little man. Keep your eyes peeled and trust your old uncle Keith.'

Titch knew from old it was Keith's way, to make light of adversity; he settled down to his search, feeling better. Better, but not safe – it was hardly that, not yet but Titch believed the worst was over. If they were not attacked by a fighter Titch knew Keith could make it to England.

There was another scare when the navigator found the unexploded incendiary that had struck the second pilot. The Canadian sergeant pilot had a serious head wound. All were relieved when the navigator reported that he had thrown the dud four pound incendiary out of a hole in the fuselage.

Cologne burned as the bomber stream drew away from the target. One thousand bombers had spread a carpet of flame over the city. Titch saw it from miles away as they droned their way home.

The English coast, when they crossed it, never

looked better. Black and grim-looking though it was. Blacker than the sea that beat against the shore but welcoming; it was home. Keith made an emergency landing in Suffolk. The second pilot was rushed to hospital unconscious. Six subdued aircrew licked their wounds and blessed their luck. All agreed it had been a rough night.

'C' Charley was a wreck. It had a thirty pound unexploded incendiary jammed in the starboard wing. Most of the fabric in the centre section of the plane, aft of the bomb bay, was burned away. Luckily, the burning incendiaries had fallen through the holes they burned so it was easy to extinguish the burning cloth. The port engine had received a direct hit from something that had bent the airscrew and wrecked the engine. Keith believed it was a five hundred pound bomb. He was sure he saw one pass close. A flight sergeant fitter opined that the old Wimpy would never fly again.

'Good only fer scrap she is. Been a good kite in its day. Bloody marvellous you brought her home at all skip.'

He was right. Keith had done a wonderful piece of flying, coaxing that wreck of a plane along the way he did – and single handed.

The second pilot died on his way to hospital; a fractured skull the report said. There were other losses from the Unit, Roy Ellis among them. Poor Roy. His mother had just died and he was to be married in a month. Another old comrade 'bought it', 'got the chop', 'gone for a burton', 'gone for shit'. Phrases that fitted the mood or the vocabulary of the speaker. The oft-sounded phrases repeated themselves in the reargunner's mind. Titch wondered if it was flak or a collision that had killed him; at least he knew Roy was not in that Whitley.

Back at the Unit, Keith's promotion to Warrant Officer came through, backdated six months. Why? A bureaucratic bungle? There was no explanation given then or later. They continued in the dreary round of training with resignation. In mid June, Keith was awarded the Distinguished Flying Cross for his magnificent effort over Cologne. The citation spoke of courage and dedication to duty; it was all an understatement. No words could tell of the effort it called for. Five men owed their lives to Keith. Titch pondered, if ever there was material for a Victoria Cross, Keith Gale is it. But whoever took notice of a sub-human reargunner? Titch smiled grimly and ordered another half pint to wet Keith's medal ribbon.

Months went by. Keith and Titch knew they would be recalled for a second tour at any time and talked of volunteering before they were ordered back to operational flying; perhaps they could choose a crew and their own squadron? There were a lot of Australians coming through the Unit. Noisy lads, with loud voices and dark blue uniforms but keen to get onto squadrons. A Wellington crashed on the air field; an all Australian crew lost their pilot and reargunner in the fire that burnt the Wimpy to pools of molten aluminium. It was Leo Lewis, the tall navigator of the crew that approached Keith and Titch in the sergeants' mess.

'Stiff shit losing old "Bluey" Randle. A bonzer bloke Bluey. Bloody good pilot. And "Tiger" Catlin, our reargunner.'The navigator swallowed. "Ad a beaut Sheila back 'ome did Tiger. Got married just before we left Aussie.' The tall thin Australian had a full pint of beer in his hand and was about to take a swill of it. 'We called 'im "Tiger" 'cos 'e flattened three cops in a fight at the Cross before we left Sydney. Fought like a bloody tiger 'e did. Only a little bloke too.'

'Yes. I remember him.'

And Titch did. He was a good gunner; pugnacious and aggressive.

'Do yer now? But you wouldn't 'ave seen 'im fighting. Some experience that was. I'll never ferget that fight outside that pub in the Cross. Better than the flicks it was. Made Errol Flynn look like a bloody poofta.' He took a long pull at his beer.

"Ere. You blokes drinkin'?'They were, but were on their usual half pints. 'Let me buy yer both a man's size grog.' He went to the bar and returned with two brimming pint tankards. 'Get the other side a these bastards. Cheers.'

The three raised their glasses.

'You jokers ready fer another tour? 'Eard you were expectin' ter be recalled.' He took a pull at the drink in his hand. He eyed them uncertainly as he lowered the glass. 'What about joining up with us?' He paused and looked from Keith to Titch, then back to Keith. 'We're all Aussies but we like Poms. Well, some of the bastards. I've talked it over with the mob and they're keen.'

331

The words came out with a rush as if he had rehearsed them. He continued when he saw they were listening.

'We want to get with 460 Aussie Squadron. They're in Lincolnshire some place. Binbrook. Ever 'eard of it?'

Keith and Titch exchanged looks. Leo saw this as a sign, perhaps of them weakening to his proposal. He took heart and added, 'a mate a mine is there already. Reckons it's a bonzer joint.'

It was that that convinced them. They applied for a posting to 'Operational Duties' and with the Wing Commander Flying's connivance, Keith and Titch found themselves captain and reargunner of an Australian crew; they were all N.C.O.'s and that suited them all.

The Australians' rough exteriors concealed hearts of gold and an enthusiasm of operational flying that the two Englishmen found embarrassing. They could not hear enough about squadron life and operational flying. They wanted to know about their tours on Defiants and Wellingtons; even their abortive adventure in France came in for examination and the appropriate lurid expletives.

An initial posting to Heavy Conversion Unit, a few rounds of the hostelries of the city of Doncaster preceded the crew's arrival at Royal Airforce Station Binbrook in June 1943; in time to join in yet another Battle of the Ruhr.

To say Titch was happy to be with Mary again was an understatement, he was ecstatic. All thoughts of operational flying; the fear, cold, danger and loneliness were as nothing to his joy.

To celebrate their good fortune at being reunited, Titch took Mary to an expensive dinner at the 'Saracen's Head' Hotel in Lincoln. An expensive establishment that was affectionately called 'The Snakepit' by aircrew of all squadrons. It was noted for the frequency of visits by the street ladies of the cathedral city. In their many calls at the bar over the months, neither Titch nor Keith ever saw anything but aircrew of one sort or another propping the bar and sinking their noses into large English pint glasses of ale; so much for rumour.

Mary and Titch sat in the corner of the dining room oblivious of their surroundings. Their hands were clasped across the candle-lit table and their eyes locked. Impulsively Titch removed the gold signet ring from his finger and taking Mary's hand, placed it on the second finger of her right hand. The ring was too large for the small finger. He said nothing; his heart was too full of love for this dark-haired girl. Mary looked deep into Titch's eyes and he saw a tear forming in her hers.

'You don't have to give me this Rupert.'

'I want to. I want you to have it ... until we can have a wedding ring. My wedding ring.' He paused and thought for a moment. His eyes clouded and his voice faltered. 'I gave this ring to Judy too ... I think I said very much the same words. She was killed wearing it. I hope we will have better luck.'

It was a spontaneous gesture on Titch's part. The ring was his greatest treasure; his only treasure. All he had ever possessed were but ashes in the conflagration that had consumed the house and treasures of Ma and Bert James. Mary knew this and was grateful.

'Please Rupert. It means so much to you... You told me about Judy and I understand.' Their eyes held each other and their hands were tight clasped.

'But I will be proud to wear it. I will just mind it for you.'

'I know. I think that is why I want you to have it,' he smiled. 'Just for safe keeping. I hope one day to take it to Wales and maybe give it to my cousin.' Mary looked at her hand and made no attempt to remove the ring.

'I'll keep it safe for you. Just for the time being. It will be yours again on our wedding day.' She wanted to say more but an elderly waiter came for their order and the moment was lost.

Their marriage plans were privy only to themselves and Keith. They were afraid if higher authority heard, one or other of them would be posted away. The Command discouraged close romantic involvement between aircrew and W.A.A.F.s on the same station. 'Bad for morale' and 'too distracting for personnel concerned' was the rational and the wording of the Air Council Instructions; the bible for the R.A.F.

Warrant Officer Keith Gale and crew were attached to 'A' Flight of the three flight squadrons and given Lancaster 'D' Dog as their aircraft. The aircraft was known as 'The Dog' – so named by its former crew who had finished a tour of thirty operations in it. Twenty six small bombs were stencilled in yellow paint on the fuselage below the pilot's window. Three had a key neatly painted in black in the centre of them denoting that the crew had 'the key' of the German city bombed on three or more occasions. There were two carrots denoting mine laying operations, code named 'gardening' and three ice cream cones to show the aircraft had bombed Italian cities on three operations. On the nose was painted a large and fearsome hound of indeterminate breed. It was inescapably male – it had in its teeth a realistic looking bomb. It's hind leg was raised over a facsimile of an agitated Adolf Hitler. A stream of noxious looking urine gushed from the oversized penis of the dog dousing the unfortunate Fuhrer's face. It was an undignified mascot but the crew were unanimous that it remain as theirs. To change the mascot might mean a change of luck for the aircraft that was obviously lucky. Two weeks of waiting for their first operation was taken up with training and familiarisation. They caught up with the latest intelligence information, played cricket and Australian rules football, drank a lot of beer in the Marquis of Granby public house and Titch introduced the crew to Mary.

Number 460 Royal Australian Airforce (Lancaster) Bomber Squadron was made up largely of Australian air and ground crews, officers N.C.O.s and airmen. The balance, mainly N.C.O. aircrew, were personnel from the R.A.F., Royal Canadian and New Zealand airforces. The crew of The Dog trained hard ready for their first operation together. Fate ordained the target was Essen. It was a beginning.

Chapter Thirteen

Essen was completely covered with cloud. The bomber force bombed using 'Wanganui' sky markers; a method of marking used when the target was obscured by cloud. Markers, or T.I.s, (target indicators) were dropped to burst above or in the clouds by Path Finder Force. A 'master bomber', a pilot and crew of exceptional skill and experience in navigation dropped a cluster of white marker flares that exploded by a barometric fuse just above the cloud ceiling. His 'backers up' (other Path Finders) followed with similar clusters, but of reds. The main force of four hundred, all four engine bombers, Lancasters and Halifaxes, bombed the centre of the red T.I.s. The master bomber radioed his instructions of change of aiming points to P.F.F. – main force bombers corrected any error and bombed accordingly. It was a technique that had devastating results; not as accurate as Parramatta, a method used when the target was clear of cloud. In the case of Parramatta, the T.I.s were dropped directly onto the target after a visual identification by the master bomber, sometimes at very low level. With both methods the main bomber force bombed the centre of the pattern of marker flares. Colours changed nightly, combinations of two from a choice of four, white, yellow, red or green. That night on Essen they were on red on white. The

Dog bombed the centre of the red T.I.s.

It was a dark night and no moon. Black would be a better name for it. 'Black as the inside of a Red Boomer's arse,' was how Aussie Meldrum, The Dog's mid-upper gunner described it. Aussie had a good turn of phrase.

It was a 'der Zahm Eber' (the Tame Boars) nightfighters' dream. Twin engine planes equipped with a bomber searching radar and positioned into the bomber stream by ground controllers. It was black – so black it was difficult for gunners to see the matt black ME110s or JU88s. So black, the enemy defenders could detect targets with little fear of being seen.

Flak over the target was as intense as ever it was on their first tour. Heavy and medium calibre shells reached to their height. Great flashes of light ruined Titch's night vision as shells exploded in flesh shredding bursts of high explosive and shrapnel. Flashless 88mm shells burst around him, invisible but were no less deadly. Titch quietly thanked God The Dog could get to an altitude where the deadly tracer of the rapid firing 40mm flak could not reach them; he remembered the Whitley over Cologne.

Searchlights played their beams onto the cloud base and lit up the sky to an opaque brilliance. Bombers were silhouetted against the glare of searchlights and fires burning on the ground. A setting made for the single engine 'cat's eye' fighters; ME109s and FW190s; the Luftwaffe's 'der Wild Eber' (the wild boars). Aptly named, their technique was to charge courageously through their own flak and attack from above the bombers silhouetted.

'Christ! We must stand out like a country shit house.' Aussie had a phrase for every situation.

They saw no fighters. The old Dog was buffeted by the flak; they bombed on time and their target photograph showed the centre of the T.I.s as their aiming point. The flight home was uneventful – others were not so lucky; over the target or on the way home. A bomber was shot down into the North Sea within sight of the English coast. Not a flak hole in The Dog to show as evidence they had been to the most dreaded target in the Ruhr.

'Whak'o you bastards. Number one under the old belt. Who said Ops were bloody dicey. Piece a bloody cake, if yer ask me.'

Keith and Titch looked at each other. Aussie Meldrum's remark was worrying. He was cocky; over confident? Over confidence killed aircrew. Was Aussie's opinion shared by the rest of the crew? It was not a comfortable thought.

Word spread through the crews waiting for interrogation that a 100 Squadron aircraft had made an emergency landing at Binbrook; the aircraft shot up, some of the crew dead and wounded. Titch was talking to Mary and saw Keith in conversation with their flight commander. Squadron Leader 'Poppa' Higgins looked over his shoulder at Titch and the rest of the crew yarning, waiting for their coffee. After a minute he nodded and said something to the pilot. Keith abruptly broke away and walked to the table where Titch, Mary and the five crew members were.

'Leave your gear fellows. Come with me.'

'Hey! Break it down Keith. I 'aven't 'ad me bloody coffee.'

Leo and Merve the flight engineer looked indignant.

'Leave it and come with me. And no argument!'

The first time Titch had ever heard Keith give a direct command. He stomped out of the briefing room – out into the dawn half light. Titch saw Mary looking askant at him; he shrugged and followed the others.

They clambered into the Flight Commander's utility. Keith gave the W.A.A.F. driver orders to take them to the 100 Squadron aircraft.

'It's at the end of number three runway. And hurry please.' The car drove off; seven crew of The Dog sat huddled in the back, silent. All but Keith puzzled. It took only minutes – minutes when the silence was unbroken.

From a distance in the poor light of a July dawn the plane looked normal. Even the cluster of ground crew around it was not unusual. The utility swung to a stop under the starboard wing. The seven tumbled out. Silent ground crew parted to allow them through. The seven too were silent as they looked at the shot riddled Lancaster. There was a gaping hole just forward of the rear turret. The turret's Perspex was shot to pieces. A series of tears in the skin of the fuselage shone a bright silver against the drab black of the regulation paint; like bloodless wounds, Titch thought. The H2S radar blister beneath the fuselage was a shattered wreck.

A round pool of blood-smeared oil looked black in the poor light; it was dripping slowly

339

from under the rear turret. Keith Gale climbed into the Lanc, followed by his crew. Titch was the last. The floor of the Lancaster was slippery with congealed blood and hydraulic oil from the gun turret's pipe leads. Ammunition tracks to the rear turret were bent as if a giant hand had torn them apart. A burst parachute lay soaking up gore. Titch looked forward and saw the shattered mid-upper turret and flare chute. A flying boot lay on the floor of the turret. Aussie took it and held it by the foot; blood dripped from the inside. The Australian's voice exploded with a softly spoken 'Shit!' The word exploded from his lips in a hiss. The rest just looked and made their way deeper into the plane. Further forward was a mess of shell-shattered radio equipment and blood. Morning light cast insipid beams through holes in the fuselage. No abattoir could have looked more gory. Titch heard someone vomiting. He felt sick himself. An oath came from the half light around him.

'Holy fucking cow. I 'eard they washed gunners out a their turrets with a bloody hose. I thought it was all bullshit.'

Titch didn't know who said it. It didn't matter. Keith swung himself to the direction of the voice.

'No fellers. Not bullshit. What we are looking at is what is left of a badly shot up aircraft. Both gunners dead, and the Wop dying.' Keith was able to see Aussie Meldrum in the gloom. He raised his voice and addressed himself to the Australian.

'The mid-upper bought it, Aussie. He wouldn't agree with you that it was a piece of bloody cake tonight.'

Keith Gale pushed past his crew to the exit door. He stopped, turned and held onto the smashed gyro compass; he had his foot on the door's step. The pale light shone on the young pilot. Titch saw he was white with anger and shaking. Keith turned and looked back at the six standing in a state of shock.

'Just remember this you dumb bastards. We were damned lucky tonight. You treat every Op as if it is your last. One day, one way or another, it will be. Only by vigilance and being afraid in the knowledge that there are people out there whose only ambition is to kill you. Will your last Op be the happy end of your tour?'

He turned and swung himself out of the door opening onto the concrete apron of the dispersal and marched to the waiting utility. Six chastened N.C.O.s followed him. When they were seated he turned to them and smiled wanly.

'Now let's get back and enjoy our coffee.'

A week later they went to Nuremberg – again nothing, or almost nothing. Titch sighted a night-fighter; it was out of range and was flying away from them. The Dog collected a few holes from flak over the target and was coned by searchlights for a minute when they got off course and flew over a defended area; otherwise, nothing.

A three day stand down was declared and they relaxed in their own ways. Keith, Mary and Titch went to Lincoln and had a quiet dinner at the Snake Pit. There were several of the squadron there and Keith discreetly said goodnight to the lovers after dinner and joined the crowd around the bar. Mary and Titch sat on drinking and talking quietly until closing time when twenty of them walked to the bus and returned to the Station. Mary and Titch left the bus at Binbrook village and walked across the water meadows to the W.A.A.F. quarters.

There was a moon and the night was warm. They walked with their arms around each other and allowed the night noises and the moonlight to wash over them. They did not talk until they reached the gate to the huts that housed the girls. Only then did Mary turn to face Titch and they kissed. They talked for minutes of the things that lovers have talked of over the ages and swore eternal love.

It was after midnight when Titch reached the sergeants' mess. There was pandemonium. A group around the piano were singing lustily. Other groups were playing the boisterous mess games that were a feature of stand downs. The bar was cluttered with N.C.O. aircrew in varying stages of intoxication. He saw Keith among a group playing 'High-Cock-a-Lorram'. A suicidal game involving no little violence. Keith grinned at his reargunner as he sat on Leo Lewis' head. Titch was about to wave when Aussie Meldrum and Merve leapt on Keith's back. The four of them were lost in a heap of twisting limbs as other aircrew fell, or jumped, on top of them.

Titch smiled and crept out of the building to his bed. He was in the glow of Mary's kisses; he had no wish to spoil his evening by being bashed and bruised. Certainly not when he was sober.

At Broadstairs a westerly wind blew on the wild

willow herb growing between the graves. The doctor hovered despondently over his plot. Otto Meyer was the first to notice that the old cavalry colonel was missing. The German pilot drew Titch's attention to it. The ornate family crypt that was the old man's resting place was devoid of his spirit. Tom Higgins noticed it too.

'Looks as 'ow 'e's been a sent fer now.' The former policeman looked puzzled. 'I'd give a lot to know just what do 'appen to us in th'end. That I would.'

'Don't 'e be daft. What 'ave 'e got ter give. About as much as I do 'ave.' Sid Mathews shifted his tin hat to the back of his head. He was right, none of them possessed a thing. They all wondered what happened to 'people' when they were 'sent for'. The R.E. sapper chatted on.

'The more I do see o'this y'ere. The more I do believe wot my ol' granny used ter tell us nippers back 'ome. When you do die, she used ter say, when you do die you all go to a place where that there Jesus bloke a sorts out all they things you 'ave a done wrong. N'all they things you 'ave done right. 'E adds them all up she said. If you 'ave done more good things than bad, then you goes to 'eaven, she said. If you 'ave done more bad things then you go to 'ell.'

He put his helmet squarely on his head. 'I do reckon as 'ow Jesus be a workin' at 'is sums fer us this very minute. An' wot's more, I do believe 'E won't keep us a waitin' a moment more than 'E 'as to.'

'What happens to people who do not believe in Jesus… Jews, Moslems and Buddhists? And all the other religions? What did your granny say about them?' The doctor smiled his ridicule at Sid's simple beliefs.

'Ah… My ol' gran a said as they be 'eathens. All on 'em. There be no place fer them in our 'eaven, she said. She did say as 'ow they 'ad their own 'eaven somewhere else. Sounded reasonable to I. A seein' as 'ow they never comed to our church when I was a lad. Not never they didn't. Not at Christmas, Easter or th'Arvest Festival. Like she did say, 'eathens, the lot on 'em.'

Who were they to say Sid's old grandmother was wrong. None of them knew, though Titch could not see God being discriminatory. He recalled one of many discussions with Keith he had on Jesus and the prophesy that He would come again. He was quite vocal.

'I believe it is a matter of faith Rupert. A belief. Some would say that it is time for a second coming. Their argument is that God gave Moses and the people of Israel Ten Commandments as a guide to live by. Simple words with no ambiguity. Over the centuries grey areas of doubt have crept in. The simple people of the tribes consulted their wise men who began to twist the Commandments for political expediency. Three thousand years later there was such a hierarchy of High Priests and Pharisees that simple men were bewildered. It is argued God sent Christ at that time to cut through the mumbo jumbo. Cut through all the doubt and wondering and give two Commandments. Just two. He thought that ten were too difficult for us to remember. He said, "love God and love your neighbour as

344

thyself." What could be simpler?'

Titch remembered they were looking around the small red sandstone cathedral at Lichfield. They had visited the site in the city where one thousand Christians had been massacred in the year 286 for no other crime than their beliefs. Titch began by asking why men killed each other so readily in the name of religion. Their discussions continued as they sat in the sun out of the wind in the shelter of the old shrine. Keith spoke again.

'Over nineteen hundred years man has built up another hierarchy of Priests, Bishops Cardinals and of course the Pope. All with their own book of rules. Canon law, theology, ecclesiastical precedence and dogma. Modern day mumbo jumbo. Today, in 1942, people are bewildered. Love God? That is straight forward. It is loving our neighbour we find difficult. Especially today. Britons loving Germans? Germans loving Russians? Japanese loving Americans? Us all loving one another and so on.' Titch recalled he smiled and looked at him.

'So you see Rupert, perhaps it is time for the second coming. Some people believe the second Christ is already among us. Who knows? There are lots of cranks and genuine Christians waiting, convinced it is so. If, and when, he does come, perhaps he will again cut through all the learned teachings and arguments. All the mumbo jumbo and give us just one commandment. Something like...' Titch recalled Keith paused and looked into the distance as he often did when he was thinking. 'Something like... To love your neighbour is to love God.' He smiled sadly and looked back at Titch. 'Who knows. And perhaps the establishment will crucify him again as a rebel or pillory him as a crank.'

It was a topic the two friends had discussed at length but could come to no conclusions. It was the same at the moment in the church yard of St Peter's Church in Broadstairs. What was going to happen to them? All the talk among themselves solved nothing.

The bomb load that July morning told them little – the petrol load told them less; the target could be anywhere in central Germany. The cardboard cartons loaded into The Dog puzzled the crew; they had to wait for the briefing to satisfy their curiosity.

It was a 'Goodwood Effort', a maximum effort. The Australian squadron was putting twenty-six aircraft in the air. Every serviceable plane. The wall map in the briefing room showed the target to be Hamburg; a new target for Keith and Titch. They listened to the Wing Commander saying his piece.

'Until now it has been our custom to take evasive action. We call it weaving, from four degrees east.' The silence in the briefing room was broken by the scraping of a match as somebody lit a cigarette. The tall squadron commander's eyes tried to penetrate the tobacco smoke to take in all of the two hundred men sitting in rows. He braced himself and continued.

'Tonight you will not weave.'

There was a gasp from two hundred throats. A

murmuring broke out

'I repeat, you will NOT weave!' The Wing Commander's voice broke through the murmurings. 'You will fly straight and level. All the way in. Over the target. And all the way home.' He paused to allow this information to sink in. He held up his hand for silence as the aircrew began to fidget uneasily. Titch was as amazed as any of them. Not weave? Unthinkable! We will all be sitting ducks for the flak and the fighters. His dread fed his imagination.

'Don't be alarmed fellers.' The squadron commander's voice broke through Titch's wild thoughts.

'The boffins assure me that it is perfectly safe.'

There were snorts of disbelief from many of the two hundred aircrew. The Wing Commander ignored it.

'Loaded into your aircraft are cartons. No,' he held up his hand apologetically, 'sorry fellers, they are not cases of grog.' There were hoots of laughter from a hundred nervous throats. 'They are cartons of "window".' He saw through the fug the look of mystification on their faces for he repeated the word.

'Window. A code name for packets of metalised paper strips you bombaimers will throw out at regular intervals. These strips will, I am assured...' He smiled as derisive laughter broke out. When it subsided he continued in a more serious voice. 'These strips will confuse the enemy's radar defences to such an extent that flak, searchlights or fighters will be unable to see whether they are firing at an aircraft or a piece of

Window. It will make their radar totally inoperative.' There was a silence in the room. He continued.

'By flying straight and level we can pack in tighter throughout the operation. It will give a greater accuracy and concentration of bombing. Give better "window" coverage.' He paused for a moment, smiled at his crew and added, 'and be a damned sight more comfortable.'

A voice from the back shouted. 'Good on yer boss. I'll buy that bastard.'

There was laugher. After more details the briefing broke up.

The Dog was next to the last Lancaster to take off. Twenty-four fully loaded planes were already airborne. Titch had watched from his turret as one after the other roared off into the sunset.

Keith had The Dog taxiing along the perimeter track; the Lanc swung onto the runway and stopped on its brakes facing into the wind. The rear turret was to beam. Titch saw the caravan flash a 'Green'. He saw the figure of a W.A.A.F. waving frantically. It was Mary Golding. Titch Wilkins returned the wave; a gloved hand came to his lips and he blew her a kiss. Did Mary do the same? Titch was not sure. He wasn't sure she saw him clearly.

Keith and Merve eased four throttles forward. Four Merlins began their powerful roar. The Dog began to shake as the power built up. Four airscrews clutched the air to draw the Lancaster forward against the anchor of the wheel brakes. Four engines roared power; the kite shook enough to shatter the rivets free. The tail lifted a little under Titch. Only then did Keith ease the brakes. The Dog began to roll, all thirty tons of it; half were bombs and equally explosive high octane petrol.

'Here we go lads. Good luck.'

There was no reply. The crew were braced for take off; holding their breaths for fear of the worst. Bracing themselves uselessly against the crash and explosion of a failed take off they knew was possible. A failure that would mean a holocaust of flame; a vapourising fireball of men and machine.

Titch saw the ground beginning to move under him. Faster they went as the airscrews bit into the wind. Faster. The tail of The Dog came up; it was in a flying posture. The concrete became a blur of greys and blacks, long dark streaks stretching away behind. The Dog was still on the ground tearing along at one hundred miles an hour. One hundred and thirty. The caravan and hangars were small in the distance as they tore down the long runway. Titch knew they needed every yard of concrete for a long take off, so heavily laden were they. The rumble and vibrations of wheels on concrete ceased. The Dog was airborne, but only just. The perimeter track, then the barbed wire defensive fence shot beneath the plane only feet away. A farm building was close – too close for comfort.

'Wheels up!' Keith's breathing was laboured as he strained at the controls. 'Keep the flaps as they are Merve.'

There was no reply from the flight engineer; he

spoke only when he had something important to say. Titch watched the last Lanc take off behind them. Twenty six Lancasters of 460 Squadron were airborne. Part of an eight hundred bomber force heading for the German city of Hamburg.

The ground was far below. Airfield and hangars, like a child's toy in the late evening light. Farm houses and sheds with cows and sheep grazing on the hill sides like models he had dreamed of having as a boy. How he had longed for one of those. Titch watched them getting smaller and knew Mary was watching them climbing to get to operation height.

'Course 087° for the coast Keith.'

'Roger, Leo.'

Lancaster AR 'D' Dog banked gently as it came on course. Titch saw dimly the Norfolk coast below him; night was drawing in.

Four Merlins droned power and carried The Dog across the North Sea. It was completely dark as it crossed the Dutch coast. Seven souls were tense and alert. Two gunners strained optics, searching for friends and foe. Collision was as likely as a fighter attack. The moon rose out of Titch's sight ahead of them as they flew over Holland, it was going to be full, a mixed blessing. It made it easier for him to see the nightfighters but it gave the 'wild boars' light enough to attack.

'You OK Titch?'

'Great. This straight and level flying beats weaving.'

'Too bloody right it does. My guts are staying in place for a change.'

It was Aussie. Titch looked along the fuselage and saw the bottom of the Australian's turret moving from side to side as he searched the sky from the horizon up. Titch had seen other Lancasters as they crossed the sea, but none had ventured too close.

'Flak to port.'

Bombaimer Dave was on the ball, looking forward as he threw out 'window'. Someone was off course and flying over Rotterdam.

Mile after mile of Germany passed beneath the bomb-filled belly of The Dog. Occasionally it slurped as it got in the wash of another Lancaster's slipstream. An ambivalent feeling. The crew knew they were not alone; that too could be dangerous with another bomber close ahead. What if he...? Titch's thoughts jerked to the here and now. A P.F.F. track marker dropped at the turning point simultaneous to Leo, giving a course alteration. Their navigation was spot on.

'We are half a minute early Keith. Time to target ten minutes. Course out of target 180° for five minutes. Then 270° until the first dog leg. Got all that mate?'

'Roger. Thanks Leo.'

It was only minutes before Titch heard the dreaded, 'Flak and searchlights ahead.' Another minute, all Titch heard was the roar of the engines and the thump of his heart. He felt fear like ice in his veins. His gut churned; he felt a familiar dryness in his mouth. In a word, he was terrified. Through it all, he felt gentle puffs on his face as oxygen was pumped into his mask and he began to sing, a ludicrous song, 'This is a lovely way to spend an evening'. Titch screamed the lyrics into a dead mike.

'Christ! Look at those searchlights. They've gone crazy.' The bombaimer's excitement passed through to all of them. Titch stopped singing, as much because of what Dave said as the realisation of the song he was singing.

'Must be the bloody Window. They haven't a fuckin' clue.'

It was all happening behind Titch. He couldn't see a thing, other than the blackness astern of him. He wanted to ask what the hell was happening but they were coming up to the target. There were more important questions.

Titch began to feel the crump and thump of flak. A flash or two as shells burst. The flashless 88mm he didn't see – he just felt it. Jarring thumps that could blast the life from him, or explode flesh-tearing steel in his direction to cut his body to a pulp.

He recalled a nightmare he'd had. He was in his turret, naked; his body translucent. A shell exploded behind the turret. A piece of steel emerged from the smoke and was coming straight at him; long and barbed, like the head of a fishing spear, glowing red hot in the darkness and moving in slow motion. The shaft come through the turret and touched his stomach just above the navel; the skin dimpled and singed, slowly. He smelled burning flesh. The red hot point punctured the flesh and turned to rip open the white translucent flesh. A gash opened crimson and bleeding, like the cut throat of a pig, contrasting vividly with the pale skin. His intestines were exposed, a revolting blue-black, streaked with red and yellow. Red, blood red. There was no pain. The slippery mass slithered onto the turret floor; then it hurt. He screamed with pain and woke up sweating.

'I'm going back to the flare chute now Keith.'

'Roger Mac. Remember your oxygen bottle.'

'Too bloody right mate.'

'Keep an eye on him Titch.'

'Will do.'

No unnecessary dialogue. Say what has to be said then 'button up'; it was a standing rule in The Dog.

Titch turned his turret to beam as Mac went down the fuselage. The Wireless Operator had the lonely task of waiting by the fire chute and pulling the manual lever that released the 'photo-flash', a pyrotechnic fused to explode when their bombs struck the ground; sometimes the automatic mechanism failed. He did this as the bombaimer said, 'bombs gone.' Nobody wanted to fly with a pyrotechnic with the explosive power of a five hundred pound bomb primed with a barometric fuse for a moment longer than necessary. The 'flash' was synchronised with the aircraft's camera; a photograph of their aiming point told Intelligence the success or otherwise of their bombing.

Flak bursts and waving searchlight beams gave enough illumination for Titch to see Mac dimly; he saw him picking his way aft. He checked in when he was at station.

The Dog was among the flak now but there was no co-ordination with it. It was haphazard firing but there was a lot of it. The plane was thrown around and the crew felt the crump of near misses. Searchlights were all over the place. The blue radar-directed lead lights waved erratically; no two lights were in the same place. Several swept over them, none held; 'window' was working.

'Bomb doors open!' Dave's voice loud in Titch's ears. 'Keep her coming Keith. We're right on track.'

Titch felt a jolt and heard the crash; a shell burst close to him. The Germans may be firing blind, but they were chucking it up at them.

'Right.... Steady... Steady... Steady. Keep it coming cobber.' There was a pause. Titch was holding his breath. His gut felt tight and the size of a pin head. His anus sphincter threatened to collapse. His throat hurt as he screamed some stupid song into a dead mike.

'Bombs gone! Let's get out of here.'

'Photo-flash gone!'

Mac had done his job. Titch swung his turret and watched for a second as he made his way forward.

'Bomb doors closed.'

The worst was over; now for home. Titch popped another barley sugar in his mouth and sighed. It was a mistake. There was a crash that shook the whole plane. A thick cloud of oily black smoke was sucked into his turret and stung his eyes. The Dog lurched as if it had been kicked with a giant boot. They were turning and losing height.

'Hang on chaps.' Keith was breathing hard as he fought the controls. Slowly The Dog came on an even keel. It banked a little in the opposite direction and was flying more or less normally.

'Get up here Dave and navigate. Mac, see to Merve and Leo. You OK Titch? Aussie?'

'Shit yes. But I've had a lump blown out of my turret. What the fuck happened? One of the engines is buggered.'

Aussie's voice was an octave above normal. Keith's was as calm as ever.

'Merve and Leo are hit and the starboard inner is out. But we'll be OK. Just keep your eyes peeled back there.'

Neither gunner replied. Titch should have done. He looked hard at the flak-studded sky astern, looking for fighters, and prayed. After a minute Keith called again.

'You OK Titch?'

'Fine Keith thanks.'

'Good. We'll make it OK old friend.'

It was all he said but Titch knew he had been worried. The moon was bright above and behind them. The target fires were bright beneath. Titch had never seen such a blaze. The master bomber's red markers were invisible against the fires. Only the greens of the 'backers up' showed. The combination of fires, ground markers, searchlights and moonlight lit the sky as bright as day. Smoke was billowing up towards them. For a moment Titch's heart bled for the people down there, but only for a moment. Other more pressing, more personal considerations filled his mind; things like survival. The flames on the ground were a bright orange red, even seen from twenty thousand feet; smoke billowed to fifteen thousand. Hamburg was ablaze.

The target was well behind. They flew over cloud as they headed west. Titch could see the fires in Hamburg, but soon the cloud obscured everything. It stretched like a white linen tablecloth as far as he could see. The Dog was flying well on three engines but Titch was sure all was not well up front. The pilot's voice cut through the silence.

'How are Leo and Merve, Mac?'

'I'm no bloody expert but I reckon they've just about bought it, Keith. Whole bloody sides shot away. Both of 'em. Merv's got his back shot away too. I can't stop them bleeding. Oh shit! What a fuckin' mess.'

Mac's Sydney accent came as a sob. Leo was a great friend of his. That random 88mm shell had near blasted the life out of the engineer and navigator as it had the starboard inner engine.

Titch began to look above the horizon. It was the most likely place for a fighter to attack. From the dark side of the sky; to get The Dog silhouetted against that white moonlit cloud. Even to dive out of the moon.

The thought was no sooner out when he saw it. A dot at first; a single engine plane, right in the eye of the full moon. As it got closer, Titch recognised the snub nose of a Focke Wolfe 190. It was well away; out of range for his Brownings. He told the crew, 'Prepare to corkscrew port. Look out for his mate Aussie. These bastards hunt in pairs.'

'Sure thing cobber.'

The fighter was well out of range. Perhaps he hadn't seen them. Impossible. Evasion was

356

useless. It was too light; the cloud was too far away. Titch knew it would have to be a shoot out. The 190 was closer. It's wing tips touched the dim red circle of his reflector gun sight; four hundred yards and closing rapidly.

'CORKSCREW PORT GO!'

Four Brownings spoke as one; they rattled and jarred. Titch's gun sight quivered, his turret shook as he fired a long continuous burst into the F/W. Four streams of tracer snaked into the enemy's fuselage, around it, under it, over it and behind it. Tracer bounced off the engine cowling and cockpit canopy and still the fighter pressed home its attack, following The Dog's manoeuvres. Flashing lights heralded the stream of tracer from the fighter's wings. Titch was sure they were goners. The tracer missed The Dog by inches and still the gunner fired at his enemy. Titch was screaming profane obscenities; willing the German to die. Willing him to go away and leave him in peace. His breath came in agonising gasps.

He corrected his aim and fired again. The Focke Wolfe disintegrated in a ball of flame. It had fired that one burst of cannon fire. WHY! Titch had no time for an answer. 'Keep fuckin' weavin'.' It was Aussie Meldrom's urgent command.

AR 'D' Dog continued its corkscrewing combat manoeuvre. On a roll, beginning another diving turn, Titch saw a second 190 swooping into attack. A twin stream of tracer passed over the reargunner's head as Aussie opened up simultaneously to the starlight flicker of lights from the muzzles of the Wild Boar fighter's cannon. Titch laid off the appropriate deflection automatically and fired. For seconds the sky around the F/W. was filled with tracer, but only seconds. As the reargunner peered through his gun sight, the fighter's fiery tracer shells were coming straight at him. The enemy was close. Very close; less than two hundred yards and closing. Titch's nerve was at breaking point. He was near panic when there was a shattering, jarring, ripping crash heard above the cacophony of six machine guns and three racing Merlin engines, then the turret controls in his hands went slack, lifeless. The tracer from Aussie's turret continued for seconds until the stream was way off the target. It ceased abruptly when pressure in the hydraulic accumulator ran out, the fighter rolled and exposed its oil streaked belly. It swooped past them in a dive, trailing a wisp of smoke. In that moment Titch distinctly saw the black crosses on the under surface of the wings.

'We got the bastard!' Aussie's shout came over the intercom in a burst of sound. Titch was shaking from exertion and the reaction from the combat. His heels beat an uncontrollable tattoo on the turret floor. His stomach heaved. In a fumbling rush, he removed his oxygen mask and vomited.

'Resume course Keith.' Titch's voice was weak. He was speaking through convulsions of spitting and gut heaving nausea. There was no response from the pilot. The Dog continued in a diving turn.

Titch's turret was on the port beam. By

standing and leaning forward, he was able to see smoke coming from the port engines. The Dog was on fire and losing height at an alarming rate.

'KEITH!' Titch screamed into his mike; he fought against the Gee and manually turned his turret fore and aft prior to an exit to assist his friend. The exertion was exhausting. The Dog's wing came up, the dive steadied to a gentle angle and the nose pointed to the west.

'Sorry Titch.' Keith's voice and heavy breathing crackled over the intercom after what seemed an age.

'I was busy. Sorry. You OK?' A typical understatement. Keith's voice, though breathless, was conversational, even confidential. The reargunner could have cried with relief. That great childhood loneliness had come over him for a second but now he was not alone. Keith Gale was alive.

'Fine.' It was a lie of course. Anyway, it was all relative. 'You?' Titch fought to keep his voice steady.

'I'm OK but the kite is a mess. Both port engines are stuffed but the fires blew themselves out, thank God.'

'I know. My turret is as dead as a Dodo.'

'Mine too… What a bastard.' Titch didn't need Aussie's confirmation but he was pleased the mid-upper gunner was unhurt.

'How are Merve and Leo?' Titch was pulling a few rounds of ammunition up the servo feed mechanism, just enough to fire one gun manually; a burst of tracer might deter another fighter.

'Not too well. Things are a mess up here. We are flying but losing height.' Keith laughed his short, nervous laugh. 'Just don't find any more fighters, old friend. My nervous system won't stand it and we are running out of engines and blokes this end.'

Keith was far from feeling the humour his voice portrayed. Things were bad on the flight deck. Two wounded men near death. A shattered aircraft, flying gamely on a single engine. The altimeter crawling down the dial. Two hundred miles to go for home and no guns to fend off attacks. Not encouraging.

The young pilot's mind was racing. Logic told him to abandon ship. Bale out while there was still sufficient altitude.

'Bale out? Unthinkable! I have to get these wounded home but the rest can go. I can fly The Dog on my own and make for Manston or the flat land of Kent. Romney Marsh! Flat as a pancake there.' His decision cemented into action.

'Give me a course for Dymcurch, Dave. It's on the coast of Kent.' Keith's voice trailed off. Titch wondered if his pilot had been wounded and was saying.

'How are you Mac?'

'Pretty crook, Keith, but I'll be OK mate. These poor bastards are the ones that we should worry about.'

'I know.' There was a pause. The only sound over the wires of the intercom was Keith's deep breathing and the faint crackle of atmospherics.

'Look here all of you.' The pilot's voice seemed close. 'I can see the French coast. All of you bale out. It will lighten the kite. I can get these poor blighters home then. Otherwise we might all finish up in the drink.' He paused as if to regain his breath. 'OK everyone?'

They said their farewells and wished each other luck. Titch sat in his turret and watched three parachutes billow white silk astern and below him. They looked beautiful in the moonlight. The memory of Pat Tilson parachuting into enemy held France flashed through his mind. Surf lined beaches appeared as he lost sight of the last canopy into the black shadow that was Nazi occupied Europe. Titch estimated the Dog's altitude as two thousand feet. Not much and they were losing height.

Minutes later, the single Merlin was gamely pulsing power, taking then nearer home. The sea was close, moonlight glittered on corrugations of polished silver that stretched to infinity. The scene was beautiful but Titch was scared. He was afraid to break the silence of the intercom. He did – his voice was hoarse, and he was embarrassed. Embarrassed that his friend would be offended at him not obeying his order to bale out.

'Sorry Keith. I was too scared to jump.'

The Dog lurched noticeably. The intercom was silent. Titch wondered if it was unserviceable. It crackled into life; Keith's voice held a note of anger.

'You lying little bastard Titch Wilkins. I always said you were a sub-human reargunner. Now I know you are just a bloody fool.'

The pilot was angry but Titch couldn't help that. He couldn't leave his friend to fly that machine and the two wounded men home alone. Besides a patrolling nightfighter might jump him over the drink, not that Titch could do more than warn him, perhaps fire a short burst from a single Browning. Another minute passed. Titch could see white caps on the waves below him. Keith's voice crackled over the intercom.

'Thanks Rupert.' He paused, the intercom hissed and crackled quietly. Titch could hear his friend breathing. 'Sorry I blew up but you really should have baled out, you know.'

It was all he said. Titch heard a break in his voice, or perhaps it was a fault in the intercom. There was a silence. Neither needed words to telegraph their feelings; the bond of comradeship was set in concrete. There was silence until Keith turned and saw the navigator and engineer were dead. He looked at the altimeter and pressed the intercom button on his control column.

'The blokes are dead Rupert. Both of them. Their eyes are open and staring at me. They look bloody awful. What do you think?'

It was sad news. Their gesture had been a waste of time. It was too late to bale out now. The water looked most unfriendly and close. They were too low anyway; just keep going and hope England came up quickly. And pray.

Titch tried to pump some humour into the situation.

'Don't ask me. I'm just a stupid sub-human reargunner, remember? Just drive this bloody thing and get us home. I want my mum.'

Keith laughed, his old laugh; they were together. It was like old times. Like being at

Speke in the old Defiants; just the two of them but for how long. Would they make it? The thought steadied Titch.

A full minute passed in silence. Titch could see the white caps on the waves breaking; the French coast was miles astern. Titch searched the sky for a lurking nightfighter. Keith's voice exploded in his ear.

'We won't make the coast, Rupert, though I believe I can see it. I'll make a "Darky" call then we'll have to ditch.'

'Whatever you say old chum. Just make it gentle. Remember I am only a little man and very delicate.' Titch was more than that, he was mortally afraid; he couldn't swim.

'DARKY! DARKY! This is…!' Keith's words sped over the ether on the distress frequency. In a moment's vision, Titch saw Mary and she was smiling. He wished he had baled out with the others. Life in a prison camp was better than… He stopped mid thought. 'I couldn't leave Keith.' The thought was comforting. They had been through so much together in their three years of friendship and he had done so much for Titch in ways the gunner found hard to analyse. Snatches of discussions they had had crowded Titch's mind. Discussions about life, the future, religion and God. Titch relaxed, his dread was under control. A peace came over him that reached down to the depth of his being. Mary would approve of what he was doing, and Judy. They would understand and Bert and Ma and the Wilsons and Scrapper Morgan, even crippled little Molly. Yes, they would understand. They would know what he felt for the man piloting the stricken bomber.

What of his parents? The mother he hardly remembered and the father he never knew. What would they have thought? Titch would never know but he hoped he was doing what they would have wanted him to do. He smiled a sad smile. 'Funny I should want their approval.'

A vision of Freddy Silk fused itself into Titch's thoughts. The dead chum of his orphanage days, what would he have thought and Miss Cuthberson? The world was so different then. Titch felt very close to them all.

The sea was just feet below him. It seemed to reach up invitingly. Titch wound his turret to beam and prayed. He didn't pray for wisdom, it was too late for that. He prayed for strength and courage. Strength and courage to survive. To have another chance at life and fulfil the hopes his friends, living and dead, had for him. He promised nothing in return; there wasn't time for that either.

Titch blew two lungs full of air into his Mae West life jacket; the turret doors slid open at his touch. His parachute harness disintegrated at the press of the release button and he was able to jettison it and the attached parachute into the sea by thrusting his backside out of the turret into the slipstream. No sense in impeding his movements for a quick exit once they hit the water. The memory of screams of a reargunner friend who had been trapped in his turret as flames consumed him was a recurring nightmare. Titch was determined that would not be his fate.

He was as ready as it was possible to be; he grasped the turret's struts with nervous hands ready for the crash that was coming. Oddly, he held the Mae West inflation tube in his mouth like a cigar.

Water was rushing past, just inches away. The note of the single Merlin changed as Keith throttled back. Titch saw a wave advancing on them from the beam. It looked huge.

'HOLD TIGHT RUPERT!' Keith's voice cut through the intercom like a sword thrust. Ice cold dread surged through Titch's veins.

The Dog bounced. Titch heard an unintelligible exclamation from Keith. An oath? A cry? A last appeal? It was the last Titch heard from him. The crash, when it came, sent a mind-smashing light through Titch's brain in an explosion of pain. He knew no more until he saw his body floating face up in the swell of the grey waters of the English Channel with the word T I T C H painted on his flying helmet and a pair of seagulls fighting over his corpse.

Chapter Fourteen

'It is all very well saying that Adolf Hitler had no alternative but to go to war. I know the Treaty of Versailles made it hard for you Germans but you started the Great War, you know. You invaded Belgium.' The old doctor was getting wound up. Since the disappearance of the old cavalry

365

colonel, Otto Meyer had been the foil for the medico's arguments. He looked across his grave to the young Luftwaffe pilot he was addressing; the doctor was giving Otto a run for his money.

'And after all, you lost the wretched war. What is more. I believe you deserved to lose. And you deserved to pay for it. How would you have treated us if you had won? Eh?'

The young Luftwaffe pilot would not agree. His answer was heated.

'Ach. You smug Englanders. How foolish you are. You believe everything that drunken pig Churchill tells you. How little you really know. Every good German child knows it was world Jewry that lost Germany the war in 1918. It was their greed and covetousness that sapped the life blood from the nation and made millions in the process. Every German knows it is only by abolishing the hold Jew finance has on the world, will we get peace. Through "Der Fuhrer" we can be free of Jews and other useless peoples and bring prosperity and peace to Europe and the world.'

It was another of those arguments that none could settle. Prejudices ran too deep. Police Constable Tom Higgins and Titch had heard them before over the months, many times. They looked at each other now. Titch smiled, he shrugged. His attention wandered as the argument went back and forth. Titch saw the young woman next to Tom's grave and the baby beyond. He was always sorry for both of them, especially the young woman, hers was a sad story. The baby, they could only guess at its history. A childhood disease?

366

Perhaps an accident?

Titch Wilkins felt nothing – he had no warning. He was half listening to the two arguing, not thinking that anything could happen to change his circumstances. He saw a vivid white halo of light that had all the colours of the spectrum around its periphery. It was brilliant but not dazzling. Titch was able to look into it but without amazement. A wonderful peace was upon him. There was a deep shadow at the centre of the light; almost a hole. Titch seemed physically to move, to float. Slowly. Drawn by the magnetism of the ring of light. It was an odd sensation that lasted for... Titch didn't know how long. He had no way to measure time. His ethereal existence was beyond calculation, it was infinite. Slowly and painlessly he was drawn through the eye of the circle of brightness.

The light left him and receded slowly. The colours dimmed and the circle went further and further away. As it travelled from him it got smaller until it was a pin point of light that faded to nothing. Like a ship's light that disappeared over a horizon. It was there and then it wasn't. Titch was alone; or thought he was. When he assembled his thoughts he saw he was in a spacious bedroom in an old house. There was no sign of the Broadstairs church yard, or St Peter's Church or his erstwhile spiritual companions.

The room was furnished with old Jacobean furnishings. Solid unvarnished oak wardrobes and chests, a dressing table with a modest mirror. A coffin-like oak chest stood beneath a wide window. It had cushions on it and an open book, as if someone had sat there reading until recently; a knitting bag and a ball of white wool with knitting needles through it lay on the floor. A paper brochure of knitting patterns lay where it had fallen. Titch saw the patterns were of baby clothes.

The room was spartan, except for a vase of daffodils that adorned a small oak writing desk. Photographs of groups of young people were scattered around the walls. A log fire burned in the stone fireplace. There was a calendar standing on the mantlepiece, the date showed it to be February 21st, 1945. A large plain four poster bed dominated the large room. Austere woollen drapes hung from a canopy. The bed covering was a bed-spread, composed of dozens of badger skins. A line of fox furs edged the borders. The auburn red of the fox contrasted pleasingly with the grey and black of the badger furs. Homespun woollen rugs were scattered over the unpolished oak floor and the skin of a black bullock stretched in front of the fireplace.

On a bed-side table was a large black draped photograph of a young officer in the khaki uniform of an officer of the Royal Marines. He was in an oblique pose and was smiling. The Marines' emblem of a globe on each of his lapels were a dull bronze. He wore the three 'pips' of a captain on his epaulets over a shoulder flash that boldly said, 'Royal Marine Commando'. Beneath it was the anchor and tommy gun emblem of the Combined Operations Command. Scrawled across the bottom of the photograph was written, 'To Elizabeth, my wife. On our wedding day. All my love, Monty. January 1st 1944.'

An official Admiralty Message Form was pasted on the glass. Titch was able to read.

'HIS MAJESTY'S COMMISSIONERS OF THE ADMIRALTY REGRET TO INFORM YOU OF THE DEATH OF YOUR HUSBAND CAPTAIN RUPERT MONTGOMERY APP-LUGUS. D.S.C. ROYAL MARINES.

YOUR HUSBAND DIED GALLANTLY SERVING HIS COUNTRY ON 6TH JUNE 1944 WHILE LEADING HIS MEN IN THE STORMING OF THE BEACHES AT NORMANDY.'

Titch could not read the signature. It finished with the words 'SUPREME ALLIED COMMANDER. OPERATION OVERLORD.'

Titch saw instantly it was his cousin Rupert, or Monty as he liked to be called; heir to the Manor of Cuffty Mawr. The cousin he had met and fought with that day in… When was it…? Some years before the war. Poor Monty. Titch recalled their long talk on that day. Was this his widow?'

Propped up on the pillows on the huge four poster was a beautiful young woman. Her shoulders were bare and revealed a glimpse of full breasts under a thin night-gown. Her dark hair hung over her shoulders and her brown eyes told of worry and sadness, and something Titch could not define. He looked closer. A swelling under the covers told the former reargunner the young woman was in an advanced stage of pregnancy.

Titch was embarrassed. He was an intruder. He looked about for a means of escape but his feet were glued to the floor. He turned away from the intimate scene and looked out of the window. He saw the neglected terrace gardens of the old house; the wooded valley stretching into the distance to the slate roofs of the little Welsh hill town visible in the February afternoon light. Beddgelert, Titch supposed it was. He saw patches of snow above the tree line on the distant mountains. A yellow haze of newly emerging daffodils ranged over the floor of the woods close to the house. It was all very beautiful. Titch realised with surprise he was in Cuffty Hall. The master bedchamber of the Lord of Cuffty Mawr. He smiled wryly to himself.

'This would have been my inheritance if...'

As if she sensed Titch's presence, the young widow cried out.

'Daddy!'

The bedroom door burst open and a woman appeared; an elderly man followed. The woman looked at the young girl and laid a hand on her forehead. The man stood uncertainly at the girl's side, holding her hand. The young woman allowed a groan to escape her lips, then a cry.

'Quick Herbert. I believe it is her time. Fetch that old witch Megan Evans. And ask Montgomery to telephone the doctor.' The man left the room hurriedly and almost collided with an old woman pushing her way into the room.

'Don't you worry about me my lady. Y'ere I am indeed.' There was a rustle of skirts and shuffling of old feet. 'Witch you call me? I don't know 'ow you would all get along without Megan Evans.'

A tall, bent, wizened crone of a woman was hurrying into the room. There was no telling how old she was; suffice to say, she was ancient. Her sharp features, snarled old hands and twisted posture gave the appearance of a witch. A long black dress of severe cut added to the illusion. A snow white apron covered the front of her dress from scrawny neck to the ground; toes of heavy, black polished boots peeked from beneath the hem. Strands of white hair ran wild from a lace dust cap. She carried a bundle of towels in her arms and a bowl of water in her hands. Her sing song country Welsh accent was rich and loud.

'Go to your step-daughter woman. Or daughter-in-law is it? Whatever she is, she needs a mother now. 'Old 'er hand, I tell you. Do what every mother should do. Don't stand there like a sheep. Comfort her! The poor wee lamb.'

The old midwife laid the bowl of water on the dressing table. She looked at the girl's mother-in-law standing over the bed.

'She will need us both over this next hour indeed. There will be tears a plenty before today is over, I tell you. God willing, we'll be smiling later on.' She leaned over the mother to be, with a damp cloth mopped the young woman's brow. 'Poor little thing you are indeed. So young and so pretty, and your 'usband dead only these eight months. Terrible it is. Killed 'e was, they tell me.' She straightened her old back and looked at the middle aged woman holding the hand of her daughter-in-law.

'This is something you never see in those fancy drawing rooms of yours down in London. Or Birmingham. Or wherever you live. I am sure you never 'ave you know. Much too fancy for me you are indeed.'

'Shrewsbury. We live in Shrewsbury.' The former mistress of Cuffty Mawr sounded indignant.

'I don't care where the 'ell you come from. Just 'elp that child, if you can.'

Old Megan Evans had her chin thrust forwards in her agitation – the cleft in it nearly touched the tip of her long pointed nose. Her thin lips parted, and exposed toothless gums, a long pointed tongue shot out to wipe away a stream of saliva running down her chin.

The girl's mother-in-law. Titch's cousin's mother; his uncle's former wife, looked at the old midwife with a look of distaste. Titch recalled his cousin Monty telling him his parents were divorced and his mother had remarried. And wasn't there a girl? Elizabeth? The daughter of her new husband?

Titch's cousin Monty's mother was a plump, attractive woman in her late forties, who had lost her youthful comeliness and beauty. She was fashionably dressed in quality materials and had a fortune in jewellery on her neck and wrists. A diamond brooch of the Royal Marines' emblem glittered on her expensive blouse.

'It will soon be over, Elizabeth dear. The doctor is on his way.' The words were no sooner out of the lady's mouth when there was a commotion at the door. It burst open without a knock; a short stout man entered. He was perhaps sixty or more years old. A clipped crop of grey hair stood on his head. A dog like moustache drooped, untrimmed, over his mouth; pale watery blue eyes peered through thick lense spectacles. He approached the bed and Titch saw he had a withered leg, a hunch back and walked with the aid of a stout ash stick. Titch Wilkins recognized him as his Uncle Montgomery. His dead father's twin.

'The doctor was not at home but I left a message.' He addressed no one in particular. Titch's uncle had no chance to say more.

'Out with you man! This is no place for you!' Megan Evans gave a high pitched shriek.

'Don't speak to me like that Megan Evans. I'll have you whipped for a querulous old witch. This is my daughter-in-law. And the child is the heir to Cuffty.'

'I don't care if 'e's the Lord Almighty and you are Saint Joseph 'imself. This is no place for you. Be off and 'urry before I throw this water over you.' Her voice rose to a shrill and she took hold of the bowl of water. Old Megan looked hard at the lord of the manor, willing him to do his worst. He could not meet her gaze and retreated through the door, dragging his crippled leg. It was not until the door closed that she turned her attention to the girl in the bed. Old Megan Evans looked again to her work. She muttered in Welsh under her breath and looked at Elizabeth.

'Sorry I am my lamb. I am forgetting you don't speak the Welsh. I was sayin' if I am a witch, then we make a good pair, 'im and me. He is the most wicked old warlock that ever came out of the brimstone of a mountain cave. That 'e is. The old sinner doesn't remember. It was me that brought his son in to the world. Your 'usband that was, that is.'

'And I will lay that old devil out in 'is coffin I

373

shouldn't wonder indeed.' The crackling laugh came from her thin lips again. 'And I will enjoy the task, indeed I will.'

There was silence, except for the rustle of skirts and the crinkling of Megan's starched apron and the occasional click of her booted heel on the oak floor. The old woman busied herself about the room. For one so old, she moved remarkably quick. Her hands folded towels and she brought numerous oddments out of the copious pocket in her apron. The girl gave a cry from the bed. Titch saw perspiration on her brow. In an instant the old midwife was at her side.

'Scream girl bach, if you want to. Old Megan is used to it. Only God and us three can 'ear you. We women know something of the pain Christ suffered on the cross for us. Indeed we do now.'

She did something with the girl that Titch could not see. Bed-clothes were removed and there was a flurry of towels.

'Ah… Everything is fine downstairs girl bach.' She stood and went to the girl's head and gently mopped her perspiring brow again. Elizabeth lay back on her pillows. Her hair was matted with sweat; her eyes glazed with pain.

'Forget your pride little one. The Lord 'ears you and understands. Only us women know the pain 'e suffered. 'E cried on the cross too you know. Or so the preacher at Chapel tells us. So scream my little lamb. It will make you feel better.' The old woman spoke gently. The girl cried out; a spasm of pain wracked her body.

'The next time that 'appens, push as if your life depends on it. Do you 'ear me now?' It was a

374

command, given with authority. The girl's mother-in-law looked at the old woman in surprise.

As if a cry had been held in her breast all her life, an anguished call came from the young mother's lips. 'Monty!... Oh!'

There was more. With every cry Titch winced, unseen by the three. With every groan of agony, the old midwife encouraged the young widow.

'Just one more, girl bach. The babe is nearly ours. Push little one. Push for old Megan.'

The old crone's voice whispered encouragement and hope. There was another cry. A call again to her dead young husband. A cry to God to hear her; and the child was born.

Old Megan Evans, midwife and the layer out of the dead, mother of twelve children, wife to four husbands, called witch and angel, saint and sinner by the people of the small Welsh mountain town of Beddgelert stood and held the red, slimy morsel of humanity by the feet and looked at it with a look of triumph.

'That wicked old wizard Gwydion 'as an heir. The name and legend of "Lleu Llaw Gyffes" will live for another generation, damn his wicked old soul.' She raised her hand and slapped the babe's red, thin and withered buttock. There was no response. Titch saw the new grandmother rise as if to protest; there was a cry from the tiny form.

A red explosion of light burst before Titch Wilkins. The brilliance seared his eyes and his mind. In an instant he was transformed.

Titch Wilkins, or the babe held by Megan Evans,

375

was cold. Very cold. It was as though he had been thrown into a tub of ice. He cried in protest; red lips parted, toothless gums allowed a small pink tongue to protrude stiffly. His eyes were closed and his wrinkled red face was puckered with pain. With every inhalation of breath, his lungs screamed agony. Briefly, he opened his eyes; it hurt. In that moment he saw what he learned to call a face. It was what he learned to know as old; old and wrinkled. Pale thin lips parted in a smile and he saw toothless gums. A sharp pointed tongue shot out and curled around the lips. A droplet of crystal clear moisture hung on the tip of a long pointed nose. As the babe watched, it disappeared into a cavernous nostril with a sniff.

But Titch was cold until he felt warmth that was somehow familiar. It was what he learned to call water, warm water. It flowed over him soothingly and did something to ease the agony he felt. It was like it was before ... before he was born. Soft and warm in his mother's womb.

Everything was huge and strange. Giant gnarled old hands caressed warmth into him. Titch felt a roughness cover him tightly. He couldn't move. His arms and legs that, until then had been free, were bound yet he felt comfortable, secure; for a moment. Cold air passed into his lungs. Everything was pain, every breath was agony.

Titch was passed through the air. He felt a warmth and the smell of sweat and a sweetness that he learned to love. It was warm and friendly. He breathed the warmth; the agony in his lungs eased to a gentler pain. The warmth was comforting – he was rocked gently. Titch wanted to cry but he hurt too much. He tried to open his eyes again but the pain was too great. His eyelids were like lead. The tiny morsel of humanity who had been Titch Wilkins was exhausted. He fell asleep in the strange soft warmth of his mother's arms.

A sound woke him. He felt the comfort of arms and the softness of a naked bosom. He had a discomfort inside him. Before he could manifest his need, a nipple was placed in his mouth. He sucked – he didn't know why, it seemed the natural thing to do. He kneaded the soft flesh of his mother's breast with tiny fingers and sucked. It was very satisfying. He felt warm fluid in his mouth. It was sweet and altogether pleasing.

Faces looked down at him. He saw double and struggled to focus. Great eyes stared at him; huge teeth grinned through thick red painted lips. A voice spoke an unintelligible tongue. The face of who he later knows as his grandmother turns to a person close to her. Her voice has a sharp edge to it.

'You have your heir Montgomery. Be kind to him. The App-Lugus' have a history of losing their first born. Look at your grandson. Rupert Montgomery App-Lugus the 21st. Guard him well.'

A face larger than the others appeared above Titch. It came close. Two enormous watery eyes looked at him through thick lenses. They were a pale blue they looked cold and unfriendly. The face was all hair and wrinkles. Titch felt afraid. The lips under the hair were wet and saliva drooled; they did not move. Titch heard no noise but he smelt an unpleasant odour. It frightened him. He felt another sort of pain; a weight, a foreboding, a dread deep inside him. He was glad when the grotesque image went away.

The tone in the voice changed but it was the same voice. Titch felt a hand on him. It uncovered his face; his eyes hurt as the light from the ceiling lamp shone on him.

'Elizabeth my dear. I am so happy for you. The baby is so like his father was when he was born. Your son is so perfect it hurts me.'

Titch opened his eyes and looked for he knew not what. He struggled to focus on the image above him. He found he was looking into brown eyes that were looking deep into his. They were moist with tears. They were the eyes of the person he learned to call mother.

Titch sneezed. Liquid overflowed from his mouth and ran down his chin. The nipple fell away from his mouth; he reached for it with eager lips. A soft cloth in a gnarled old hand gently wiped the drips from his chin. He sneezed again. Titch Wilkins heard a soft laugh and felt a gentle pressure on his body – it felt good. All the pain had somehow gone away. A tear fell on his face; a finger stroked his cheek. He heard a gentle voice say soothingly,

'Sleep Rupert my darling son. Sleep my angel.'

The voice was very close. Sweet-smelling breath blew onto him, warm and scented and already familiar. Titch closed his eyes; the dark pink of his eyelids felt warm and secure. It changed to black as a darkness came over the room around him. He heard a voice say,

'Sleep now my lamb. Get you strong again indeed. Old Megan is 'ere if you want 'er. All night if I 'ave to. Believe me girl bach.'

A voice vibrated through Titch as his mother spoke wearily, 'Thank you Megan.'

Erstwhile Titch Wilkins relaxed in the warmth and gentle pressure of the arms about him. Suddenly he was tired and happy. Gone was the former loneliness, fear and cold. There was no more dread of eye-searing fire coming at him from the night sky. The soft rise and fall of his mother's breast soothed him. Her breath coming in soft sighs, comforted him. Mother and son settled themselves to sleep.

Life had begun for Rupert Montgomery App-Lugus the 21st, heir to the Manor of Cuffty Mawr.

Chapter Fifteen

An Epilogue 1996

Mary Golding never remarried. She was at R.A.F. Station Binbrook until after the war. The Australian Squadron left for home and she enjoyed their boisterous farewell. She was there to welcome 12 Squadron to its old home and drank the health to 'The Shiny Twelve'. Four engine Lincolns, big brothers to the Lancaster, replaced the war horse of Bomber Command. Peaceful cross-country navigation exercises, passive practice bombing and gunnery exercises replaced 'Operations'. Phrases like 'get the chop', 'bought it', 'wizard prang', 'gone for a burton', 'pucker gen' and 'that'll teach the stupid bastards to smoke in the aircraft' faded into history.

Mary left the W.A.A.F. in 1947 with the rank of Flight Sergeant. She wore a crown over her chevrons on her arms and Titch Wilkins' signet ring on her finger; the same finger he had placed it on that night in Lincoln; the second finger of her right hand. In fact she never took it off. Never. She claimed it was her most precious possession.

Mary qualified as a librarian and worked in the Rochdale town library until her father died in 1952. She then took up a post as librarian in the Lincoln City Library and was there until she retired in 1983. She had a small house in the city near the Cathedral, in Cathedral Close. A small Georgian terraced house with a tiny garden that she tended with loving care. She claimed was just big enough to sleep two, eat four and drink eight in comfort. She collected miniatures and wrote poetry. Two books were published under the pseudonym of Mary Wilkins. They were poems of what she called 'waiting'. When asked by the publisher what she meant, she said, 'we are all waiting for something, aren't we?' She refused to say what she was waiting for.

'I leave that for my readers to sort out' was her evasive reply.

After retirement she travelled. She visited the battle-fields of Europe and Africa. She went to Thailand and saw the infamous railway and the bridge over the River Kwai, built for the Japanese at the cost of many Allied lives. She visited the Ruhr, Berlin, Hamburg and Dresden and spoke to survivors of the bombing. She took a trip to Japan and visited Hiroshima and Nagasaki. In 1986 she travelled to Australia and attended a 460 Squadron reunion and met many old friends among the veterans. She was guest of honour at the reunion dinner. In her after-dinner speech, she recalled the days of 1943-45, the good and the bad, the ugly and the sad. She posed the question, 'If they could rise, what would the dead think of the peace they died for?'

The hall buzzed with different opinions for an hour. She marched with the squadron veterans on the Anzac Day Parade and through it all she became a peace campaigner. She wrote to members of parliament and the press. Mary abhorred violence, war, communism, party politics and any form of bigotry and was a devout Anglican.

When Her Majesty Queen Elizabeth II unveiled at Runnymede, the Airforce's memorial to British Commonwealth Airmen, 'Who Have No Known Grave', Mary Golding was within touching distance of the Queen. When the crowd thinned she searched for the name of Titch Wilkins. It took her an hour and another thirty minutes to find Keith Gale and the others of Titch's crew who died that night. It was at Rupert's name she said a prayer. She stood and looked up at the name carved in stone for all to see.

FLIGHT SERGEANT R.M. WILKINS, D.F.M. 156282. R.A.F.V.R. MISSING. JULY 1943.

She smiled at the sight of it. It was a sad smile as she thought of Titch. How pleased he would be if he knew. An orphaned boy, a bastard from the slums of London, immortalized in stone, seen by thousands from all over the world every year who visited the historic site of the signing of the Magna Carta. Was it a coincidence, she wondered, that his name looked over the very site of the signing. Lines from a war-time poem came to mind as she stood in the evening light. John Pudny wrote them in 1941 watching a thin stream of twin engine bombers heading east. He called the poem 'For Johnny'. It was easy for Mary to substitute Rupert for Johnny as she said the words.

Do not despair
For Johnny (Rupert) head in air.
He sleeps as sound
As Johnny (Rupert) under ground.

Spare not a shroud.
For Johnny (Rupert) head in cloud,
But save your tears.
For him in after years.

Better by far,
For Johnny (Rupert) the bright star.
To keep your head,
And see his children fed.

A tear formed when she whispered the last line. Titch was childless but if he had lived…? In their whisperings together they had planned a family of three. Not their own of course – that was impossible, but wartime orphans in need of loving parents.

From that year, she made a pilgrimage to Runnymede on Titch's birthday. Every Christmas morning she placed sprigs of holly and mistletoe beside his name. She fixed them with transparent adhesive tape – it made a fine splash of colour against the pale grey of the granite. The red berries of the holly looking like drops of blood; the pale opaque mistletoe berries like a woman's tears. It all seemed so appropriate in the winter weather. The small token of her continuing love stayed for weeks before a diligent gardener or a winter storm removed it.

In 1988 she motored up to Beddgelert in her new Morris Mini car. She didn't know it but she ate a sandwich sitting in the same window seat in the little pub 'Gelert' that Titch had sat drinking his beery shandy and eating a sandwich all those years before. She walked the path to 'The Grave of Gelert'. She leaned on the same post that Titch had leaned on as he read the old worn plaque; she didn't know that either.

Her heart beat faster as she drove through the well-kept gates and passed the neat lodge at the entrance of Cuffty Mawr. She recalled what Titch had told her of the drive, how unkempt it had been. The clean yellow gravel she drove on was crisp under her tyres. She found the clearing and the rail fence where Titch and his cousin had sat and talked after their fight. The legend of 'Lleu Llaw Gyffes' and the dog Gelert flooded her mind.

Mary drove slowly up the hill until she saw the old manor house sitting four square and overlooking the valley and the woods. She stopped her car and soaked in the scene. She did not know that it was in the exact same spot that Titch had stopped to get his breath and gather his courage for his approach to the house.

Mary was enjoying the minute of quiet reverie; the colour of the well-kept terrace gardens, the woods and the hills. Details of Titch's story came back to her. His crippled uncle, the old man's rage and his cruelty. The estranged marriage and the boy who was Rupert Montgomery App-Lugus the 20th, instead of Titch. If only Titch's father had not been killed. If only he had married Titch's mother. How different things might have been – if only... But then... Wishes? It was all past now; all buried with her lover Rupert in an unknown grave.

She was so lost in her memories she did not hear the crunch of footsteps on the gravel behind her.

'Excuse me madam. This is private property. Have you business here? Or perhaps you are lost?'

Mary Golding looked at the man standing beside her small car. The breath caught in her throat. He was short and muscular, about forty years old. He had fair hair and eyes that were so like those that had once looked into hers. The way he stood looking at her was the way Titch stood.

The figure wore a pair of work-worn dun-coloured corduroy trousers and a brown tweed jacket that was patched with leather; it looked comfortable on his muscular frame. He was bare headed and his face was tanned a healthy brown.

The man was in fact an incredible likeness to Titch Wilkins.

Mary pulled herself together.

'I'm sorry. You must be...' her throat was tight and would not allow her to say the words that tumbled through her mind. She swallowed hard and tried again. 'You must be Rupert.' She said the words in a rush.

'I'm sorry. I feel I know you. I'm sure I have seen you somewhere but frankly...' he shrugged his shoulders. 'Frankly, I cannot recall meeting you. I am Rupert, yes. Major Rupert Montgomery App-Lugus.'

'Royal Marines?' It was a question that took the man by surprise. He laughed.

'My goodness, does it show?' He stifled his laugh and looked closely at Mary.

'Who are you Madam? And what do you want?'

As an answer, Mary extended her hand through the window. Her hand was bare and the heavy gold signet ring glittered in the summer sun. The man looked at it.

'Dear God. Where did you find that?'

'I didn't find it. It was given to me a long time ago.' Mary smiled at the look of surprise on the man's face.

'It's a long story. Come and sit in the car and I will tell you.'

'No... No. Come up to the house. It is lunch time. We run a strict schedule. We are always very busy. Come. Join my wife and I for luncheon.' He began to walk briskly towards the house. 'Follow me.' It was a command and Mary started the motor and obeyed.

Rupert App-Lugus strode off at a brisk pace, Mary followed. As she drove, she studied the man's back. 'He even walks like Rupert. He has the same lithe step. The same swing of his shoulders. The way he opens and closes his hands as he walks. Incredible.'

It took about five minutes to cover the distance along the curved drive. A woman of about thrity-five ran down the stone steps to meet them. She was attractive, with dark curls and was dressed in comfortable country tweeds. She was as tall as her husband and her lithe figure told of good living, country air and exercise. The major embraced her warmly. Mary put on the hand brake and got out of her car. She looked at the couple standing close, waiting for her. The visitor's eyes took in the large old entrance and the family crest of the griffin and the lion on a shield with crossed swords. She tried to read the motto 'I ddyru sydd enill'. It was impossible for her. Mary recited the English translation aloud as Titch had taught her. 'To strive is to achieve'. Major App-Lugus broke into her thoughts. He addressed her in an astonished voice.

'You know the Welsh?'

Mary laughed.

'Gracious no!' She looked at the facsimile of Titch. 'But that is part of the story.'

'Curiouser and curiouser.' The Major snapped himself out of his fascination of Mary's words and looked at his wife.

'My dear. I don't know what to say. I have invited this lady to lunch. She has a ring. I believe it is THE ring. The one we believe great uncle

Rupert wore when he was killed in 1916. There is a story here and I want to hear it. Every word. But let us have a drink first. Then you must tell us all.' He looked to Mary. 'I am sorry, I don't even know your name but this is my wife Penelope. Penelope this is...?'

'Mary Golding. Mrs Mary Golding. I am widowed. I live in Lincoln.'

'Please come in Mrs Golding. Or may I call you Mary?'

The younger woman offered her hand to Mary. The ex W.A.A.F. took it. The two women eyed each other critically. Each liked what they saw.

'Mary please. I would like you to do that.' She laughed a short nervous laugh that caught in her throat. 'I was almost part of the family once.'

The word threatened to choke her. Major App-Lugus saw her distress and took her arm. His wife said kindly.

'Then if we were nearly family, please call me Penelope.' Her husband came between them.

'Come. We will have that drink. Then you may tell us what this is all about.' He put his arm on Mary's and gave a puzzled look to his wife.

They passed through the large oak door into the hall. Like Titch before her, Mary gazed at all the portraits. She saw the coat of arms over the great fireplace, and the ancient weapons hanging on the stone walls. The sun was shining on the portrait of Titch's father as he had described it to her. Like Titch she saw the ring on the little finger of the right hand.

Everything came to life for Mary. She could feel her lover standing close to her. But it wasn't

Titch – it was his likeness, older than she remembered him; and so like him. And the portrait? It could have been the reargunner himself in the uniform of an officer in the Royal Marine Artillery.

It was four in the afternoon before Mary had finished her story. She told it frankly and honestly, not sparing herself, her lover or the families that had disowned him. Tears came to her eyes and ran down her cheeks as the story unfolded. Her host and hostess hardly breathed during the whole time. Coffee went cold in their cups. Table napkins fell unheeded to the floor. The telephone rang and nobody answered it. A car came up the drive, the loud knock on the door went un-noticed; the car drove away and none of them heard it.

During the whole time Mary twisted and turned the signet ring nervously on her finger. Her hands were wet with her tears from wiping her eyes during the long telling of the story. Perhaps it was because it was just meant to be, Mary could never decide when she thought about it afterwards, the ring simply fell into the palm of her hand.

Mary Golding turned her tear-filled eyes on the lord of the manor of Cuffty Mawr.

'This is yours. Please take it. Rupert would want you to have it. He intended to bring it back here. It belongs here. With you and your son and later his son. That is what Rupert would have liked. My Rupert, I mean.'

She passed the ring to Rupert Montgomery App-Lugus the 21st. She took his hand and placed it on the little finger of his right hand. The same hand, the same finger she had seen on the portrait of Titch's father; the same finger on the same hand she remembered Titch wearing it before he gave it to her.

The spell was broken by the telephone ringing again. Penelope rose to answer it. Rupert and Mary looked at each other.

'Thank you Mary. I appreciate the courage it took for you to come here. And even more for telling your story. Or rather, my father's cousin's story. He died in the war too, my father I mean.' He looked from Mary, to the ring on his finger and then back to Mary before he continued.

'We keep an accurate family record here. I will see that your Rupert is mentioned with all the honour he deserves. He will get all the recognition that is his due as a son of the family. Thank you again. For the ring. And for filling in the gap in the family's history.'

Penelope returned with a tray of tea things.

'Come. We will have tea on the south terrace. I am sorry about the mess. It's our maid's day off. The house is much too large for us these days, especially with the boys away at school.'

Mary followed them both out of tall French windows onto a sunny terrace that looked down the slope of the woods in the valley to the town of Beddgelert in the distance. The two rivers that met at the town were plainly seen in the clear mountain air. The sun shone down on the slate roofs and grey granite walls of the houses; old oaks dotted the streets and gardens; it was all quite lovely. Again Mary realised this might all have been Titch's, but fate, or God, had meant otherwise. She sighed sadly. She might have been the mistress of Cuffty Mawr.

The three sat and talked. A young man with an arm amputated at the elbow passed below the terrace after emerging from the woods. He waved the stump at the trio sitting in the summer sun. The major returned the wave.

'Young Evans seems happy enough these days. A bit of a shock for him at first. Working for the estate I mean.' He laughed a short laugh. A laugh that tore the heart out of Mary Golding; it could have been Titch Wilkins laughing. Mary stifled the cry that came to her lips and looked at her host. The Royal Marine major mistook Mary's look for one of surprise and added.

'His family hated us up here. I believe it all started with his great grandmother. Megan Evans her name was. A funny old biddy, by all accounts. The local maid of all work. Midwife, layer out of the dead, practitioner of herbal remedies for everything from an ingrown toenail to cardiac arrest.' He laughed again. 'And everything in between. And very effective it was. Her medicine, I mean. She brought me into the world. There was animosity between her and my grandfather. He claimed she was a witch. Many of the locals would agree. Others say she should be canonised. She was a funny old thing. Only died a few years ago. No one knew her age. Some say she was over a hundred. Died on the mountain returning home from laying out an old lady on a mountain farm. Dickens of a night apparently; snow and wind, a terrible combination on the mountain. Anyway they found her dead in a snow drift days later.' He looked pensive as he spoke, as if he believed in her magic.

'People say that my grandfather was a warlock. Every twin in the family has been called that. There have been several over the generations. Seems to be a bit of a family curse. Part of the Lleu Llaw Gyffes legend. And grandfather was a cripple too, poor old chap. He had the image of a warlock, poor devil. Even had a hunch back. He was your Rupert's father's twin. Something went wrong at birth I suppose. One brother normal, the other grotesquely crippled. His physical deformity warped his mind, I should think. I didn't know him well. He died when I was very young. Mother had to move away. Couldn't stand his moods and vile temper. We went to live in Shrewsbury, close to my grandmother. She still lives there. Grandmother is quite frail now.' He paused and reached for a cup cake and bit into it. He chewed for a minute, swallowed and continued.

'Grandfather is the only App-Lugus who has not a portrait hanging in the hall. Pity really. We should have us all there.' He looked at his wife and smiled. 'Anyway, he and old Megan Evans were at logger heads all their lives. Mother told me that grandfather threatened to whip her on the day of my birth. The old lady stood up to him. Threatened to throw a bowl of water over him. Must have been a fiery old thing.'

He stirred his second cup of tea and tapped the teaspoon gently on the cup. The sound made a gentle ring in the silent sunshine.

'Young Taffy Evens there was with me in the Falklands. He was a corporal in charge of one of my assault teams. Splendid young leader. Would have gone far in the Marines. Had a reasonable education. He told me once his old great grandmother had seen to that. Had the stuff it took, if you get my meaning. I had recommended him as sergeant just before he had his arm blown off by an Argentinian grenade. It landed among his team as they advanced. Young Evans didn't hesitate. He picked it up to hurl it back to the "Gauchos". The blasted thing exploded in his hand. Lucky he wasn't blinded. Splendid action. Saved several lives. I recommended him for the Distinguished Conduct Medal. Got no further than Brigade, I'm afraid. Seems several of the chaps were being brave that day and Taffy lost out. Sad really.' He drank from his cup and continued. 'When we got home I looked him up in hospital. He was upset that he was out of the Corps. Wanted to make a career of it. Anyway, when I knew he wanted to come back to the valley, I offered him a job as a game-keeper. More of a ranger really as we have phased out the shooting and hunting on the estate. He works at his own pace and what with his disability pension and the lodge cottage and the wages he gets, he manages quite well. He is getting married soon to a local girl.'

The three sat talking until late in the evening. Mary talked about herself; Penelope talked about her sons away at boarding school. It was a pleasant time that had to come to a close. Mary had an hotel room booked in Llandudno for that night and had over an hour's motoring ahead of her.

The three parted with the hope that they would meet again. The major was about to return to his post with the Defence Ministry in London. He extracted a promise from Mary that she would come and stay with them the following summer. Mary accepted happily. It became an annual event. Mary Golding became part of the family. When she spoke of this to Penelope some years later, the kindly mistress of Cuffty Mawr smiled and said 'It is as it should be Mary. You have more right to be here than I have and Rupert agrees. Besides, we all love you and love having you.'

The winter of 1995-96 began mild. In mid-December it froze. On Christmas Eve it snowed. Mary Golding left Lincoln for Runnymede early on Christmas morning. Snow had stopped falling – the sky was overcast but not menacing when she left home. The ancient cathedral sparkled white in the early morning half light. It was dark when she joined the A1 motorway at Newark-on-Trent heading south; the snow had turned to brown slush. There was a hint of fog as she drove on the lower land. The weather forecast was 'fog patches and snow clearing.' Mary was making good time and there was little traffic. She kept her speed to a steady 50mph. There was no hurry. The carols on the car radio were festive and she sang with the choirs. This was her Christmas pilgrimage and she was happy; it was Titch Wilkins' birthday.

Fog came in patches as the road dipped into

low ground. Stamford was by passed. The road was clear so she accelerated. A bank of fog suddenly came up in front of her. She slowed; there were no rear lights on the articulated lorry stopped in the slow lane. Mary struck the vehicle at a speed of forty miles an hour. Her face hit the steering wheel of her Morris. She was hurt but not unconscious. Her seat belt came unclipped at the touch of her thumb. She was halfway out of the door of her Mini when the full laden lorry with a shipping container towering over its rear, ploughed into the two stationary vehicles. The Morris Mini was crushed between the two. Mary Golding was killed instantly.

When the police found her she was sandwiched in her car. As they lifted her clear, a sprig of holly and mistletoe fell into the snow slush at the side of the highway. A large black boot of a young police constable trod it deep into the mush.

Patricia Tilson, secret agent code-named Cherry Ripe, was captured by the Gestapo in 1943. She was caught when hundreds of agents and partisans were rounded up after a betrayal by one of their number. Pat suffered a period of severe and barbaric interrogation and was later interned in Buchenwald Concentration Camp where she died as the result of a particularly bestial medical experiment. It was poor consolation to her friends that the perpetrator of the surgery was hanged for his crime.

Tom and Mrs Wilson survived the war. They lived through the Blitz – their flat only suffering broken windows from a near miss. In the summer of 1944 a German VI Flying Bomb demolished their flat and the pork butcher's shop below. Two of their sons died in the explosion.

The parents and their youngest child Molly, the little girl with a club foot were away visiting their eldest son Corporal 'Billy' Wilson of the Royal Tank Regiment in hospital after he had arrived back from Normandy where his tank had been blown up by a land mine just inland from the beach. He was a double amputee with both legs blown off above the knees – he was blind too and his face a ruin from burns received when his tank's fuel tank exploded.

The family live in a new house in Paddington, just a stone's throw from their old home. Molly is unmarried; she writes children's stories for radio and television and looks after her old parents and her blind crippled brother, doomed to the solitary confinement of his disfigured and mutilated body. There is a permanent sadness in the home. The empty places around the table – an enlarged photograph of Titch Wilkins and their daughter Judy with their bicycles, the sight of Billy's scarred face and his wheelchair in the little hallway are constant reminders that life will never be the same.

Aussie Meldrum survived the war. He evaded capture by the Germans and was sheltered by French Resistance Fighters. He later joined them in fighting the Nazis in the countryside of France. He was liberated by Canadian troops outside the Normandy city of Caen in July 1944 after he was wounded in street fighting that was characteristic of the battle for the city. He lives today quietly in Sydney, Australia, in sight of the beach, with his French wife and five daughters. He spends his leisure hours fishing and breeding French poodles. 'Them and the missus are the only French connection I 'ave, sport. Them an a liking fer French grog. Bloody marvellous stuff it is,' is a favourite comment.

The old mid-upper gunner-cum-resistance fighter is content to see his life through with only memories of 1943-44. When pressed for a story from his war days, he dismisses it with a joke.

'Put it this way cobber, I never suffered from bloody constipation.' As ever he has a quip for every occasion. He neither saw nor heard of his bombaimer Dave or his wireless operator Mac after leaving 'The Dog'. There is no record of them surviving their parachute descent. Their deaths are still a mystery. Aussie believes they were captured by the SS and shot out of hand. The French underground fighters could find no trace of them; their bodies were never found. They are just two of the thousands of airmen, friend and foe alike, with 'No Known Grave'.

Miss Cuthberson returned to Broadstairs years after the war. She stayed in Africa until the Missionary Society insisted that she retire. Sadly she said farewell to the mountain mission school and her African pupils, young and old, and sailed home for a former fisherman's cottage overlooking the English Channel. On her sideboard stands the ornate silver-framed photograph of a young man in the uniform of the Royal Flying

Corps. To the left of the mantlepiece, is a smaller one of the same man. To the right, a photograph of a boy of twelve. He is grinning a happy grin; his hair stands short and stiff on his head and his clothes are too large for his small figure. Underneath the picture in a neat scholarly hand are the words 'Rupert. My cockney sparrow. 1930.'

Miss Cuthberson attends morning service at St Peter's when she can. At ninety-odd years, she is frail and relies on the goodwill of parishioners to get her to and from the church. She is totally unaware that her favourite pupil lies a stone's throw from her kneeling figure.

St Peter's Church in Broadstairs flies the cross of St George on the Saint's feast days. The choir stalls ring out with the voices of small boys and the church bells ring a carillon every Sunday calling the faithful to church. There is a stretch of lawn around the old flint stone church and a new wicket gate leading to the rectory but the graves beyond are overgrown with a jungle of weeds and briars. Elms and ash saplings compete with tombstones for space, light and air. If you walk the single track among the graves and look hard, you will see what had been the gravel path between Titch Wilkins' and Constable Tom Higgins' graves. There is a clear patch of well-clipped lawn there and three white tomb-stones erected by The Royal Graves Commission. The first bears the crest of the R.A.F. and reads, 'AN UNKNOWN R.A.F. FLIGHT SERGEANT AIR-GUNNER. D.F.M. JULY 1943.' Beneath are the words, 'Lest We Forget'.

The other two are for Sapper Mathews, Royal Engineers and Luftleutnant Otto Meyer, but don't look for their spirits or for others that are surely there – they are invisible to us living breathing folk. And be careful of what you say, remember they can see and hear you, as this tale has shown.

> The thundering line of battle stands,
> And in the air death moans and sings.
> But day shall clasp them with strong hands,
> And night shall fold then with soft wings.

Rupert Grenville 1915

The publishers hope that this book has given you enjoyable reading. Large Print Books are especially designed to be as easy to see and hold as possible. If you wish a complete list of our books please ask at your local library or write directly to:

Magna Large Print Books
Magna House, Long Preston,
Skipton, North Yorkshire.
BD23 4ND

This Large Print Book for the partially sighted, who cannot read normal print, is published under the auspices of

THE ULVERSCROFT FOUNDATION